Outdoor Life
COMPLETE HOME
TAXIDERMY

Outdoor Life
COMPLETE HOME
TAXIDERMY

by Tim Kelly

Photos and drawings by the author
unless otherwise credited

OUTDOOR LIFE BOOKS
New York

Published by

Outdoor Life Books
Grolier Book Clubs Inc.
Sherman Turnpike
Danbury, CT 06816

Distributed to the trade by

Stackpole Books
Cameron and Kelker Streets
P.O. Box 1831
Harrisburg, PA 17105

Produced by Soderstrom Publishing Group Inc.
Designed by Jeff Fitschen

Library of Congress Cataloging-in-Publication Data

Kelly, Tim, 1935–
  Outdoor life complete home taxidermy.

  Includes index.
  1. Taxidermy.   I. Title.   II. Title: Complete
home taxidermy.
QL63.K45   1987   579'.4   86–31153
ISBN 0–943822–87–4

Manufactured in the United States of America

Second Printing, 1989

To my darlin'
Rose Malone Kelly

CONTENTS

PREFACE

Doing taxidermy is a lot like eating liver: Some people wind up enjoying it, and some don't. But everyone should try it at least once.

This book is the culmination of my life-long infatuation with taxidermy. My skill as a taxidermist helped me offset college expenses and paid for flying lessons when my GI Bill expired. Then my ownership of taxidermy studio gave me the background to serve as editor of *American Taxidermist*, a trade journal for the profession. But most important, after I enrolled in a taxidermy correspondence course in 1948, taxidermy has given me thousands of hours of enjoyment.

As a fledgling taxidermist, living in the city and still too young to drive, I had to be resourceful and so collected specimens whenever possible. I became adept at catching common pigeons at night in the railroad yards, using a flashlight and net, before carrying them home on a bus. My first "rare" trophy was a starling that I bagged with an air rifle while my father was visiting a bootlegger on the outskirts of the city. My first mammal mount was a fox squirrel killed by a car in front of my home. Fortunately, though, my father was an avid hunter and included me on many of his trips that yielded a variety of game for mounting.

Two significant changes have occurred in taxidermy since I mounted my first pigeon. First, there have been tremendous improvements in the quantity and quality of taxidermy supplies. Second, the exchange of information and "secrets" among taxidermists is freer now. Both of these changes have helped taxidermy. The handful of taxidermy supply companies of the late 1940s and early 50s have become a hundred or more. This healthy competition has encouraged research and development that have resulted in vast improvements in the quality of supplies. Many of these products are so good that even the most inept or talentless "taxidermist" can turn out a reasonably acceptable mount.

Some taxidermists consider themselves artists, while others think of themselves as craftsmen. I think taxidermy requires a bit of both. It does require an artistic eye as well as skills acquired through a lot of practice. It occasionally requires the precision of a watchmaker but also the brawn of a butcher. Yet I believe that almost anyone can master taxidermy as long as he doesn't try to depend on just a video tape and a week's practice. Also taxidermy has no sexual preference. In fact, some of today's leading taxidermists are women.

In this book I have described commonly accepted techniques that can be easily understood by the beginner. As an individual progresses, he can make improvements and modifications suited to his own style and needs. As these adjustments are made, skills should improve rapidly.

I hope that the absolute beginner can read this book and follow the step-by-step descriptions and then, with a lot of practice, recapture the beauty of nature in the animals he mounts. As well, I hope this book will plant the seeds for many a full-blossoming taxidermy career.

ACKNOWLEDGMENTS

It is difficult to know where to begin and end the acknowledgments for this book. Through the years a vast number of people have contributed to my knowledge of taxidermy. In fact, I have included many of the contributions to my trade journal, *American Taxidermist*, in this book.

First and foremost, though, I want to thank my wife Rose, who has tended the daily chores of journal subscriptions and correspondence so that I could concentrate on the editorial duties and the taxidermy featured in *American Taxidermist* as well as write this book and take its photos.

Four taxidermists made major contributions to this book. Richard Christoforo of Revere, Massachusetts, taught me the fine points of deer-head mounting while a hurricane raged outside. Jim Hall of Idaho Falls, Idaho, showed me that it was really possible to mount a trout that wouldn't shrink. Jack Wilson of Brockville, Ontario, has made major contributions to bird taxidermy and the international relations among taxidermists. Ralph Garland of Roxboro, North Carolina, got me off the hook by describing his snake-mounting techniques. Each of these men is without equal in his specialty, and each has made major contributions to the taxidermy profession.

When I became interested in taxidermy in 1948, the field was in the "dark ages." This was before the boom in large taxidermy studios, and most of the trophies were being mounted by little old men working in dark basements and garages who were secretive and refused to discuss their work. Help for the beginner was nonexistent. All of this was changed in 1970 with the establishment of the National Taxidermist Association by Charles E. Fleming, the late Charlie Haynes, and a handful of other farsighted individuals. Wm. Lee Birch, assisted by his wife Mary, served as the first Executive Director and held the Association together during its formative years. Over the years, most of the officers and members of the Association have contributed to my knowledge of taxidermy and indirectly assisted in the preparation of this book.

Joe Kish, always the maverick and always innovative, proved that taxidermy competitions were possible. This tradition has been carried on by the N.T.A. and numerous state and regional taxidermy groups. These competitions have become one of the greatest teaching aids available, and many of the award winners have been an inspiration to me. Kenny D. Asproth had more first place ribbons than birthdays at the age of 20. At the other end of the age spectrum were Paul and Esther Mae Provenzano who began winning ribbons at retirement age. In addition, mounts by Tony Gilyard, Sallie Dahmes, Frank Newmyer, Roger Martin, Ron Reynolds, Henry Wichers Inchumuck, and many others have given me inspiration and encouragement.

Two other people deserve special thanks. James J. Houston, president of the Northwestern School of Taxidermy, granted permission to use some of the material and illustrations from the school's renowned correspondence course. And D. L. Gruben, of

American Wildlife Studio in Albuquerque, graciously loaned supplies and equipment when I suddenly found myself under-equipped.

Finally I would like to express my appreciation for three nontaxidermists who made this book possible: Kay M. Collins, who edited and typed the manuscript; Neil Soderstrom of Soderstrom Publishing Group, who edited and produced this book and offered encouragement; and John Sill of Outdoor Life Books, who published it.

Tim Kelly

INTRODUCTION

Taxidermy is the act of preserving parts of wildlife in a lifelike manner. The word "taxidermy" is derived from Greek, with *taxis* meaning order or arrangement, and *derma* meaning skin—thus, the arrangement of skin.

Most people become interested in taxidermy through their interest in hunting, fishing, or their study of wildlife. Frequently a hunter or angler will take a prize specimen and decide to preserve the trophy himself. Others are looking for a hobby, a source of extra income, or the ability to reduce their own taxidermy expenses. Whatever the reason, as many as 10,000 people begin the study of taxidermy each year.

For whatever reason a person begins the study of taxidermy, he will find many hours of enjoyment. Not only is taxidermy a relatively inexpensive hobby, it is also educational. Also taxidermy is a tool of conservation because taxidermist-hunters often become more selective and ultimately harvest less game.

The desire to preserve wild game is as old as mankind itself. Stone Age hunters preserved the hides of their kills for clothing, and antlers and horns were frequently preserved as tools and implements. The Indians of North America preserved the heads of buffalo as headdresses and ornaments, and the Aztecs wove cloth from turkey feathers.

The ancient Egyptians preserved dogs, cats, and even birds, which were then left in the tombs with the pharaohs. But this was more a form of embalming than taxidermy. Still, it indicates the very early interest in preserving life forms. One of the earliest museums of record was founded by Ptolemy I in Alexandria, Egypt, in the third century B.C. Elephant tusks and rare animal hides were displayed there.

During the Middle Ages, trophies were commonly displayed on the walls of European castles. Many of these trophies are still in good condition. L. J. Van Dyke of Van Dyke Taxidermy Supply Company described a stag head that is still on display in the Meersburg Castle in the Bavarian Alps. The head had been carved from wood and the antlers of a red deer set in the carving. This provided the hunter with a lifelike representation of the animal before modern techniques in taxidermy had been developed. In other European castles, the entire skull and antlers were preserved much like a modern antler mount that I describe in Chapter 9.

Like the other arts, taxidermy had its modern beginnings during the Renaissance. The oldest mounted specimen in existence today is a rhinoceros prepared in about 1500 for the Royal Museum of Vertebrates in Florence, Italy. The rhino skin was tanned and then stuffed with gravel. A collection of bird skins from the East Indies was stuffed and displayed in Amsterdam in 1517. And the Sloane collection, which formed the nucleus of the British Museum in 1753, illustrates that a form of taxidermy was practiced in England before that date. The first published work describing collection and preserving techniques was R.A.F. Reaumur's *Treatise* in 1749.

During the 19th century many examples

Shown with a golden eagle mount, J.W. Elwood founded the Northwestern School of Taxidermy in 1903. The school has since become the primary source of taxidermy instruction for millions of students and is still highly respected. Elwood's taxidermy studio was located in Omaha, Nebraska, on the Union Pacific's main line, which carried many wealthy sportsmen to and from the Rocky Mountains. Elwood's clients included Theodore Roosevelt, Buffalo Bill Cody, and members of the English nobility. (Northwestern School of Taxidermy photo)

of British taxidermy were displayed in exhibitions, and a special taxidermy section was prepared for the Paris Exhibition in 1865 by Edwin Ward. In the late 1800s the Rowland Ward taxidermy studio was established in London, and for many years it was the foremost commercial taxidermy studio in the world.

Some of the earliest works of taxidermy in the United States were prepared by John Scudder for New York's American Museum, which was established in 1791. Mounts by Titian Peale were displayed in the Philadelphia Museum in 1821.

Probably the greatest advancement in North American taxidermy resulted from the founding of Henry A. Ward's Natural Science Establishment in 1861 at Rochester, New York. As a supplier of scientific goods to schools and museums, Ward's became the source for many of the early taxidermy mounts displayed in American museums. Ward's was also the training ground for many outstanding taxidermists of the 19th and 20th centuries. These included Wm. T. Hornaday, Frederic S. Webster, Wm. J. Critchley, and Carl E. Akeley. Many of these men have been elected to the Taxidermist Hall of Fame.

When the rest of North America was wallowing in the depths of the Depression in

Considered to be the father of American taxidermy, Carl E. Akeley was also a well-known African hunter and explorer. Much of his taxidermy work is now on display in the American Museum of Natural History, in New York. Akeley died in Africa in 1925, a year after this photo was taken. (American Museum of Natural History photo)

the 1930s, the Northwestern School of Taxidermy had a staff of more than 100 persons, and students began to enroll at a record pace. In addition to the Northwestern School, which was founded in 1903, there are now several other correspondence courses being offered and taxidermy curriculum is being taught at various private and public institutions.

Vast changes have occurred in the taxidermy profession since World War II. This is due to the development of modern plastics, tools, and chemicals that were not previously available. They have enabled the modern taxidermist to produce more lifelike and longer-lasting mounts than had previously been possible.

HOME TAXIDERMY

In order to be a competent taxidermist, you must develop a variety of skills. You must develop the skills of a surgeon, sculptor, and painter. At times you may also need to be a welder and a carpenter. As a result, the taxidermy studio of today resembles a butcher shop, an auto body shop, and an artist's studio all under one roof.

Most modern homes contain all of the tools necessary to begin a career in taxidermy. In fact few specialty tools are required by the beginning taxidermist. Some special tools have been developed to simplify the work, but most of these are not necessary. For example, most skinning is done with a scalpel, but a single-edge razor blade or sharp pocketknife is adequate for the beginner. Many taxidermists prefer dental floss for sewing small mounts instead of using waxed nylon thread. Table salt can be used as a preservative by the beginner, and such common

tools as pliers, saws, and hammers come in handy too. Since special tools may occasionally be required for a particular type of taxidermy, I have included a discussion of special tools in each of the chapters.

LAWS

Taxidermists in the United States are regulated at the federal and sometimes at the state level. The Fish and Wildlife Service of the Department of the Interior requires that all persons doing taxidermy for others, and who are at least 18 years of age, must apply for a Taxidermist's Permit *if* they intend to mount migratory birds. These permits, which are available for a few dollars, must be renewed every two years. The purpose, as stated on the permit, is "To authorize the acceptance, temporary possession, and mounting or other preparation of migratory birds for other persons." Since a professional taxidermist may have 50 to 100 migratory birds in his possession at any given time, the importance of the federal permit becomes obvious. It prevents a poacher from operating under the guise of a taxidermist.

In order to obtain a Taxidermist's Permit, write to the Director, Bureau of Sport Fisheries and Wildlife, Department of the Interior, Washington, DC 20240, or the nearest regional office. These are: Region 1 (Northwest), P.O. Box 3737, Portland, OR 97208; Region 2 (Southwest), P.O. Box 1306, Albuquerque, NM 87103; Region 3 (North Central), Federal Bldg., Ft. Snelling, Twin Cities, MN 55111; Region 4 (Southeast), Peachtree-Seventh Bldg., Atlanta, GA 30323; and Region 5 (Northeast), U.S. Post Office and Courthouse, Boston, MA 02109.

Some states also require that taxidermists

obtain licenses. This varies from state to state, both in requirements and cost. Some states require no permit; others require a small annual fee. Pennsylvania is unique; there a taxidermist must pass a test of skill and knowledge before being granted a permit. For additional information, contact your state wildlife agency. For the address, check with your local game warden or with a sporting goods store.

You can't legally mount all birds and animals. For example, it is illegal to possess any endangered species. While this may seem rather logical, the distribution of endangered species is not. For example, the pine marten is endangered in Wisconsin and may not be mounted by a taxidermist there, but the marten can be mounted in Canada, Maine, and many other states. Predatory animals can be mounted without restrictions in most states, but a fox may be classed as a predator in one state and a furbearer in another. Therefore, you should investigate the laws in your own state before embarking on taxidermy professionally.

Virtually all birds in the United States are protected by law. The only exceptions are the common pigeon, the English sparrow, and the starling. These three species were imported into North America from Europe and are not considered to be natives. All other birds are either considered migratory birds and are protected by various treaties, or else they are upland gamebirds that are protected by state laws. Consequently the beginning taxidermist should practice on pigeons, domesticated fowl, or legally taken gamebirds. An exception would be gamebirds that are raised by a licensed dealer; in this case, you must obtain a certificate at the time of purchase.

A word of caution: Protection of birds varies from one country to another, and laws in the United States are more restrictive than in Canada, Mexico, or Europe. So the purchase of a specimen outside the United States does not make it legal when returned or imported to the States.

SUPPLIERS

Although the taxidermist may not require special tools, he will need special supplies. For example, glass eyes, tanning oils, artificial bodies and headforms must be obtained from taxidermy supply companies. These companies have developed a wide range of tools and supplies that simplify the taxidermy process and greatly improve the quality of the finished mount. Listed below are some of the companies that offer a complete line of taxidermy supplies. Each of these offers a catalog for a modest fee. In addition, there are a large number of suppliers of specialty items that are advertised in taxidermy trade journals (see "Journals" below). Here are the full-line supply companies:

American Pacific Supply
5036 E. Jensen
Fresno, CA 93725

Buckeye Mannikins
3002 S.R. 83, Rt. 3
Millersburg, OH 44654

Blomquist Taxidermy Supply
P. O. Box 2945
Hammond, LA 70404

Chase Taxidermy Supply
Rt. 2, Box 317A
Baker, LA 70714

Clearfield Taxidermy
P. O. Box 870
Clearfield, PA 16830

Elwood Supply Company
P. O. Box 3507
Omaha, NE 68103

Jonas Bros., Inc.
1037 Broadway
Denver, CO 80203

McKenzie Taxidermy Supply
P. O. Box 480
Granite Quarry, NC 28072

A. Phillips Supply
205 52nd St.
Fairfield, AL 35064

Quality Taxidermy Supply
Rt. 4, Box 715
Salisbury, NC 28144

Research Mannikins, Inc.
315 W. Sherman St.
Lebanon, OR 97355

Van Dyke Supply Company
Dept. ATM
Woonsocket, SD 57385

JOURNALS

Like all professions, taxidermy is ever changing. Therefore the beginning taxidermist should subscribe to various trade journals, which keep their readers advised of the latest changes in techniques and supplies. In addition, the National Taxidermist Association attracts members from throughout the world to its annual meetings for seminars and taxidermy competitions. These addresses are listed in column two:

American Taxidermist
P. O. Box 11186
Albuquerque, NM 87192

Breakthrough
P. O. Box 1320
Loganville, GA 30249

National Taxidermist Association
18626 St. Clair Ave.
Cleveland, OH 44110

Taxidermy Today
119 Gadsden St.
Chester, SC 29706

HOW THIS BOOK CAN HELP

Taxidermy is a wonderful hobby and a satisfying profession, but it requires skill, practice, and patience. Taxidermists are not born. They develop through years of study and experience. Therefore, in this book, I don't attempt to teach all of the fine points used by professionals. But the book does contain enough authoritative information to enable the beginner to become a proficient taxidermist.

The ultimate quality of your work will depend on your skill and aptitude, and your ability to recognize and reproduce the wonders of nature. So avoid beginning with a record bass or trophy buck because you will probably be disappointed. Begin with any specimen that is available and *expendable* so that you are not afraid to make mistakes. In fact, it is best to experiment and not worry about the final results. Proficiency on average specimens will ultimately lead to success on real trophies.

1 CARE PRIOR TO MOUNTING

The ultimate quality of a mounted trophy begins prior to the trip, and the mounted trophy's maintenance never ends. Unfortunately a vast number of trophies are lost each year because hunters and anglers do not know how to care for them before mounting.

This chapter outlines the basic steps of trophy care, from planning the trip to the actual field care, whether you mount your own trophy or turn it over to a professional taxidermist. Field equipment and techniques here described will enable you to get your trophy from field to your home shop or to a taxidermist with a minimum of damage. I'll here cover preliminary skinning techniques for game heads and big-game trophies, as well as proper care of small game, birds, and fish. In most cases, though, taxidermists prefer to do the actual detailed skinning in their own shop.

CARE OF GAME HEADS

Each year more whitetail deer are bagged in North America than any other big-game animal. Unfortunately a large percentage of the trophy animals are ruined. One of the big-

Since dragging an animal will damage the cape, a game head should be caped-out at the kill site and packed to camp. If you use ropes to lash the cape for packing, tie to antlers or horns, rather than allowing the rope to damage the fur or skin. To ensure that the cape doesn't acquire additional bullet holes while you are packing it out, conceal it with hunter-orange fabric.

gest losses of trophies is the result of the old-fashioned practice of throat cutting. Fortunately this practice is on the decline, but it is still a terrible waste. This custom stems from the early woodsmen who often dropped the quarry with a large bullet from a muzzleloader that broke an animal down without killing it. Then, to prevent escape and to save ammunition, the woodsmen cut the throat of the wounded animal. Consequently, many of today's hunters believe that some magic transformation occurs in the quality of the venison when the throat is cut. Because modern bullets produce tremendous shock and hemorrhaging, animals often bleed to death internally within a matter of seconds. Also, since the heart is nothing more than a pump, once the heart stops beating, the animal is dead and the head can be completely severed without effectively draining more blood. So nothing is effected by cutting the throat—except to damage the neck skin of the trophy.

Marksmanship, both good and bad, has ruined its share of trophies. Some hunters pride themselves in neck or head shots. "It saves meat," they claim. They are right, but it also ruins the cape (head and neck hide) of the deer. Naturally you'll want to bag your trophy humanely, but head and neck shots should be avoided if at all possible. One reason is that the cape may be damaged beyond repair; another reason is that the Boone and Crockett Club will not accept a trophy for official recognition that has skull damage. The late Jack O'Connor, well-known author and hunter, told of rejecting a neck shot at a Dall sheep from 75 yards in favor of a chest shot from 200 yards in order to protect the cape and trophy. That was a wise decision. It is sometimes possible for a taxidermist to obtain an extra cape to replace a damaged one. But a damaged skull is almost impossible to work with.

Ropes do their share of damage to trophies. It is best to cape the deer as soon as you field-dress it. Take the head and cape to camp and return later for the meat. The hair of most big-game animals is rather brittle and easily damaged by ropes. So if you use rope on the head of an animal, always tie it around the antlers or horns and not around the throat.

It is common practice for a hunter to drag hoofed game long distances using the antlers or horns for pulling. Since the shoulders of a field-dressed animal are the heaviest part, the hair there is often totally destroyed by dragging. Since the shoulder skin is needed for a quality head mount, you should normally skin and quarter the animal, rather than drag it by the antlers or the horns.

The skinning job is much easier when the proper tools are available. This requires a

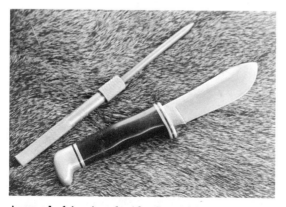

A good skinning knife should have a short, curved blade of high-quality steel. Also always carry a sharpening steel or whetstone to maintain a good edge on the blade.

little prehunt planning. Items you might need include skinning knife, whetstone or sharpening steel, steel tape, keyhole saw, and salt. Naturally the type and length of your hunt determines which items you will need.

A good skinning knife and whetstone are essential on any trophy hunt for big game. But beware—a good hunting knife is not necessarily a good skinning knife. Your old faithful hunting knife with the straight, 10-inch blade might be the greatest all-around camp tool in the world, but it is a poor skinning tool. The best skinning knives have a curved blade, as shown, that is 4 to 6 inches long, made of top-quality steel. Such a knife is essential for the delicate skinning that must be done on the face and ears of a trophy head.

A steel tape allows you to make the measurements needed later for mounting the head. Carry a small piece of note paper for this purpose, but if worse comes to worse, you can always record the measurements on the back of your license.

A keyhole saw can be real effort savers. The take-down models are light and easily carried. You will only need the crown of the skull with antlers attached for your mount, so you can leave most of the skull in the field and save yourself the effort of carrying out an extra 10 pounds or more of bone.

Salt is extremely important in preserving your trophies. However, its use depends on the trophy, weather, timing of the hunt, and many other factors. Salt is inexpensive, so take at least 5 pounds for each deer cape. Ten pounds would be needed for each elk or caribou. And 15 pounds should do for moose. For a full-body skin, triple those amounts.

As soon as you've field-dressed the animal, remove the cape. Make an incision completely around the body in line with the back

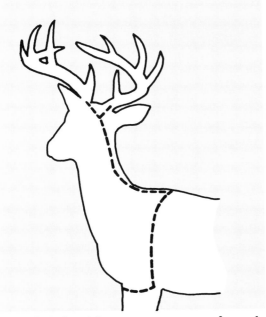

For a full-shoulder mount, you need nearly a third of the body skin. The incision should extend around the body and the front legs. The second incision follows the back of the neck to the top of the skull. At the back of the skull, the incision should fork to the base of each antler.

back of the neck. Use this as a guide for making your incision. At the top of the skull, make two short incisions to the base of the antlers. All of these cuts should be made by inserting the knife point beneath the skin and cutting upward. In this way very little hair will be damaged.

You can detach the skin from antler burrs by prying the skin away from the burr with a blunt instrument such as a screwdriver or the back of the knife blade. However, on horned game such as pronghorn, goats, and sheep, the skin must be cut away from the base of the horn.

After you have freed the skin from the antlers, work the neck and shoulder skin toward the head by cutting the membrane that holds the skin to the muscle. If you work carefully, you will be able to remove the bluish-white skin cleanly from the shoulders and neck, and at the same time you will not cut the cape.

It is not necessary to skin the entire head at the kill site if the head and cape are small enough to carry conveniently. Cut through

of the shoulders. The incision should pass around the top of the front legs. This will be nearly one-third of the body skin, and all of it is needed for a top-quality mount. The caping incision is shown in the accompanying drawing. Remember, it's better to take too much cape than to take too little.

If possible roll the trophy onto its belly in order to make the next incision. This cut extends along the back of the neck from the shoulder incision to the top of the skull. Many big-game animals have characteristic color patterns down the back of their neck that can be used as a guide. For example, whitetails have a dark band of hair down the

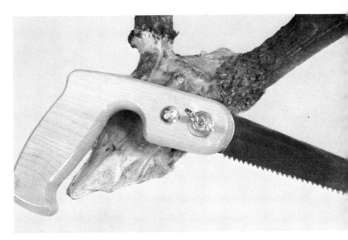

A take-down keyhole saw allows removal of the skull crown in the field.

the neck muscle at the base of the skull; then by twisting the head, you will break the head and cape free from the spine. If the spine is too difficult to break, use the keyhole saw and cut through the spine at the base of the skull.

Now is the time to record some measurements. First record the distance from the tip of the nose to the front corner of the eye. A medium-size whitetail will measure approximately 7 to 7½ inches from nose to eye. The second measurement should be made from the tip of the nose to the back of the skull, or about 12½ inches for the average whitetail. Both of these should be straight-line measurements against the unskinned face; do not follow the curvature of the head. The third measurement is the circumference of the neck at the base of the skull—the

smallest part of the neck. Because of the thick hair on bucks, this measurement should be made against the neck muscle after you pull the cape forward or remove it. This measurement will be a minimum of 18 inches, but might be considerably more for a heavy-necked, rutting buck. The locations of these measurements are shown on the accompanying drawing.

As I will describe in Chapter 2, some taxidermists take considerably more measurements than I suggest here. But these three measurements are essential for mounting the head, and you should record them in the field. You can take other measurements later in camp or in your shop where the final skinning of the head is done.

If the daily temperature is below 40 degrees, and if the head can be returned to

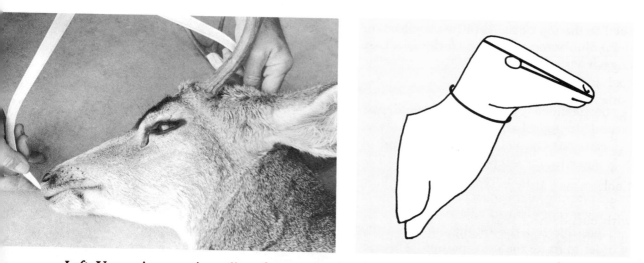

Left: Use an inexpensive caliper for accurate head measurements. The nose-to-eye and nose-to-back-of-skull measurements are straight line distances and do not follow the curves of the skull. Measure the neck circumference at the base of the skull with a steel carpenter's tape after you have skinned the neck. *Right:* Make these three measurements in the field. You can make others later. Measure the distance from the nose to the front of the eye, from the nose to the back of the skull, and around the neck at the base of the skull.

your shop within two or three days, you don't need to skin the head in the field. If you simply hang the head in the shade where air can circulate freely, the head and cape should remain in satisfactory condition for several days. Otherwise, you should skin the head as soon as convenient. Your removing the cape promptly allows the skin to cool and this helps prevent spoiling of the skin. Prompt removal is especially important in moderate or warm temperatures in which the cape must also be salted to ensure that it does not spoil.

According to Mario Panattoni, Chief Tanner for New Method Fur Dressing in South San Francisco, California, there are five important things to remember in order to prevent field damage to a deer cape:

1. Don't allow the trophy to lie on the ground. The body heat is trapped between the animal and the ground. This prevents cooling, resulting in skin decay that causes the hair to slip (fall out in large patches).

2. Whenever possible, hang the freshly bagged trophy so that air circulation will cool it. Then skin the trophy as soon as possible. This is good for both the skin and the meat.

3. Don't put the cape or skin in a plastic bag.

4. Avoid direct sunlight on the trophy. Cool, shaded areas are best.

5. Don't let the trophy come in contact with outside heat sources such as the hood of a vehicle, mufflers, or camp lights.

Freezing does not hurt the trophy. In fact, freezing is one of the best ways to protect the cape from damage. If the head can be frozen in camp or at the local locker plant, so much the better.

Pronghorns and members of the sheep and caribou families have very porous hair which readily absorbs blood and dirt. If the blood dries on the hair, the resultant stain is extremely difficult to remove. So as soon as you remove the cape and head from the body, examine the hair for bloodstains, especially around the nose and mouth. Wash the hair gently but thoroughly in cold water if any blood is present.

After you have removed, cleaned, and chilled the head and cape, you can safely transport it to your home or shop for detailed skinning and fleshing. This is described in Chapter 2.

FIELD CARE FOR LIFE-SIZE ANIMALS

The pre-taxidermy care of an animal depends on the size and species. In general any animal you can conveniently carry yourself is considered a small animal. This would include any species from rabbit or squirrel to fox; anything larger than a fox is considered a big-game animal. (These classifications are used in taxidermy competitions but as you can appreciate, they are not necessarily scientifically accurate.)

A crippled small animal may be humanely killed by hitting it on the head with a blunt instrument. Never shoot the animal in the head if you can avoid it. Head wounds are difficult to conceal because facial fur is quite short. If you must shoot a crippled animal, aim for the spine and into the chest. This will put the exit wound beneath the animal. If you use a shotgun, move 20 to 30 feet from the animal to get a widespread shot pattern to put only a few pellets into the animal. In such cases, a shotgun does little damage to the fur pelt.

Trappers beware. Commonly an animal that has been taken in a leghold trap will have suffered so much leg damage that you won't be able to save the foot. If you intend to trap a specimen for mounting, use a dead-fall or some sort of killing device or trap that will kill the animal quickly. Water sets that drown animals such as beaver and mus-krats are quite effective.

Small animals do not require much field care. As soon as possible, the mouth, anus or vent, and all bullet holes should be plugged with any soft material available. This field care is practical for animals the size of a fox or smaller. For heavier animals such as large beaver or coyotes field-dressing can eliminate the need to plug openings. After an animal has been field-dressed, wash or wipe the body cavity free of blood, and rinse away any blood on the pelt with clear, cold water. If practical, wrap the animal in paper or cloth in order to keep the fur clean. Thus, it is helpful to carry a rolled burlap bag in your hunting coat if there is a chance of bagging a mountable animal. The bag helps make carrying easier in addition to helping keep the animal clean. In the case that animals such as fox and squirrel have not been field-dressed, simply keep the animal clean. Avoid putting more than one animal into each bag so that blood from one animal will not stain the fur of the other.

Keep the animal cool or frozen until you are ready to mount it. Most small animals can be rolled within a paper sack and placed in a freezer until you are ready to mount them. If this is not possible, hang the animal in a cool garage or outbuilding to dissipate body heat. Never lay the specimen down because the side that is down will not cool properly. If you don't freeze the animal soon after field-dressing, you should skin it within two or three days at the most.

A frozen specimen can be kept for several months without damage. However, freezer burn will gradually damage the unskinned carcass, particularly the face, ears, toes, and tail. So it is best to skin the animal and then freeze the skin. Complete skinning details are described in Chapter 3.

Many big-game trophies are lost by im-proper timing or handling. This failure probably occurs most often with black bear. The pelt of a bear reaches its prime about a month prior to hibernation, and within a month after hibernation the hide is badly rubbed. Consequently the hunter has only about two months during which he can ex-pect to bag a trophy in prime condition. Likewise the full-body mount of a whitetail taken during the rut is likely to be badly damaged from fighting. That does not rule out mounting the specimen by the begin-ning taxidermist. Such a buck provides ex-cellent practice but is unlikely to produce a quality mount.

Many trophies intended for life-size (full body) mounts or rugs are ruined by improper handling, owing to their size and weight. On the other hand, these factors are advan-tages in some instances. When a trophy hunter bags a brown bear, the bear's great weight dictates skinning on the spot. Al-though such field skinning takes a great deal of work, if you are careful the extra effort will contribute to the quality of the mount.

Regardless of whether the animal will be mounted life-size or as a rug, the same skin-ning method is used. As shown in the ac-companying drawing, three incisions are made on the underside of the animal: (1) the length of the body from the vent to the middle of the throat; (2) from one front foot,

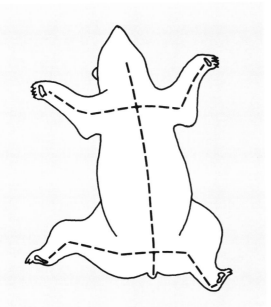

Make three incisions when skinning a large animal: from foot to foot along the inside of the legs and from tail to throat. Use these skinning incisions whether you plan to make a rug or a life-size mount.

down the inside of the leg and across the chest to the other foot; (3) across the inside of the hind legs from foot to foot.

Peel the skin back from the leg incisions, and skin the legs to the toes or hoofs. Sever the leg bones at the hoof of antlered trophies or at the last bone of the toe of animals with claws. Quite often it's more sensible to remove the pelt hurriedly in the field and return to camp to do the final skinning. In these instances, you can sever the feet at the wrists and ankles for skinning in camp. It is absolutely necessary to skin the feet; otherwise the claws or hoofs will fall off the pelt during the tanning process.

After you have skinned the legs, split the tail from the vent to the tip and carefully

remove the bone. Then skin the body from the hindquarters to the base of the skull.

If you wish to skin horned or antlered big-game animals for a life-size mount, you'll need to make slightly different incisions. The belly incision should continue only to the brisket and not up the throat. Then make an incision down the back of the neck as described for game heads, covered in Chapter 2. This will allow you to pull the skin over the head and antlers. In other words, a life-size deer or sheep mount requires four skinning incisions instead of three: a belly incision from vent to brisket; a leg incision inside the hind legs; a leg incision inside the front legs; and a nape incision.

As when skinning a trophy for a head mount, you have several choices once you have removed the skin and head from the carcass. If the hide can be frozen or skinned within a day or so, no further skinning is necessary beyond the neck. Cool the skin by laying it flat, hair-side down, in a cool place for several hours and allow the body heat to escape. Once the skin is cool, roll it up with the unskinned head uncovered, and freeze it. If you can't freeze the head and skin, continue skinning the face and head using the method described in Chapter 2.

After you have removed the hide, lay it flat and remove any fat or muscle still attached. You'll have to do most of the fleshing on the eyes, lips, and nose. Also, the ears must be completely skinned. If the hide is unusually thick on the neck or shoulders, as is frequently the case with elk or moose, you should also "score" the skin for salting because salt will only penetrate about ¼ inch. When the hide is thicker than ¼ inch, score the thick areas so that the salt can penetrate through the skin to the hair roots. The easiest way to score a hide is to lay it over a log or your knee, hair-side down, and cut a cross-hatched pattern deep enough to allow the salt to penetrate. The cuts should be about ½ inch apart and only about ¹⁄₁₆ inch deep, except on thick-skinned animals such as elk and moose for which the cut may be slightly deeper. If the scoring is cut too deep, it will seriously weaken the skin.

The pelt is now ready for salting. Pour a pile of salt in the center of the skin and work it toward the edges of the hide with your hands. Be sure that the entire hide is salted and that there are no wrinkles left unsalted. Fill the toes, ears, nose, and lips with salt. There are many places to save money on a hunting trip, but salt is not one of them because it provides vital protection and, anyway, costs little. You will need 10 or more pounds of coarse non-iodized salt for the average black bear or whitetail hide. Remember, by skimping on the salt, you might lose the trophy.

After the salt has been on the skin for 24 hours, scrape the moisture and excess salt from the skin, then give the skin another complete dose of salt. After the second salting, fold the hide double, flesh sides together. You may leave the skin folded or roll it, but in either case, allow it to drain.

If you keep the salted hide cool, it will remain in good condition for several weeks. A hide that has been well salted and dried will last indefinitely, provided you keep it dry. Salted hides are not bugproof, however, and the hair should be sprayed with insecticide if you store the hide for more than a few weeks.

Big-game animals are much like humans in that each member of a species has a slightly different size and shape. For this reason, you should record several measurements on your animal if you intend to have a life-size mount. In general, the more information you have, the more realistic and natural your finished mount will look. As I explain in later chapters, many commercial artificial bodies are available, and your field measurements will help you to purchase or construct an artificial body that will accurately fit your particular trophy. You can use your steel tape to make these measurements. Record them on notebook paper. Many taxidermists prepare a standard form for recording these measurements in the field.

The first three measurements listed below are essential; the others are desirable. The first two measurements must be made prior to skinning; all others should be taken from the carcass.

1. Length of body from tip of nose to root of tail, following curve of the back
2. Nose to back of head
3. Greatest circumference of the body
4. Height at the shoulders
5. Circumference of the body behind the front legs
6. Circumference of neck: behind the ears, near the middle, and in front of the brisket
7. Depth of chest or flank
8. Thickness of the body through the shoulders
9. Distance from point of shoulder to point of hip
10. Distance from base of neck to ear
11. Circumference of lower and upper front and back legs

The numbers on the accompanying drawing correspond to the various measurements described above. Remember, these measurements should be made for any big-game an-

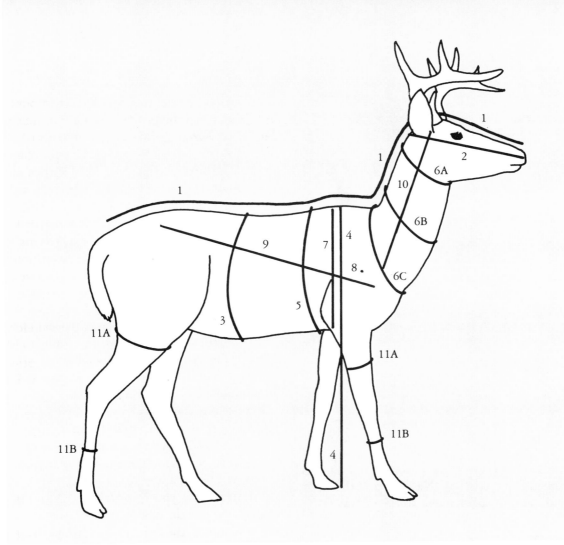

For a life-size (full-body) mount, you will need a goodly number of measurements, which you should make after you have skinned the animal. The same system for measuring applies whether you have a deer, a bear, or a cat.

imal that will be mounted lifesize regardless of the species.

CARE OF BIRDS

In general the field care of birds is simpler than that required for mammals because most birds are relatively small and are taken on hunts of short duration. Even our largest gamebirds, such as Canadian geese and sandhill cranes, do not present a major problem. However, you need to exercise some care in order to ensure that birds stay in prime condition for mounting.

Bagging a bird humanely is of primary importance, but at the same time you should strive to do as little exterior damage as possible. When you have a choice, select small

A crippled bird can be killed quickly and humanely by applying pressure on the rib cage under the wings. Never wring the neck or do additional damage to the plumage.

birdshot. By taking a pheasant with No. 8 shot, fewer bones will be broken and the 8s will not pass through the bird, leaving large exit wounds.

If the bird is crippled when retrieved, kill it humanely by firmly grasping it beneath the wings and applying pressure on the rib cage. This way the bird will suffocate quickly and any plumage damage will be hidden under the wings. Never wring a bird's neck and still expect to have a good mount. At best, the neck feathers of a bird whose neck has been wrung will be severely damaged. Also, birds that have been winged generally

do not make the best mounts, although there are times when the taxidermist has no choice. However, winged birds are suitable for practice and it is good for the beginning taxidermist to work with damaged specimens in order to develop techniques for repairing such birds for mounts.

Make every effort to prevent blood from getting on the plumage. You can prevent excessive bleeding by putting a small wad of cotton, tissue, moss, or any absorbent material into the bird's mouth as soon as you retrieve it. If possible, keep the trophy from coming in contact with other birds that have blood on them. For this reason, you should carry toilet tissue and a paper bag in your hunting coat. After you have plugged the throat and wiped away any blood or dirt from the bird, put the trophy into the paper bag, taking special care to avoid damaging the wings and tail feathers. You can then carry the bird in the game pouch of your hunting jacket without danger of its being soiled by the other birds you have taken. Don't use plastic. A plastic bag is nonabsorbent and will not allow the bird to cool properly.

Do not gut the bird. Gutting will not prevent the skin from spoiling, and it will only ruin the breast feathers. When mounting a bird, only the skin and a few of the bones are used, so it is far more important to protect the skin than the meat.

When you return to your car or camp, remove the bird from the paper bag and wipe away any blood on the feathers. A damp cloth works well for removing dried blood. (Always wash blood stains with *cold* water. Blood will wash away cleanly with cold water; whereas warm or hot water may permanently set the blood.) If the absorbent plug you earlier stuck in the mouth has become saturated, replace it. Then lay the bird away from the rest of the game on a clean piece of newspaper or on your hunting vest. This will allow body heat to escape. Unless the temperature is above 50 degrees, you can let the bird cool in that condition for up to 12 hours.

After the bird has cooled, chill or freeze it. Place it in a clean paper bag or wrap it in newspaper, before putting it in a refrigerator or freezer. The bird will remain in excellent condition for three or four days without being frozen. A frozen bird will last for six months or longer and can be mounted anytime during that period.

If you are traveling a long distance with a bird, it is wise to keep the bird in a cooler. However, you must keep the bird from becoming wet. After the bird has cooled and after you have wrapped it in newspaper, put it into a plastic bag and seal the bag tight. A plastic bread wrapper works well for this purpose. Do not put the bird into the plastic bag without wrapping it in absorbent paper. If you use dry ice, which I recommend, you won't need the plastic bag.

If you are on a big-game hunt in Canada or Alaska, you may have the opportunity to bag a spruce grouse or ptarmigan. In this case, you would be wise to wait until the end of the hunt before collecting one of these birds, even though there is sufficient ice in the streams or snow fields to protect the bird until it can be packed out and frozen for shipment. If you anticipate a delay of several days or more before you can freeze the bird, you should gut the bird promptly. This should be done as carefully and cleanly as possible. The body cavity should be rinsed and all blood washed from the feathers before you chill the bird and wrap it for shipment.

CARE OF FISH

Many anglers land a trophy fish expertly and then mistakenly clobber it to death. Pike anglers, especially, seem to excel in the kill. However, if you put a crease across the top of a pike's head, it is safe to assume that you will have creased the trophy hanging on the wall, unless you want to go to a great deal of effort repairing the damaged skull. Instead of clobbering a trophy fish, just use the club or paddle to hold its mouth open while you run the stinger through its lower jaw. Then slide the fish gently into the water. It's important to put the fish on the stringer as quickly as possible because the more the fish flops around in the boat, the more scales it will lose. Too many missing scales give the mounted trophy a rough or irregular appearance.

When landing a trout or salmon on shore, slide him up a mud bank or onto some moss. These fish have small, delicate scales that can be scratched quite easily by dragging them over a log or rocky bank. This precaution also applies to catfish, although damage is less likely because of their habitat. In general it's smart to use a landing net whenever possible, regardless of where you are fishing.

All varieties of fish begin to lose color as soon as they are taken from the water. This characteristic is especially noticeable in species such as dolphin or trout, and less apparent in others. Nevertheless this color change does occur. And by the time the fish reaches your shop, the color may have faded drastically. A color photo of the live fish, fresh from the water, will help you in restoring the natural colors.

Avoid letting the trophy come in contact

with other fish. For whatever reason, this frequently causes discoloration of skin; dark splotches may develop on the trophy that will require additional work on the final mount.

At the first opportunity, and if possible while the fish is still alive, spread some newspapers or plastic on a flat surface and pour out a layer of powdered borax. (Powdered borax can be obtained from taxidermy supply companies or your local chemical dealer, and it is sold as a detergent by your local supermarket.) Roll the trophy in the borax, working the powder around the base of each fin, under the gill covers and jaws, and onto the tail. Since the fish will be wet,

In order to preserve the skin and protect the color of a fish trophy, apply a coat of powdered borax as soon as possible. Then wrap the fish in paper and keep it cool until you can freeze it or mount it. If a fish is boraxed and kept on ice, it will last as long as a week without gutting.

the borax will form a protective coating that should be allowed to remain on the fish until you are ready to mount it. The borax helps to stabilize the natural colors in the skin, it removes the mucus or "slime" from the fish, and it also acts as a preservative. I cannot overstress the importance of applying the borax coating. After you have applied the borax, wrap the fish in newspaper or butcher paper.

Keeping the fish cool is very important when the fish cannot be frozen or skinned immediately. Cooling has two advantages: (1) it keeps the fish in good condition; (2) it doesn't alienate the other members of your party against you and your trophy. The best method of cooling the fish is to put it, now boraxed, wrapped, and in a plastic bag, on crushed ice. A fish that has not been cleaned will stay fresh for a week or longer if kept on crushed ice. If you happen to be in the backwoods where ice is not available, wrap the fish in wet moss or grass and keep it moist. Evaporation will keep the trophy cool and in good shape for several days provided you keep it out of the sun.

The gills are the first part of the fish that becomes "ripe." If you wish, you can remove them individually by cutting them loose at the top and bottom with a sharp knife or wire cutter. Don't attempt to tear them out because that may damage the skin.

Freezing the fish is the best method of preserving it; however, this should be done with caution. First, protect the tail from harm by attaching several pieces of cardboard to it with rubber bands or string. Place the fish into a plastic bag, wrap with newspaper, and then store it flat. If you must move the frozen fish, take special care to protect the tail and the fins, which are brittle when

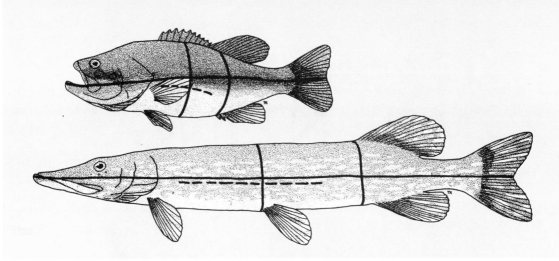

Measure the length and girth of the fish while it is still fresh. These measurements will help you ensure the accuracy of the eventual mount. If you must gut the fish, make the incision on the more damaged of the two sides, as shown by the dashed lines. *Do not* make the belly incision you would routinely use for a fish you'd plan to eat.

frozen and so are easily damaged. Once a fish is frozen, you can keep it indefinitely.

If you are not able to freeze the fish within four to five days, you'll need to gut it. But before you start cutting, be sure that you have accurately measured your trophy. You will need at least two measurements and possibly three or more. This is discussed more fully in Chapter 7. For trout, bass, and panfish, measure the length from the tip of the head to the end of the tail along the side of the fish. Measure the girth (body circumference) midway between the gill cover and the anus, or where the body is largest in girth. When measuring a pike or marine fish, you will need the length of the fish and its girth at the anus. In addition, the girth should be measured at the base of the pelvic fins. Generally, the more measurements you take, the better, because later you will be happy with all of the measurements you can get. These measurements will assure you of a more natural looking trophy.

Before gutting the fish, examine it carefully to decide which side has the fewest scars

or defects. This should be the "show" side of the trophy when mounted. Then make an incision on the *opposite* or *back* side, slightly below the spine or lateral line of the fish. Naturally if a fish has been gaffed, you will want to make your incision on the gaffed, damaged side. The side incision should be long enough to adequately clean the fish, but it also should be as short as possible. The incision should *not* extend to the anus. *Do not split the belly*! When mounting the fish, you will be able to use the incision along the side; whereas a belly incision is very difficult to conceal.

In summary, care of a specimen in the field is the same for brown bear, birds, and bass. Keep the trophy clean and cool. Since field work on a trophy is much more difficult than home shop work, your principal goal should be to protect the trophy as well as possible, while keeping it cool and clean. Remember that even the best taxidermist has only the trophy at hand to work with. Only God can replace scales, feathers, or fur.

2 GAME-HEAD MOUNTING

The late outdoor writer Jack O'Connor once wrote, "The whitetail deer is the most widely distributed big-game animal in the United States, the most plentiful, and the smartest." Perhaps these are the reasons that a whitetail buck is the most sought-after North American trophy animal. Nearly a million whitetail deer are bagged by hunters each season, not because they are an easy target but because this species of deer is widespread and plentiful. Good game management, coupled with adaptability of the whitetail, have produced sufficient numbers of whitetails to allow their being hunted in nearly every state and province in North America. As a result, the whitetail is the bread and butter of the taxidermy profession.

In this chapter, I introduce game-head mounting techniques, using the whitetail as the subject because of its popularity. The mule deer is the second most common big-game trophy in North America, followed by the elk, the blacktail deer, and the pronghorn. The same mounting techniques—a taxidermist never "stuffs" a specimen—are used for all of these species. An elk and a whitetail are mounted identically, except that

The Jordan buck (bagged by Jim Jordan in Burnett County, Wisconsin, in 1914) was recently remounted by the noted taxidermist Richard Christoforo, based in Revere, Massachusetts. The alert, ears-forward pose enhances the appearance of the high, massive antlers that make this the world-record, No. 1 Boone and Crockett whitetail deer in the typical (symmetrical) category. (Duncan Dobie photo)

you do a lot more grunting when you mount an elk. In fact the same methods are used to mount an elephant head, except that the taxidermist must deal with tusks instead of antlers. Some variation in methods is required when mounting open-mouth game animals such as bears. And the horns of sheep and goats require different preparation than for antlers. But in general, if you can mount a whitetail deer, you can mount any game head no matter how large or small.

To a first-class taxidermist, it is the quality of the mount and not the size of the antlers that counts. Any taxidermist who attends a state or national taxidermy competition will learn that a quality mount is judged by its anatomical accuracy and life-like appearance and not by the dimensions of the rack. Unfortunately the average hunter sometimes does not understand this, and he consequently may accept a terrible mount with a huge rack. At a recent Boone and Crockett competition, a high scoring non-typical mule deer was mounted like a whitetail deer, and the proud hunter obviously did not recognize the difference. Unfortunately in this case, an inexperienced taxidermist had created an anatomical freak.

In this chapter, you'll find the methods for mounting an anatomically accurate whitetail. Although the methods do not vary significantly among taxidermists, some taxidermists have developed an international reputation for quality mounts. One of these is Richard Christoforo of Revere, Massachusetts. Christoforo has won numerous awards and ribbons in taxidermy competitions, and he is one of the few people to be given the

Distinguished Taxidermist Award by the National Taxidermist Association. He is a frequent judge of competitions and has lectured widely. From his commercial studio in the Boston area, Christoforo specializes in mounting New England whitetails. I'll describe his award-winning techniques in this chapter.

Patience, practice, and experience are needed to accurately skin and mount a game head. Therefore the beginning taxidermist is encouraged to skin and mount as many deer heads as possible. Don't begin with a once-in-a-lifetime trophy. Instead go to your local locker plant during deer season and pick up or buy any unwanted deer heads. If you are able to obtain three or four, saw the antlers off 2 inches above the antler burr and then freeze the heads. Then you can thaw them out and mount them when convenient. You will find your skills improving with each mount. Also, these heads will give you the opportunity to experiment with different methods. Don't worry about creating a poor mount initially. As you have probably found out, it is from the disasters that we learn the most.

ANATOMY OF A DEER HEAD

For many years each deer head was mounted using the entire natural skull brought into the taxidermy studio by the hunter. The skull was boiled and preserved, then it was attached to an armature on which the taxidermist sculpted a lifelike resemblance of the deer. Although the method was slow and tedious, each mount was reasonably accurate because the actual original skull was used. As taxidermy supply companies began to expand, the time-consuming skull-and-

armature preparation was replaced by commercial headforms that were made from the lifelike model of a deer head. These early headforms were made of laminated paper and have since been replaced almost entirely by polyurethane headforms.

Although the availability of commercial headforms has simplified the work of the taxidermist, these headforms have also created their own set of problems. First, not all commercial headforms are anatomically accurate. Second, not all deer are the same size and shape, so the taxidermist must purchase the "best fit" headform and then modify the form to approximate that of the individual buck. Third, not all customers are willing to accept a commercially available headform, so the taxidermist must be able to accurately modify the commercial form to the satisfaction of the customer. In order to do this, the taxidermist must understand the anatomy of a deer head.

Since it is seldom possible for the beginner to obtain the skull and bones of a mature buck in order to study the anatomy, the best source of information is an accurate, commercial headform. For comparison, I studied headforms from three different supply companies. I compared a whitetail headform from McKenzie Taxidermy Supply with a blacktail from the Research Mannikins and a mule deer form from Jonas Brothers. I selected each form described in advertising as a "medium, straight shoulder" style so the pose and size would be comparable. (Note: I selected these forms and suppliers because each is located in an area where the supplier has access to a particular species or subspecies: McKenzie in North Carolina, Research Mannikins in Oregon, and Jonas Brothers in Colorado. Also, each sculptor is noted for his anatomically accurate and award-winning headforms. My choices, however, should not be considered as an endorsement of a particular supplier or the rejection of others.)

When I compared the three headforms, the anatomical differences were quite obvious, reflecting the uniqueness of each species. The differences among the three are most noticeable between the whitetail and the mule deer and blacktail. This difference makes sense because the whitetail (*Odocoileus virginianus virginianus*) and the mule deer (*Odocoileus hemionus hemionus*) are different species; but the mule deer and the blacktail (*Odocoileus hemionus columbianus*) are subspecies and are therefore more closely related. The most noticeable differences are in the depth of the body at the shoulders, the shape of the neck, and in bone structure of the face.

In the accompanying drawings, I've shown how the silhouettes of each headform compare. As you'll see, I used the top of the shoulder as the common point of reference. Notice that the whitetail is much shallower at the brisket and shorter at the back of the skull. Clearly the body of a whitetail is not as deep through the shoulder, so the body of a whitetail appears more rounded, which is reflected in the headform. Also note that the neck is slightly shorter than that of the mule deer and blacktail.

Since the three headforms were all "me-

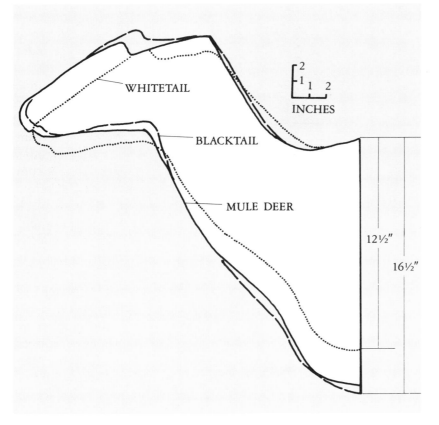

WHITETAIL

BLACKTAIL

MULE DEER

2
1   1   2
INCHES

12½"

16½"

This compares headform profiles of whitetails, mule deer, and blacktails. The whitetail is nearly 2 inches shallower through the chest. Yet, as shown in the shoulder cross-sectional drawing on page 25, thickness through the shoulders is about the same. The whitetail head is lower, indicating a slightly shorter neck.

HEADFORM DIMENSIONS IN INCHES

SECTION	MEASUREMENT	MULE DEER Jonas (3-16140)	BLACKTAIL Research Mannikins (G-230F)	WHITETAIL McKenzie (400)
A	Circumference	8	7⅞	7½
	Max. width	2½	2½	2¼
	Max. depth	2¾	2⅝	2½
B	Circumference	9	8⅞	8½
	Max. width	2⅜	2⅝	2½
	Max. depth	3¼	3⅛	3
C	Circumference	10¼	9½	9
	Max. width	2½	2⅝	2⅝
	Max. depth	3⅝	3½	3¼
D	Circumference	11½	10¾	10½
	Max. width	3	3	3⅛
	Max. depth	4¼	4	3¾
E	Circumference	13	12½	12½
	Max. width	3½	3¼	3¾
	Max. depth	4¾	4⅝	4⅛
F	Circumference	15⅞	15	16¼
	Max. width	4¼	4	4⅜
	Max. depth	5⅛	5	4¾
G	Circumference	*	16⅛	*
	Max. width	5½	4¾	4⅞
	Max. depth	*	*	*
H	Circumference	*	*	*
	Max. width	5¾	5	4⅝
	Max. depth	*	*	*

*Dimension influenced by position of neck

Reproduced from *American Taxidermist*

Manufacturer's dimensions:
   Jonas 3-16140: 7 × 12 × 17¼
   Research Mannikins
      G-230F: 6½ × 12 × 18
   McKenzie 400: 6¾ × 18

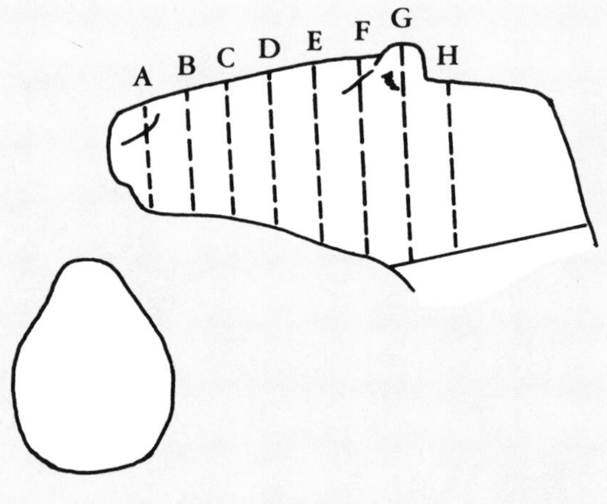

Here are headform dimensions for mule deer, blacktail, and whitetail. For comparison, I cut the cross sections from a "medium" headform of each species.

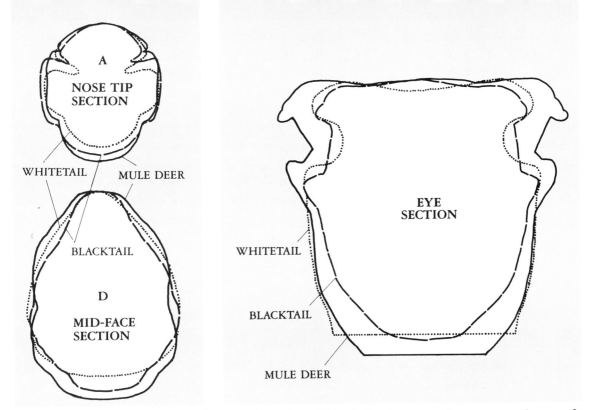

Left: When the silhouettes of face sections A and D of the three species are superimposed, all three show similar width, but the depth of the face is greater in the mule deer and blacktail. Overall, the whitetail has a more rounded muzzle than mule deer and blacktails, which are more flat-sided, rather like a horse. *Right:* I cut Section G through the eye socket to show the significant differences in head shapes at that section. The zygomatic arch, or cheekbone, beneath the eyes of muleys and blacktails is quite pronounced. This results in a somewhat bug-eyed appearance when you view these heads directly from the front. The arch is almost totally lacking in the whitetail.

These sections compare shoulders and necks. Although all three deer are nearly the same width through the shoulders, the depth of the chest is shallower in the "medium" whitetail. Yet at the base of the skull, the whitetail displays a greater neck circumference. During the rut, the neck of a whitetail may swell as much as 20 percent.

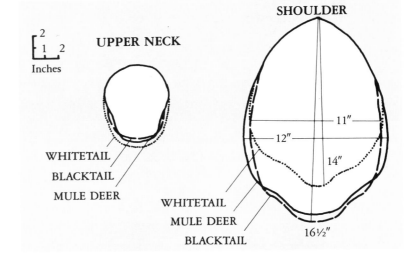

dium" in size, I cut cross sections at the same points, allowing me to compare dimensions. I severed the head from the neck at the point of smallest neck circumference and then cut cross sections of the head at 1-inch intervals beginning from the tip of the nose. I cut cross sections of the neck at the quarter, half, and three-quarter points. The points of section of the heads and the measurements are shown in the table of head dimensions on page 24.

I cut Section A one inch in back of the tip of the nose; this section shows both the upper and lower jaws and the nostrils. Notice that the circumference of the tip of the nose of the mule deer at that section is 8 inches; whereas the whitetail is ½ inch smaller. This relative size difference is maintained up to Section F, where the whitetail becomes larger than the mule deer and the blacktail. I cut Section F through the tear ducts immediately in front of the eyes. This series of sections shows that the headform of a whitetail, from tip of the nose to tear ducts, is proportionally smaller than the mule deer and blacktail heads even though all three are considered to be "medium" in size.

The greater circumferences at cross sections of the mule deer and blacktail headforms result from greater depth of the face and not from greater width. As shown in the table, the widths of the heads of all three species are quite similar. From this, it's apparent that the face of a whitetail is tapered more uniformly or cone-shaped. The muley and blacktail have heads that are somewhat flat-sided, more nearly like that of a horse.

The above comparisons are illustrated in the drawings on pages 24 and 25, with the silhouettes of sections A and D superimposed. These show that the muzzle of a whitetail is nearly circular; whereas the muley

and blacktail are rather oval-shaped. In Section D, midway between the nose and eye, the greatest width of all species is in the lower third of the face, but it is placed somewhat lower in the whitetail, relative to the jaw line. Again, we see that the whitetail's face is more conical than that of the muley and blacktail.

Section G, which is cut through the eye sockets, shows a great difference in the structure of the zygomatic arch, the cheekbone below the eye. Note that the arch is quite pronounced in the mule deer and the blacktail and nearly absent in the whitetail. This creates a somewhat more bug-eyed appearance in the western deer compared to the whitetail. Also in this section the jaw line of the mule deer is considerably deeper than that of the whitetail.

For "medium" headforms, the shape of the neck and shoulders also differs considerably between the whitetail deer and the other two. My drawings show that the three species are all about the same width through the shoulders—approximately 11 to 12 inches—but the western variety is about 16 inches deep, or about 2 inches deeper through the chest. For comparison, the circumference of the "medium" mule deer at the shoulders is 40½ inches; whereas the whitetail is 35½ inches.

All deer develop a swelled neck during the rut. Since the neck of a whitetail shows the greatest swelling near the base of the skull, the upper neck appears disproportionately large relative to the head. Mule deer and blacktails have a more evenly tapered neck, even when swelled in rut. A comparison of measurements made by taxidermist and author Fred Crandall shows that the upper neck of a whitetail will swell nearly 20 percent during the rut; whereas necks of muleys and blacktails swell only about 15 percent.

In summary, there are only minor anatomical differences between the blacktail deer and mule deer because they are subspecies. Nevertheless, the differences are significant enough that the beginning taxidermist should be aware of them. More importantly, there are major anatomical differences between these western species and the whitetail. If you don't take them into account, you may create an anatomical freak.

One other configuration of a particular deer that is not reflected in the measurements is the shape of the nose ridge. As in some humans, the shape of a buck's nose may change with age. A set of nose profiles made by Crandall are shown below. As a result of bruises during fights and the consequent gradual buildup of cartilage on the ridge of the nose, an older buck may develop a classic "Roman" nose. This is also characteristic of bighorn sheep. While the shape of the nose is not a feature that can be measured, the taxidermist should make a note of a particular shape and be prepared to reproduce this feature in the mount.

Not all deer are created equal—even within the same species. Therefore it is important to obtain the necessary measurements to properly mount your specimen. Although all whitetail deer are anatomically similar, the size of the buck can vary from region to region and from subspecies to subspecies. Obviously a large Wisconsin buck will differ in size from a large, but comparatively tiny, Arizona Coues whitetail. Within your own region there also will be a wide range in the size of bucks. Since most deer heads are mounted on commercial headforms, accurate measurements are essential for ordering the headform and reproducing the individual buck anatomically. As illustrated in the drawings on the next page, the

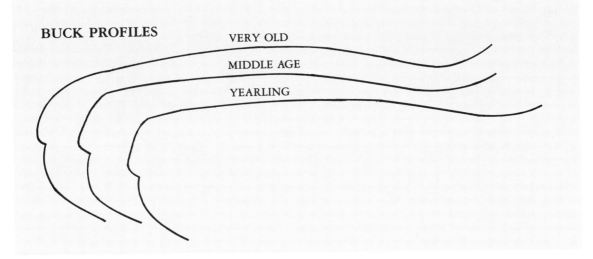

BUCK PROFILES

VERY OLD

MIDDLE AGE

YEARLING

An awareness of facial age characteristics can help you create lifelike mounts. As a buck ages, nose bruises from rutting battles may result in cartilage buildups. Also noses of younger bucks tend to be more squared than those of older bucks. (Adapted from Fred Crandall studies)

measurements recorded by award-winning taxidermist Richard Christoforo for each buck are as follows:

A. Nose to back of skull
B. Nose to eye
C. Circumference of neck at base of skull
D. Thickness of skull at front of eyes
E. Thickness of skull at back of eyes
F. Width of the septum in the nose
G. Length of the mouth
H. Depth of the ear, from the tip to the inside bottom

I. Corner of mouth to antler burr
J. Bridge of nose to each antler tip

These measurements should be recorded on a tag and attached to the antlers of the buck. Also record any anomalies about the buck; note the shape of the ears and bridge of the nose, and any other features worth remembering when the buck is ready for mounting. Measurements A, B, and C will be required when ordering the proper head-form; the other measurements will improve the anatomical accuracy of your mounts.

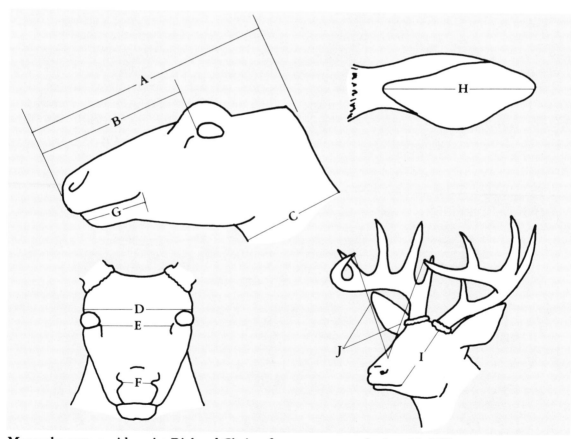

Massachusetts taxidermist Richard Christoforo recommends that 10 different measurements be taken to accurately mount a deer head. Measurements *A, B,* and *C* are made in the field, and the others are made in the shop before skinning the head.

SKINNING A DEER HEAD

In Chapter 1, I described the method of getting the deer head out of the field. The shoulders and neck were skinned to the base of the skull, and the head and attached cape were kept cool until the head could be skinned. Now, at home, is your last chance to record the head measurements if you haven't done so already.

Beginning with the Y-cut on the back of the head, as shown on page 9, skin the head forward to the base of the ears and the antler burrs. The skin can be detached from the antler burrs by prying the skin away from the burr with a blunt instrument such as a large screwdriver. Use this method for all game animals with antlers. However, on horned animals such as pronghorn, sheep, and goats, the skin must be *cut* free from the base of the horns.

After you have pried the skin from the antler burrs, cut through the muscle at the base of the ears and continue skinning along the sides of the face to the eye. The circular bone of the eye socket will be obvious on all hoofed animals; however, the carnivores such as bears, cats, and wolves do not have this circular bone. When you have skinned to the approximate position of the eye, place your finger into the eye and beneath the outside of the eyelid. You should be able to feel your knife blade under the skin. Now pull the eyelid gently away from the skull at the same time you cut the skin free around the eye. When in doubt, cut against the bone. That way you are less likely to cut the skin, and you can later remove the extra flesh.

Antlered animals such as whitetail deer have a tear duct that requires close attention. The tear duct is a fold of bare skin extending about an inch down the nose from the front corner of the eye. The skin of this tear duct is firmly attached to a channel or groove in the bone of the skull, and careful skinning is necessary in order not to cut the cape here. Sometimes it is easier to pry the duct skin out of the channel with a blunt instrument than it is to cut it free.

After skinning a short distance past the eyes, you will be able to feel the soft depression of the cheeks. By cutting against the skull at this point, you will expose the teeth. Continue to skin down the muzzle by cutting the lips free at the base of the teeth. After you have detached the cape from the lower jaw, cut the nose so that some of the cartilage remains attached to the skin. That frees the cape from the skull.

Now the cape must be fleshed. No matter how carefully you removed the cape, some muscle and tissue will be left on the skin, especially around the ears, eyes, and lips. This must be removed so that salt can penetrate the skin. Otherwise the hair will "slip" and come off in large patches, resulting in bald spots on the mount.

Begin the fleshing process by cutting the muscle away from the eye area. Be careful not to cut the skin of the eyelids. Then work your knife along the cheeks, separating the outer skin from the muscle in the lips. Skin the lips all the way to the edge. Remove the flesh from around the nose, but for the present you can leave the nose cartilage.

The ears must be turned inside out. This is relatively simple, but it must be done carefully. By working slowly around the ear butt, you should have little trouble skinning the lower part of the ear. The ear consists of a heavy cartilage which is covered by skin on the front and back. The skin is firmly attached to the cartilage in front but not on

SKINNING A DEER HEAD

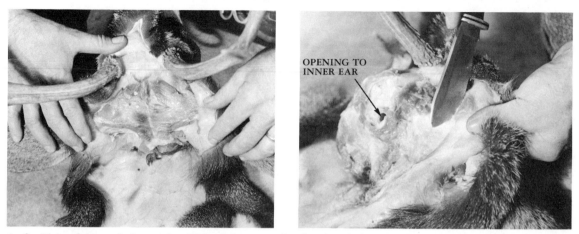

Left: Skin forward from the Y-incision on the back of the skull until you reach the antler burrs. Pry the skin away from the antlers with a blunt instrument such as a screwdriver. Then skin forward and separate the ears from the head. *Right:* In this photo the ears have been separated from the head, and you can see the opening into the inner ear at the left of the knife blade. Now with your fingers into the eye and beneath the eyelid, pull the eyelid gently away from the skull while cutting the skin free around the eye. This sounds more difficult than it is.

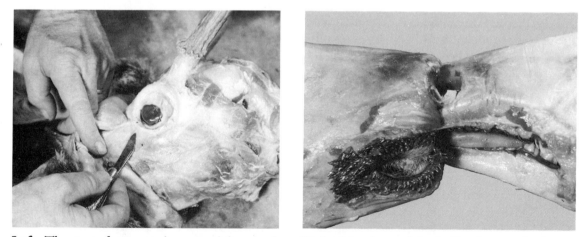

Left: The tear duct requires special attention. This thin, bare skin is firmly attached to a groove in front of the eye. Pry the skin free with a small pocketknife or even a blunt screwdriver. Only members of the deer family have a tear duct. It is not present in pronghorn, sheep, or predators. *Right:* After skinning past the tear ducts, cut into the jaws and skin along the tooth line. This will leave plenty of lip skin on the cape for mounting.

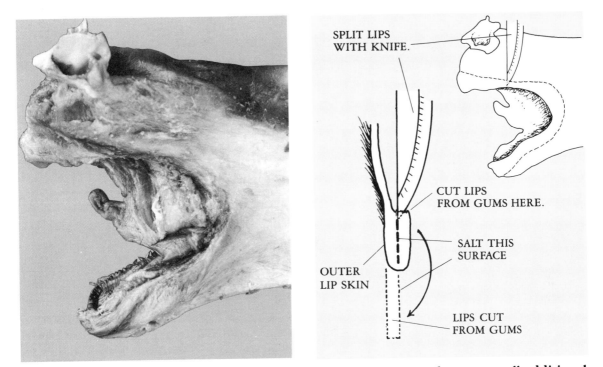

SPLIT LIPS
WITH KNIFE.

CUT LIPS
FROM GUMS HERE.

SALT THIS
SURFACE

OUTER
LIP SKIN

LIPS CUT
FROM GUMS

Left: After you skin the cape free from the skull, turn the lips and cut away all additional flesh from the nostrils. The lips are actually muscle with skin on both sides. In order to allow salt to reach all parts of the skin, "split the lips." That is, cut between the cheek skin and the mouth skin. In this photo both the nostrils and the lips have been fully skinned out. *Right:* After removing the cape from the skull, split the lips so you can salt and cure them. Insert the tip of your knife or scalpel between the skin on the inside of the mouth and the outer lip skin. This splits the lips so they lie flat and allow salt penetration.

the back of the ear. Slowly work a flat, blunt instrument between the skin on the back of the ear and the cartilage in front. The best tools for opening the ear are a table or butter knife, a screwdriver, or a smooth flat stick. When the ear has been opened, it can be turned inside out quite easily. Trim the muscle of the ear butt away from the cartilage, which remains attached to the front ear skin. Put plenty of salt on the cartilage and ear skin before turning the ear right-side out.

Set the cape aside for a few minutes while you turn your attention to the antlers. These are removed from the skull by sawing off the crown of the skull. Saw through the middle of the eye sockets parallel with the bottom of the lower jaw. Remove the brains from the top of the skull crown, as well as the meat that is attached to the skull behind the antlers. Then salt the skull crown thoroughly.

Under no circumstances should the skull plate be cut in half and the antlers separated. This is because it may be difficult to mount

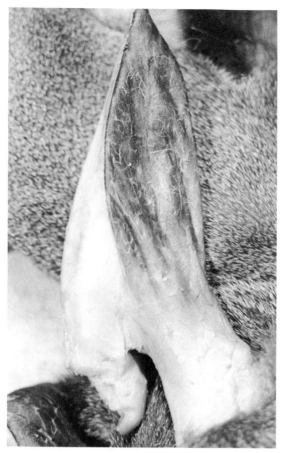

Use a small saw to remove the antler crown from the skull. Saw through the eye sockets parallel with the lower jaw. Never split the skull between the antlers.

Turn the ears completely inside out. This photo shows a completely turned ear with the cartilage on the left side and the darker-colored skin on the right. The cartilage is retained in the ear during the tanning process. If the ear is not turned, the hair will "slip"—fall out in large clumps, leaving bald spots on the skin.

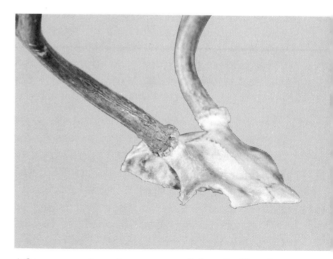

After removing the crown of the skull, trim all of the flesh from the bone and thoroughly salt the skull, inside and out. You can then set the antlers aside until you are ready to mount the trophy.

the two separated antlers at the proper angle. Besides, on potential record-book antlers, the Boone and Crockett Club will not accept antlers that have been separated.

Lay the cape flat, flesh-side up, and examine it thoroughly for additional tissue or fat that you have missed. After you have fleshed the cape clean, it is ready to be salted. Approximately 2 pounds of salt are needed for the average deer cape, and about 4 pounds are needed for caribou and elk. Spread the salt evenly over the entire fleshed surface with special attention to the lips, eyes, and nose. Be certain that there are no folds in the skin that are not salted, and you should put additional salt into the ears. Remember that you cannot use too much salt. Now fold the cape lengthwise and allow it to drain for 24 hours in a cool, shaded spot away from direct sunlight.

Most tanners recommend that non-iodized salt be used. For best results, buy salt in large quantities from your local feed and dairy supplier. Do not use one of the very coarse-grained types of ice cream salt because they will not dissolve properly.

The next day examine the cape to make certain that salt has been worked into the skin. Use additional salt if needed. Now lay the cape flat, flesh-side up, and allow the skin to dry; never expose the skin to direct sunlight or heat. When the cape begins to dry and stiffen, you can loosely fold it to convenient size, flesh-side out, for shipping, storage, or tanning.

Methods of tanning a deer cape are described in Chapter 4. Because it is seldom practical to tan a single deer cape in the home shop, I am assuming you will want to have capes commercially tanned until you have mastered the taxidermy techniques. Exper-

tise in tanning can be developed later. Normal turn around time for commercial tanning is three to six months. While a cape is at the tannery, you have an opportunity to order the proper headform and prepare it for mounting.

MOUNTING A DEER HEAD

While the cape is being tanned, obtain copies of various taxidermy supply catalogs and order the necessary supplies. You'll find a list of major supply companies in the Introduction of this book. In addition there are a number of smaller supply companies that specialize in headforms. Most of these companies advertise in the various taxidermy journals, also listed in the Introduction. In order to select the proper headform, review the measurements recorded at the time the buck was skinned. Compare these with the various sizes listed in the catalogs and select the form that best fits your particular buck. Remember, it is not the size of the antlers that makes a big buck. Headform size is based on the dimensions of the head and neck. If your measurements best fit a "medium" whitetail, order *that* form even though your hunting buddies may say that the buck is large to borderline huge.

Most headforms on the market are molded polyurethane, although a few are still available in laminated paper. The beginning taxidermist should order polyurethane because that is easier to work and modify. Also you will find that a variety of poses are available for the same size buck. These poses range from "sneak" to "upright" and come in a variety of turns. For your first mount, obtain an "upright, straight" headform. This is the most common pose and the most convenient to use. "Upright" means that the mount will have the head in a high, alert pose; "straight" means that the mount is facing straight ahead. You can learn to deal with turns and sneaks later.

For your first mount you will also need a pair of glass eyes and a pair of earliners. Most medium whitetail deer have a 26mm eye. Order a pair of these eyes from the supplier and also a pair of medium whitetail earliners. After a short time you will learn that there is a wide range in price of both of these items, depending on quality of the eye and composition of the earliners. Since your first few mounts are for practice, inexpensive eyes and earliners are adequate. Order several scalp needles also. These are heavy-duty surgical needles, three-cornered, that are best suited for sewing the cape. Although beginners often attempt to use heavy-duty sewing needles instead, they are much more difficult

to work with.

Richard Christoforo stresses the importance of good study material before you begin the mounting process. Obtain photos from outdoor magazines, posters, and various other sources. Death masks made from fresh kills are valuable; these can also be purchased from most supply companies. A fresh frozen deer head is extremely valuable. Review this material as much as possible, and then keep it handy during the mounting process.

Preparation of the Cape. When the tannery returns the cape, it will look similar to buckskin with the hair on. However, the cartilage in the ears and nose will be stiff and the cape itself will have very little stretch when dry. So you'll need to soak the cape in lukewarm water until it is soft enough to work.

Many tanneries will send you guidelines

Death masks and casts of recent kills are invaluable guides for mounting a game head. The four plaster casts at the right were made by Christoforo. The cast of the ear butt (left) is commercially available. Notice the anatomical differences between a whitetail nose/mouth (top center) and that of a pronghorn (lower left).

for soaking up the cape. Follow these instructions. Capes from different tanneries will soak differently. Some will soften quickly, while the ear cartilage remains very hard. Other capes may plump or swell up and hold a great deal of water in the skin. You want to avoid this. Generally, Christoforo soaks the cape until it is soft, squeezes out the extra water, and then rolls it up flesh-side in before storing the cape for about a day in the refrigerator. Once you have used a tannery a few times, you will know the best way to soak up their products. In general, for best results, follow the tannery's instructions.

Some people have a lot of trouble removing the cartilage from the ears. According to Christoforo, "The easiest method that I have found is to fold the ear cartilage in half and cut through the cartilage with a scalpel. Do not cut through the ear skin. Then begin peeling the cartilage away from the cut and free from the skin. Use a spray bottle of water to moisten the tissue, and this will allow the cartilage to peel easier from the ear skin. After a little experience, you will get the feel for how much you can pull without tearing the skin. When you get down to the base of the ear cartilage, you can score it and peel smaller pieces free. Don't worry about getting the cartilage out in one piece—that is both difficult and unnecessary. I prefer to use a blunt knife for peeling the cartilage because it is less likely to cut the thin ear skin."

You will need a small fleshing beam, as shown, to work around the nose, eyes, and lips. I use a tapered 1 × 4-inch piece of pine held to the edge of the workbench with a C-clamp. (A sanded 1-inch dowel also works well for this purpose.) Insert the fleshing beam through the nose and remove the cartilage. There is a small gland inside the nose which is represented by a small hole inside

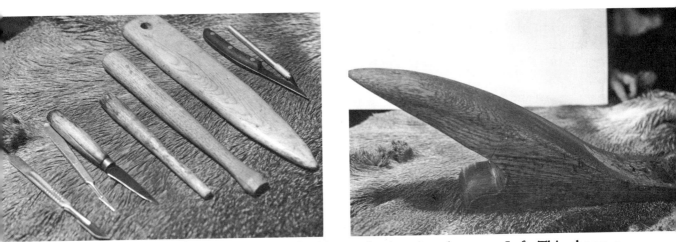

Christoforo uses a variety of tools for fleshing and trimming the cape. *Left:* **This shows a number of knives, scalpels, and fleshing beams. Each tool and beam is useful for fleshing a different part of the cape and face.** *Right:* **For much of the fleshing, Christoforo uses a carved mahogany beam, which is sturdy enough to clamp firmly to a workbench.**

the nostril. Be careful when skinning here. Keep the skin pulled tight against the fleshing beam and you will be less likely to cut the skin when removing the cartilage in the nose.

Around the lips, trim the skin thin and smooth. Split the eyelids in the same way that you split the lips. For the eyelid, you need about ⅛ to 3/16 inch of skin. The skin should be a little longer in the front of the eye than in the back. Now sew all of the small holes or damaged places with small, fine stitches.

The last step in cape preparation is a final washing. You will be amazed at the amount of dirt that can be washed from a freshly tanned cape. Wash the cape in a mild kitchen detergent, then rinse it thoroughly. At this point put the cape in the washing machine and run it through the spin cycle. The cape is now soft, clean, and ready for mounting. Set the cape aside in a plastic bag in the refrigerator, and then turn your attention to the form.

Preparation of the Headform. First attach the hanger. For an inexpensive hanger, drill two ⅞-inch holes into the top of the backboard of the headform. These should be about ⅝ inch deep and overlap one another. Then screw a flat corner iron (90°) with the point at the top. This will hold well for most deer heads. Various types and sizes of hangers also can be purchased from supply companies. Remember to put the hanger as high as possible on the backboard so that it will lower the center of gravity of the mount. This will prevent a heavy-antlered mount from tending to rotate on the wall.

The antlers should now be mounted on the form. Trim the skull plate to fit the shape of the form, then drill and countersink three or four holes in the top of the skull and into the headform. Screw the skull plate down loosely to allow use of small wedges of wood under the skull plate to obtain the proper angle, which you can determine from preliminary measurements "I" and "J," shown in the drawing on page 28, and that you made from the nose and mouth. Use potter's clay to model the final contour of the back of the head. (I describe potter's clay in greater detail in the upcoming text on face modeling.)

The headform can now be attached to your mounting stand or hung on the wall while it is being prepared. Using a small electric hand grinder tool or a rotary rasp that fits into a power drill, enlarge the nasal openings and the eye sockets. Christoforo advises, "In order to make the eye fit properly, it is necessary to grind out the eye socket of most headforms. I also make the socket deeper so that there is room for plenty of clay behind the eye."

Deepen the tear duct slot with a short-shafted screwdriver or with a knife. Also, use a heavy nail or other tool to punch a number of holes in the headform where the butt will attach. These will hold clay and give the ears a better bond with the form.

Grind out the nose slightly larger than shown in a death mask. This will give you enough opening to put a layer of clay into the nasal passage and anchor the nose skin. Shape the inside of the nose like a natural nasal passage, but slightly enlarged.

There are many ways to cut the lip slot. Christoforo describes his method this way: "I usually take a pencil and draw a line along the form where the lip slot will be cut. Use whatever tool works best for you in cutting

PREPARATION OF THE HEADFORM

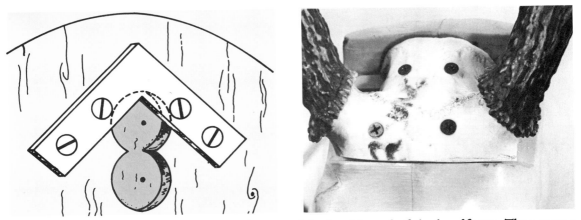

Left: Drill two overlapping holes into the top of the backboard of the headform. Then screw a 90° corner brace over the top of the upper hole. This will allow the head mount to hang flush against the wall, and this type of hanger has sufficient strength to support even the largest deer heads. If the hanger is placed too low on the headform, a heavy-antler deer head is likely to rotate or twist and fall. *Right:* The skull plate with antlers should be trimmed to fit the opening in the headform provided by the manufacturer. Countersink the holes so the screws will sit flush with the top of the skull; use wood shims to position the skull plate at the proper angle, indicated by measurements made before the skull plate was removed. The screws will anchor into the headblock of wood that is molded into the form. Use potter's clay to reshape the back of the head.

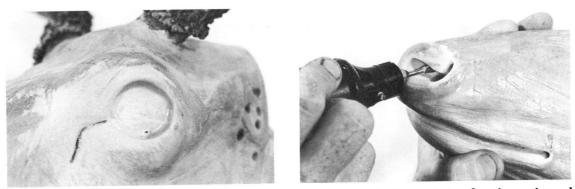

Most commercial headforms require some modifications. *Left:* Here Christoforo has enlarged the eye of a whitetail form from Buckeye Mannikins. As explained in text, he has also deepened and enlarged the tear duct gland and punched holes in the form where the clay of the ear butt will anchor. *Right:* An electric grinding tool, such a this one by Dremel, is useful in enlarging the nostril area. Do not deform the outside configuration of the form, but enlarge the nostril area so it will hold a bed of potter's clay and the skin of the nose.

(Continued)

(Headform Preparation continued)

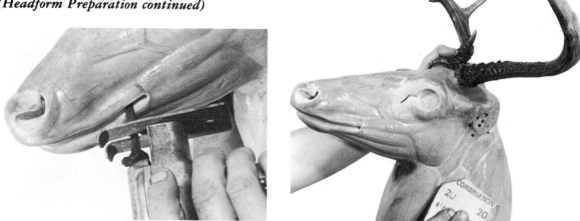

Left: After you draw a line to guide the cut, use a saber saw to cut the lip slot. Make the slot slightly larger at the back because more lip skin is present there. The cut should be just wide enough to still hold the lip skin tight. *Right:* To help the hide paste form a better bond between the form and the cape, use a 20-grit (coarse) sandpaper in roughing-up the surface. The sandpaper also removes any chemicals remaining on the form after manufacture.

the slot in the headform; my preference is a skill saw with a thin blade. Run the skill saw up into the upper jaw and cut along the line you have drawn. Make the cut slightly larger at the back where the corner of the mouth will be tucked in. Sand the mouth slot with sandpaper to give it a smoother finish. The density of the foam in the polyurethane form will have some bearing on the width of the lip slot. In general, the foam will have a little elasticity which will hold the skin once it is pushed into the slot."

Now rough-up the surface of the polyurethane form with coarse-grit sandpaper. Sand the surface of the entire form and be particularly thorough in the hollows of the form where drumming is likely to occur. (Drumming is caused by the contracting of skin, which then pulls away from a concave surface.) Look at the form from a few different angles and make any corrections needed. After you have sanded the form with

coarse sandpaper, apply a coat of orange shellac. This will result in a better bond with the hide paste.

Preliminary Modeling of the Face. Christoforo hangs the form on a wall so that the eyes can be set properly. He says, "The pupil of the eye should be parallel with the ground, regardless of the angle at which the head of the deer is held. So if you set the eyes while the form is on a mounting stand and not on the wall, it is possible that the angle of the pupils will be incorrect."

The eyes should be set at a 45-degree angle with the centerline of the headform and with the pupil parallel with the ground. Put a wad of potter's clay into the eye socket and set the glass eye in place. Use a template or compass to measure the 45-degree angle, and use a small hand level to align the pupil angle. Also, the top of the glass eye should be out slightly farther than the bottom—

MODELING THE FACE

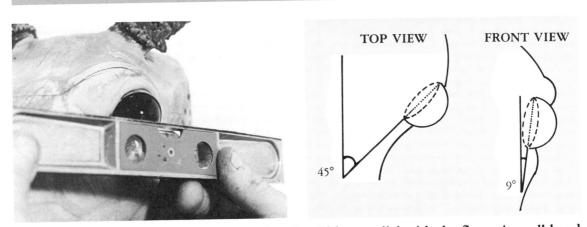

Left: The artificial eye has a blue pupil that should be parallel with the floor. A small hand level will assure that the pupil is set properly before clay is added around the edges to model the eye muscles. *Right:* In addition to the proper angle of the pupil, the glass eye itself must be positioned properly. The eye should be set at an angle of 45 degrees from the centerline of the nose. Measure this from directly above the head. The eye also angles slightly from vertical, with the upper edge of the eye set about 9 degrees out from the base of the eye.

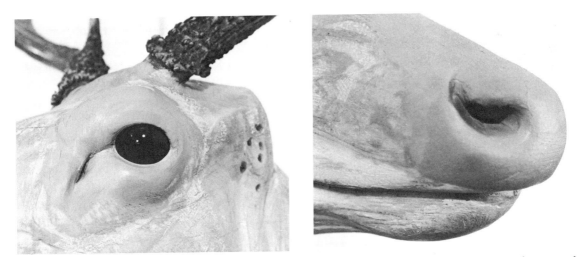

Left: After setting the glass eyes at the proper angles, use potter's clay to restore the muscle you removed from around the eye. Proper reference material is essential for shaping the eye. The eye of a whitetail is oval, with a slightly drooping eyelid at the back. *Right:* After you have enlarged the nostril of the form, as shown earlier, model clay into the nasal passage, forming the base for the nose skin, as shown here.

about 9 degrees or less. Using reference photos, model clay around the upper eyelid as needed. Good reference material is needed for setting the eye more than for any other aspect of head mounting. The finished eye should be oval with a slightly drooping upper lid at the back.

Potter's clay is the same material that is used in ceramics work; it is easy to model but dries hard in a permanent shape. Critter Clay, available from Aves Supply, Box 344, River Falls, Wisconsin 54022, was developed for the taxidermy trade, and probably is the best potter's clay available for taxidermy purposes.

"I like to put a little clay on the top of the tear duct," continues Christoforo. When mounting the cape, this clay will be worked into the duct and back to the eye. Put a very thin layer of clay on the nose, and work clay into the nostril. Put a thin roll of clay in the chin groove that you cut and a small amount of clay behind the back corner of the mouth so that the lips can be modeled better. Put a little clay around the base of each antler where shrinkage of the cape is likely to occur."

Now check the cape for a fit. The skin should fit properly around the nose and eyes. The cape should fit snugly around the back of the head and the neck. Be sure that there is sufficient cape to cover the shoulders and the brisket. When mounting a cape with short hair, you must be a lot more careful with the details that are modeled into the form with clay. Most of Christoforo's deer come from Maine where they have thick hair, so this detail is not as much a problem as it would be in the South or Southwest.

Mounting the Cape. Prepare the earliners

Richard Christoforo is shown making a final check of cape fit before beginning to mount the head. Notice that the eyes, nose, and mouth of the cape fit properly on the form, and that the cape is sufficently large to allow for sewing up the back.

now. Cut the earliners to shape according to the notes you made when the animal was fresh. Most of the commercial earliners today have some kind of release agent or film which must be removed so that the paste will hold. After the earliners have been cleaned and trimmed to shape, it may be necessary to thin down the edges if the liner is too thick. A small electric hand grinder works well for thinning plastic liners. Also, some of the plastic earliners on the market do not hold glue well, so it is necessary to punch holes through the plastic, giving the glue adequate purchase. Now insert the earliner into the skin and check for proper fit; trim as necessary and try again. It is best to work slowly, little by little, until you have the proper fit. When you are satisfied that the earliner has been cut and trimmed to the proper shape, put a small roll of clay into the tip of the ear skin.

Thicken some hide paste with plaster, whiting, or any other thickener, then add some glue to get additional bonding action. Paint a layer of glue on the earliner and slip it into place. As soon as the earliner has been inserted with glue, groom the ears with a comb or brush. This not only has a grooming action, it also presses the skin firmly to the earliner and allows you to see color patterns clearly and adjust them on the earliner while the paste is still soft. When you are satisfied that the ear looks correct, put a couple of staples in the base of the ear to hold the skin against the earliner and prevent the skin from slipping or drumming. (Again, drumming is caused by the contracting of skin that then pulls away from a concave surface.) Work the roll of clay in the ear tip to a smooth edge.

Before beginning to build up the ear butt, study your reference photos carefully. Put a ball of clay around the base of the earliner and inside the skin. The ear butt has definite muscles and a definite shape, so the more accurately it is modeled before you sew up the skin, the less problem you will have later. A study cast, such as those sold by Coombs Supply (shown on the next page) is valuable for reconstructing the ear butt. Work the clay up around the earliner, keeping in mind the desired position of the ears on the final mount. Groom the hair so you can see what the ear will look like. Most of the ear muscles are in the front of the ear, so there is not much more than cartilage in the back.

The ear butts can be modeled more accurately before the cape is fitted over the form. The table holds the weight of the cape so the ear butts can be modeled and shaped. And the ears are easier to look at and balance out while on the table. Very little then will

This profile of a live whitetail shows facial details, including cartilage buildup over the nose, as illustrated further on page 27. (Leonard Lee Rue III photo)

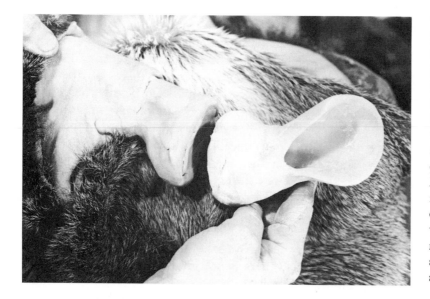

The earliners should now be inserted and trimmed for proper size and shape. Make certain that the earliners are not too large. Otherwise they will cause the ear skin to drum, wherein the contracting skin pulls away from the concave surface of the earliner, resulting in an unnaturally thick-looking ear. Model the ear butt with Critter Clay using reference materials such as this commercially-available ear butt.

Whitetail earliners from five suppliers (left to right): plastic from Jonas Bros., celastic from Bob's Supply in New York, molded plastic from Martinez, plastic from McKenzie, laminated paper from Roger Smith. The ear butts are partially or completely finished on all except McKenzie's. Commercial earliners must be trimmed to fit your mount.

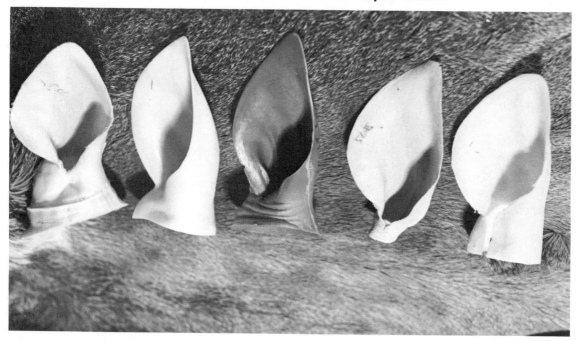

need to be done to the ears later.

Paint the form with hide paste. There are a lot of different pastes on the market, so experiment with these and find out which one you prefer. Many taxidermists have developed their own formula.

Double-check the cape. Make sure that the eyes, nose, and lips have been trimmed down properly and that all holes have been sewn. Rub some hide paste on the sewn areas of the cape. This is a double check to be sure that the sewn areas will stick well to the form. Get plenty of paste on the nose and the lips, and around the eyes.

Christoforo advises, "Slip the cape over the form and use a couple of pins near the back of the head to hold the cape in place. I usually tuck the lips in first. Tuck the top lip in first, and put a small roll of clay right at the front of the bottom lip so that it will be more full and won't have a shrunken appearance. Start pushing the lips into the slot at the front and work to the back of the mouth."

Examine the cape before cutting the slot because the lip slot in the form should be cut to the width of the lip skin. If the slot is too wide, the lips will not fit properly. If the lips are too thick for the slot that you cut, trim the skin a little or use scissors and cut the lumps off the lip skin. This should give you enough thinning to tuck the lips. Experience will teach you to cut the lip slot to fit each individual cape.

There is a natural groove in the center of the nose. Just touch this skin and press this groove into the clay film that you have put under the skin. When it dries, it will be natural looking. Tuck the nose skin into the clay-lined nasal cavities in the form. It may be necessary to trim some of the nostril skin

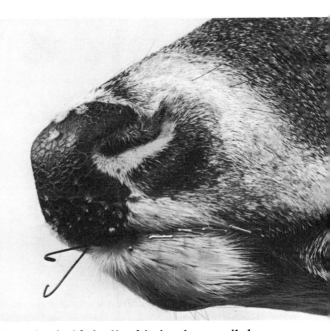

Here pins hold the lip skin in place until the hide paste has bonded properly. Pins have also been pushed deep into the nasal cavity. Instead, a small wad of foil or cotton can be pushed into the nose until the skin dries.

if you have too much remaining on the cape. The mount should now begin to take on some of its natural shape.

Now trim the eye skin as needed, leaving about ⅛ to 3/16 inch of skin around the eye. Tuck in the tear duct and temporarily pin or staple this skin into place. Then tuck the eye directly against the glass eye with the clay between the inner and outer skin around the eye. There is a crease over the upper eyelid that is apparent on the skin, so shape this in with a modeling tool. Put a fine pin or two (page 44) in the front of the eye; the back of the eye usually doesn't need any. In fact, sometimes pins aren't necessary if everything goes together properly.

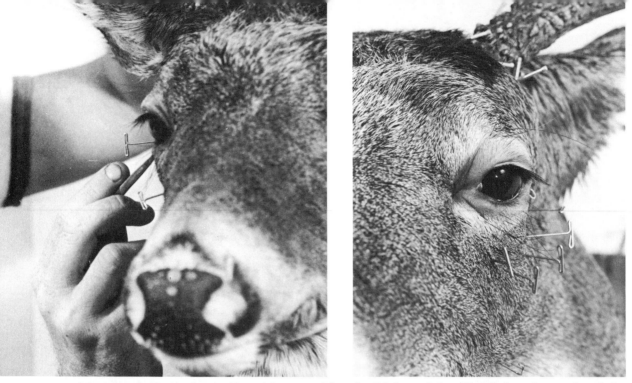

Left: Richard Christoforo adjusts the eye skin of a Maine whitetail. Notice the angle of the eyelid, which acts as a sun visor and dirt shield for the eye. Creases in the eyelids are pressed into the underlying clay base. The facial features should be checked daily for the first week to be certain that the cape is not shrinking away at the lips, nose, and eyes. If it is, reposition, glue, and pin it. *Right:* If you have properly sculpted the eye and used plenty of hide paste, few pins will be needed. Large pins below the eye hold the cape tight in the hollow below the zygomatic arch to prevent drumming of the skin across this hollow in the form. In this photo nails hold the cape around the base of the antlers while the cape dries.

The advantage of doing the facial work before sewing is that corrections can be made in the cape easier. You may even want to remove the cape to modify the cape or form. If it is sewn first, you have a major problem to correct. Worse yet, you may decide to continue mounting incorrectly rather than go to the trouble of cutting the stitching and doing a proper job.

Continue grooming with comb and brush throughout the mounting process. The hair should fall into its natural pattern. You will be able to distinguish the natural tufts and cowlicks from damaged areas.

As you are sewing, use a spatula or another tool to work some hide paste up under the seam. If you get some paste on the hair, use a spray bottle to wet the paste and then wipe it off with a damp rag.

In sewing the back of the neck, make the stitches about ¼ inch apart. Sew from the antler burr to the end of the Y-cut, then sew the other side beginning at the burr. Before starting to sew down the back of the neck, check the ear butts and make sure they have been properly modeled. If you need more clay, now is the time to put it into place. Make sure that all of the muscle is built up properly. There aren't many changes that can be made while working inside the ear because the earliner prevents it.

After the neck incision has been com-

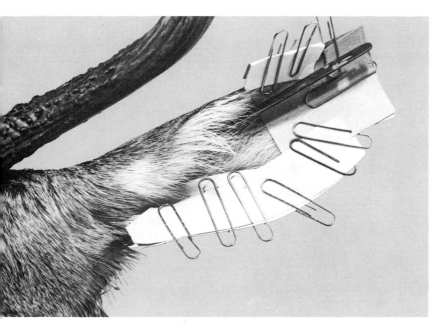

After mounting the ears, card them to retain the proper shape while drying. Pieces of cardboard and paper clips will prevent the ear skin from curling around the edge of the earliner. Notice the grooming of the hair on the ear. A large pin, as shown, or a knitting needle hold the ear at the proper angle while drying.

pletely sewn, Christoforo tacks the extra cape to the backboard with a Bostich T-22 air stapler that shoots a narrow-crown staple. Upholsterer's tacks or finishing nails also serve well.

Christoforo uses a hair-setting gel, Dryfast by Monique, and combs it into the hair of the finished mount. This grooms and sets the hair. When it dries, the hair will hold in place. (Dryfast concentrate can be purchased from a wholesale beauty supplier, but many other hair-sets will work equally well.) If you don't get the hair properly set while it is wet, you definitely won't get it set properly after it dries. So after applying the hair-set, card the ears and use gauze or other material to wrap the mount if necessary. Pin a strip of cardboard along the neck seam to hold the hair flat.

You may want to put a pin or two in the lower lip. Put these in the fleshy part; they can be removed when the mount is dry. The pinholes can be filled and then painted.

Sometimes when a mount dries, you will have an epidermis problem caused by the drumming action at the tannery. Seal around the eyes and any other place where there is exposed skin with a fungicide sealer from Master Paint Supply Company, PO Box 1320, Loganville, GA 30249.

Here are a few tips for finishing.

1. The more skin you use in the nose, the less repair and filler will be required. You may find that a piece of foil or cotton stuffed into the nostrils will hold the skin better while it is drying. Remove it after a day or two and make sure that the skin is drying properly. By this time the hide paste should hold the skin in place.

2. You can prevent some obvious shrinking by tacking the skin around the antler burrs. If you drill small holes before driving the nails, they will hold better and later can be driven all the way in after removal of the

heads. Also, be sure that you have plenty of hide paste around the antler burrs.

3. You might find that one pin in the tear duct will help to hold the skin. Check this every day and make sure that the duct is not opening up as it dries. Push down the clay around the tear duct.

4. Check the drying ears and make sure that the edges are aligned properly and not rolled over the earliners. Model in the muscles of the ear butt so that they blend smoothly with the form. A wire or knitting needle in long axis of the ear will hold it in position while drying (as shown on page 45). To paint the inside of the ear, taxidermists use an airbrush. But you could use an artist's brush, keeping the paint thin so it penetrates as a stain. If you use too much paint, the ear will look unnatural and shiny.

Finishing the Mounted Game. Be sure that the head is thoroughly dry. This will depend on the time of the year, amount of humidity, and many other factors that will vary throughout the country. As a general rule, you should wait at least two weeks.

First remove any carding on the ears or face and pull any pins that are exposed. If you plan to leave the nails at the base of the

The finished mount can be wrapped with cheesecloth to hold unruly hair in place, although this step is not always necessary. If you wrap the mount, do so while the hair is still wet. Various hair-setting agents can also be used to groom the hair. Small pieces of cardboard stapled in place will prevent drumming (unwanted pulling-away of skin from concave surfaces).

antlers, cut off the heads and drive the nails all the way to the skin. Now take a wire brush and groom the entire mount. Then, using a hair drier at *low* or *no-heat* setting, blow all of the dirt and dust off the mounted head. (Pros often use an air compressor.) Blow out the inside of the ears too.

Seal all of the exposed skin parts with Master Paint's fungicidal sealer. This should be applied on the nose and lower exposed lip, and around the eyes. Mix up a filler— Smooth-Out, Sculpall, mâché, etc.—so that it is nice and smooth. Use this to fill all of the hairline cracks on the exposed skin of the mount. Do the eyes first because the newly mixed filler is more workable at that time. Use a No. 2 or No. 4 red bristle brush to smooth the surface of the filler and around the eyes. Lacquer thinner or water can be used, depending on the filler you prefer.

Putty-in the nostrils and fill all of the pinholes with the same filler. Fill the bottom of the mounted ear with Smooth-Out or other filler. Let the filler dry overnight. Then give all of the skin parts, including the filler, another coat of fungicidal sealer.

The basic colors for finishing a whitetail deer are white, black, brown, and pink. Christoforo suggests that you first apply a little pink in the front corners of the eyes and a little in the nostrils. The next color applied is white. Strange as it may seem, give the skin of the nose a white shadow. Fade out the pink around the eyes and use white inside the ears to lighten the skin. Do this very lightly so that the paint doesn't look like wallpaper paste. Return to the pink and give each ear a few light pink highlights which should be most prominent in the deeper part of the ear.

Dip a No. 4 artist's brush into lacquer

thinner and clean any paint from the glass eyes. Also use the brush and lacquer thinner to remove any paint that might have been applied to the hair in the ears.

Now apply the brown paint around the eyes and add a few brown highlights in the ear where they belong. Sometimes the antler burr may have faded so paint this lightly with brown to restore the natural color. Shadow the skin on the nose with brown.

Mix up the black paint and color the skin of the nose until it looks neither black nor brown, but a charcoal brown. The part of the eyelid touching the eye is black as is the bottom lip.

Deer noses may be glossy or dull, so you can do whatever pleases you and your customers. Christoforo recommends a satin sheen gloss. The more that is applied, the glossier the nose becomes. Apply enough to get the desired effect, but try not to make the nose too glossy.

Finish the antlers with a mixture of equal parts of linseed oil and turpentine. This will clean the antlers and act as a sealer, preventing later drying and cracking, without giving a glossy appearance. If it is too sticky to suit you, use more turpentine. Never varnish or shellac the antlers because they will become unnaturally shiny.

Left: **Even though the forkhorns are small, this mount is a worthy one and shows the handsome, dark color patterns of a Maine whitetail. Richard Christoforo mounted the ears at a relaxed angle, allowing the antlers to appear as large as possible relative to the ears.** *Right:* **I mounted this Montana mule deer in an alert pose with a strong left turn using a Jonas Brothers Inc. headform. The mounting techniques are the same for different game species, but you must understand the anatomical peculiarities of each species.**

MISCELLANEOUS GAME-HEAD INFORMATION

Horned Game. Most people are aware of the differences between antlers and horns. Members of the deer family ranging from the smallest whitetail to the largest moose grow an antler rack each year. After the rut the antlers are shed. This is not true of horned game animals. The horns are composed of a central core of bone that grows outward from the skull. There is a thin layer of hair-covered skin that grows over the bone. A secretion from the skin bonds with hair to form the actual horn. Each year there is additional secretion and hair growth at the base, and this extends the horn length. You must understand this growth process in order to properly treat the horns of such trophies as sheep, goats, and pronghorn.

As explained in the earlier section describing the proper skinning techniques for whitetails, a blunt instrument is used to pry the skin of the head away from the antler burr. However, for horned game animals, this skin must actually be cut. Make the Y-cut to the base of each horn, then use a skinning knife to cut the cape away from the base of the horns. The rest of the skinning process is the same.

After the crown of the skull has been cut away from the rest of the skull, the horns should be boiled in clear water. Do not boil too long. Check periodically and pull the horn away from the skull plate. This may take only a few minutes for pronghorns and goats but considerably longer for sheep. After you have removed the horns from the bone core, set them aside to cool. When they are cool enough to handle, thoroughly salt all of the bone, skull plate, and horns on the inside. After the bone and horns have thoroughly cured and dried, brush off the excess salt from the horn core and the inside of the horn before spraying both with a strong insecticide. Then paint a coat of carpenter's glue on the bone core and slip the horn back into place. The horns are now ready to be attached to the headform using the same technique as described earlier for antlers.

A word of caution about preparing horns. Because of the porous nature of horn, it will readily absorb oil, which darkens the horn material. Never boil horns of sheep in a solution that has grease or fat in the water from a previous boiling. This will permanently discolor the horns, and discoloration can be disastrous on a sheep mount. Darkening is less critical for the black horns of African antelope, of goats, or of pronghorn. The grease problem can be avoided by using fresh water each time when boiling. Also, *do not* put any mixture such as linseed oil and turpentine on sheep horns.

Short-Neck Mounts. All of the discussion in this chapter has dealt with full-shoulder mounts. However, there are times when a full-shoulder mount is not possible, or in some cases undesirable. When a trophy has been cut too short for a full-shoulder mount, it is still possible to mount the neck and head. After the tanned cape has been returned from the tannery, measure the length of the neck skin available and modify the headform. This is done by sawing off the shoulders of the headform at the proper length. Then cut a new backboard from a piece of 1-inch plywood to the shape of the end of the neck. Using carpenter's cement or carpenter's glue, attach the new backboard to the end of the headform. After the glue

Horned game animals are mounted in the same way as deer, except that the horns require special attention. The horns must be boiled so that the horn shell can be removed from the bone core. After the bone has been cleaned and protected with insecticide, the horn shell is glued back into place. The massive horns of my desert bighorn ram weighed 35 pounds. And the finished mount required two-point attachment to the wall to prevent the head from rotating.

has set, attach the hanger, and the form is ready for mounting.

There are occasions when a neck mount is more attractive than a full-shoulder mount. A trophy with a small rack may look more balanced if mounted with neck only and not the shoulders. Examples of this would be a spike bull elk or a cow caribou with small antlers. In these cases the massiveness of the head and shoulders could make the antlers look disappointingly small to people accustomed to seeing larger racks.

CARE OF MOUNTED GAME HEADS

The care of a mounted game head does not end when the head has been hung on the wall. Continued care is necessary to maintain its beauty over the years.

When properly used, a vacuum cleaner is the most efficient tool for cleaning game heads and big-game trophies of all kinds. Short-haired species such as deer, sheep, pronghorn, and caribou should be vacuumed using the furniture attachments. Always move the vacuum in the direction in which the hair lies. After the hair has been thoroughly cleaned, remove the attachment and carefully vacuum the eyes, ears, and nose. Remember that the short mane on a pronghorn and some African specimens should stand up.

Long-haired species such as goat, bear, and wolf may be vacuumed *against* the hair, reversing the direction in the final pass to lay the hair down properly. A coarse-tooth

Christoforo preferred a neck mount for this cow caribou so that the otherwise massive shoulders would not dwarf the small antler rack. The same pose can also be used effectively with spike elk or any large animal with a small rack.

comb will help to fluff the hair before vacuuming. This method may be used whether the long-haired trophy is a head mount, life-size mount, or rug.

Clean the eyes with a soft, lint-free cloth, being careful not to apply so much pressure that you disturb the eye.

If the trophy was properly mounted and has received adequate care, the eyes and nose should not require additional care. Occasionally hairline cracks may develop from shrinkage and should be repaired. If the cracks are very obvious, use potter's clay or auto-body putty to fill the cracks. When this has dried, restore the colors using Richard Christoforo's methods described on pages 47 and 48 for deer heads.

The headgear of trophies needs little attention. Antlers (deer family) may be brightened up with a light coat of furniture polish, but nothing else should be applied to the antlers. Since sheep horns will absorb polish or wax, simply wash them with warm water. Some hunters prefer to have the horns of pronghorn and goats darkened with black paint. If this needs a second coat, be certain that "flat" or "semi-gloss" is used.

3 MOUNTING ANIMALS LIFE-SIZE

$\mathbf{T}$his chapter covers the mounting of small game, medium-size game, and big game. Here, I explain most of the techniques for the mounting of game of any size, using a medium-size animal—a coyote—as my subject. Once you have mastered the techniques for mounting a coyote, you will find that a life-size deer or brown bear is no more difficult, except that larger animals are heavier and require a lot more sewing.

Small mammals are among the most challenging subjects. In fact, many professional taxidermists refuse to mount animals as small as squirrels and weasels. Even the cost of a professionally mounted fox may be shocking. The reason is simple: The detail required to make a small mammal appear lifelike may be more trouble than the professional can recoup in his fees. In other words, the professional can make more money mounting deer heads than mounting squirrels because they take about the same amount of time—when properly done.

Yet you should not avoid mounting small mammals. Although not as impressive as a big-game head, a mounted squirrel is a pleasing trophy that can be proudly displayed anywhere. In fact, squirrels are ideal for beginning taxidermists. Squirrels are

A squirrel is an ideal animal for the beginning taxidermist. Besides being commonly available, squirrels are large enough to grip easily. Also, relative to the skin of rabbits or other small animals, squirrels have very strong skin that does not damage easily. This fox squirrel won a blue ribbon for William Crawford of Transfer, Pennsylvania, at a National Taxidermist Association competition.

abundant throughout most of North America and the hunting seasons for them are long enough to allow your taking several for practice. Also, squirrels have tough skin, which is helpful to the beginner using a scalpel for the first time. By contrast, rabbits have tissue-thin skin, causing difficulties for even the most skilled taxidermists. In addition, small mammals such as squirrels offer a means of improving your skill as a taxidermist without danger of ruining a once-in-a-lifetime big-game mount.

DISEASE HAZARD

Caution: Small mammals frequently are carriers of disease that can be transmitted to you by handling them. This is not the case for big-game mammals, birds, or fish. So taxidermists should practice normal hygiene and use caution in handling certain game animals. Since most infected animals die quickly in the field, they are not usually bagged by hunters. However, if there is ever any question about the health of an animal, *DON'T TOUCH IT!*

Many furbearers are hosts to fleas and ticks. Fleas are carriers of bubonic plague in the Southwest. Ticks can transmit spotted fever and Lyme disease. In the case of animals hunted in cold weather, these insects usually have been killed by cold temperatures. But, animals that are found dead or are taken in warmer seasons can be trouble.

Rabies, tularemia, and leprosy are three other diseases often associated with animals. Skunks and foxes frequently carry rabies, but fortunately the disease kills fairly quickly in nature. So an animal that appears healthy when bagged is probably not infected. The same is true of tularemia, or rabbit fever. Leprosy has been a dreaded disease since Biblical times and has recently been found in the Texas nine-banded armadillo. Since little is known of leprosy, it is best to avoid all contact with the armadillo.

Some taxidermists use rubber gloves when skinning small mammals, but this may instill a false sense of security. Again, if there is any doubt about the health of an animal, you should get rid of it.

Odor. This caution also may save you and your family some grief. All of the members of the Mustelidae family have scent glands at the base of their tail. This family includes skunk, weasel, ferret, mink, marten, wolverine, badger, and otter. It is doubtful that any would-be taxidermist would consider skinning a skunk indoors. But some reportedly have attempted skinning badger and mink in an enclosed room with poor ventilation, with resultant marital strife!

POSES AND ANATOMY OF MAMMALS

Selecting the proper pose for a mammal is essential. Although most mammals are primarily land dwellers, you should know the habitat and the pose characteristics of the animals you mount. For example, a squirrel can be posed sitting on a limb or on the ground, but a limb is probably more characteristic and interesting. On the other hand, a coyote usually has his feet on the ground and probably should be mounted that way. Of course, a coyote may occasionally cross a

log. But the better taxidermists try to reproduce wildlife accurately and in its most common poses—not the anomalies.

Most taxidermists keep a scrapbook of animal photos clipped from outdoor magazines. These photos of various animals and birds are invaluable when posing an animal. The beginning taxidermist should start a photo collection as soon as possible. In preparation for mounting a squirrel, assemble as many good photos as possible. Then select a pose that is both pleasing and realistic. Now pick up the squirrel and manipulate it into the desired position. If the body moves smoothly into position, you probably have a natural pose. But, if there is some resistance from the bones and muscles, they are telling you that the pose is unnatural.

Select your base (perch) at this time. Assuming that you plan to mount the squirrel on a stump or a limb, use a real one. Since the size and shape of the limb will affect the pose, it is important to have the base on hand early. To give yourself a stable base during the mounting, you can temporarily attach the limb to a flat piece of wood. Later, you can replace the temporary base with a finished panel. If the limb mount is to be hung directly on the wall, you can replace the wood piece with a wall hook. If you want a flat base simulating ground, a temporary flat base or single board will be sufficient during the mounting. Remember, once the glue dries, holding the skin of your animal to its body form, you cannot change its position. So whenever possible, begin the fresh mounting on the desired finished base.

Studying the anatomy of a mammal is an ongoing process that should begin before hunting and continue through the field-dressing and skinning. Before skinning, hold the animal in the desired pose and note the shape of the muscles, the angle of the head, and the position of the legs. Examine the mouth closely to see how the teeth are exposed behind the lips. Notice how the stomach sags as the angle of the body changes from a walking position to a sitting position. Note that the muscles flex when a leg is extended or contracted. Record any information about the anatomy that will be helpful in reproducing the natural shape and character of the squirrel. If you have photo equipment, take some close-up shots of the head from front and side in order to have a record of the positions of the ears, eyes, and mouth.

Remember, in humans, as well as animals, the skeleton provides the structural frame which is then moved by the muscles. So any change in pose means a change in muscles. In short, the more you learn about mammalian anatomy, the better your chances of creating a lifelike final mount.

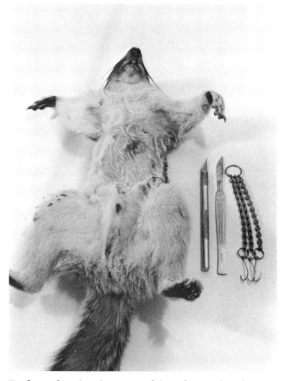

Before beginning to skin the animal, examine it closely and make notes of the anatomy and other physical features. Note the shape of the legs, the exposure of the teeth, the color of the eyes, and any other characteristics that will help you later achieve a more lifelike mount. In order to skin the animal, you will need an X-acto knife, a scalpel, or a sharp pocketknife. The hooks and chains simplify the skinning process but are not essential. You can obtain them from a taxidermy supply company.

SKINNING A SMALL MAMMAL

The Incision. Stuff a cotton ball or other absorbent material inside the throat and the anus of the animal. This will prevent blood and other body fluids from soiling the skin during the skinning process.

The ventral incision is most commonly used for skinning a small mammal. This incision begins at the center of the chest, continues down the abdomen, and stops at the anus. In your first few attempts at mounting a squirrel, you may want to begin this incision at the base of the neck. Such a long incision will simplify both the skinning and mounting process, and it requires only

a few more stitches to close. As your skinning and mounting techniques improve, you can begin using a shorter incision. The incision can be made using a sharp pocketknife and a single-edge razor blade or a scalpel.

Begin where the ribs will prevent you from cutting too deep. Peel the skin back from

VENTRAL INCISION

DORSAL INCISION

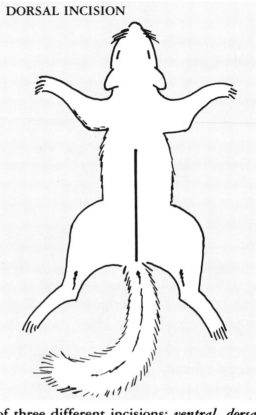

Small mammals can be skinned using any one of three different incisions: *ventral, dorsal, or cased.* Each has its advantages and disadvantages. The pose you select for the final mount will determine the type of incision. Be sure to make the incision long enough for easy skinning. As you become more proficient, you will be able to shorten the length of the incision. Your first mounts should utilize the ventral (belly) incision because it is the easiest to work with. The dorsal incision along the back might be used when you want to avoid the musk gland of skunk. The cased incision, which was originally developed by trappers, is easy to conceal but difficult to work with.

CASED INCISION

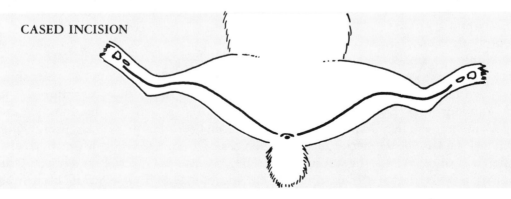

the incision and notice that the skin is somewhat bluish-white; whereas the underlying muscles are dark red. As the incision is extended downward across the abdomen, avoid cutting through the abdominal wall and into the intestinal cavity. Simply make the incision deep enough to cut the skin but not the dark muscles of the abdomen. Stop the incision at the anus.

Two other incisions are sometimes used by the taxidermist for skinning a small animal. The dorsal incision is made along the center of the back from the shoulders to the base of the tail. This incision is used when the stomach hair is very short and the ventral incision would be difficult to conceal. You can also employ the dorsal incision when you are using a one-piece artificial body.

Some taxidermists prefer to "case" the skin with the same incision used by trappers. This incision extends from the pad of one hind foot, inside the back leg to the anus, and out to the other hind foot. When a small animal is mounted sitting on its hind legs, the case incision is almost impossible to see. However, some artificial bodies are difficult to insert and wire through this leg incision. Experience will teach you that each incision has its own advantages and disadvantages, depending on such factors as pose and type of artificial body.

Skinning the Body. After you make the incision, separate the skin from the body along one side of the cut. You will need to use the scalpel or a scissors occasionally to cut the tissue that connects the skin to the body. Work the skin free around the lower abdomen until you reach the attachment of the hind leg with the body at the hip joint. Now using a scalpel or knife, cut the flesh at the hip, and pop the leg bone out of the

hip socket. Then continue cutting around the upper part of the hind leg until it is free from the body. Repeat this process on the other hind leg.

After you have severed both hind legs from the body, skin under the anus to the base of the tail. Work your fingers under the skin of the lower back so that the base of the tail is completely exposed. With a knife or even a wire cutter, cut the tail free from the body, leaving the tailbone in the skin.

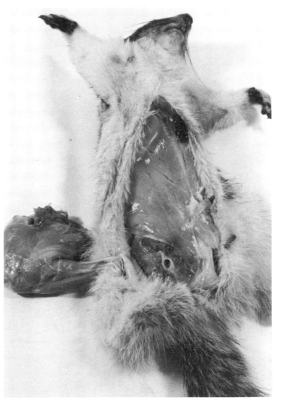

After making the incision, work your fingers under the skin and cut any tissue that holds the skin to the abdomen. When you reach the rear leg, work the skin loose from around the upper part of the leg and cut the leg muscles from the body. Notice here that the hip socket is exposed and the leg is free.

Left: Working slowly and carefully, cut both legs and the tail free from the body. The legs and tail will remain attached to the body skin until the skinning is completed. The bones of the legs remain attached to the skin at the feet throughout the mounting process. *Right:* Skinning of the body, front legs, and head is most convenient when you hang the animal from hooks and chain. Yet a stout piece of twine will work just as well for your first attempts at skinning a small mammal. Work slowly, cutting the tissue between the body and skin with a scalpel or scissors. When skinning the head, be careful not to damage ears, eyes, and lips. After completing the skinning, skin close to the skull to remove extra flesh.

With the hind legs and tail detached from the body, you'll find it most convenient to hang the carcass to continue the skinning. Most supply companies sell "hooks and chains" for this purpose, but a length of stout cord will serve the purpose. With the animal hanging, gradually work the skin down over the body and the front legs. Sever the front legs from the body at the shoulders, and continue skinning down the neck to the base of the skull. When you have skinned to the base of the ears, cut against the skull through the muscles at the base of the ears. After you have cut through the ear canal, continue skinning until you reach the eyes. Again cut close to the skull, being careful not to cut the eyelids. Then continue skinning past the cheeks by cutting the lips free from the skull along the jaw line. When you reach the nose, cut through the cartilage. The skin will now be free from the carcass.

During the skinning process, you will notice that there are body fluids and blood that must be absorbed. Wipe these away with rags or paper towels. However, the skin will be easier to handle if you apply powdered borax as the skinning progresses. Borax is the most common preservative used in taxidermy. This dry powder is available from all taxidermy suppliers. It is also sold in supermarkets under the trade name of 20 Mule Team Borax. The borax will begin preserving the skin immediately, and it will simplify the skinning process. If the squirrel is fresh and you want to eat the meat, use corn meal instead of borax as the absorbent substance.

Skinning the Legs and Tail. Now skin the legs and tail. Simply work the skin down each leg by turning the leg skin inside out. This is simplified if you hang the animal from the hooks and chains. Skin the legs all the way to the last joint of the toes; that last joint remains in the foot. Since the toenail or claw is attached to this last bone in the toe, it should remain in place. Otherwise the claws will fall out. The small amount of flesh in this last joint will later be penetrated by preservatives from the outside; whereas salt will be applied to the remainder of the skin on the inside. Skinning the feet and toes is both slow and tedious, but it is the only way to properly remove the flesh in the feet and to preserve the skin.

Begin skinning the tail the same way you skinned the legs. After you have exposed an inch or two of the tailbone, firmly grip the root of the tail in a vise or pliers and slowly work the skin off the tail. If the tailbone pulls apart, you may need to split the skin sufficiently enough to expose more of the bone. Gradually the bone will slip out of the tail skin. You will be surprised how firmly the skin is attached to the tail, so be patient and work slowly. Removing the tail is probably the most difficult part of skinning a mammal. For larger animals such as fox and coyote, it is more practical simply to make an incision the length of the tail and remove the bone that way. Also a split tail is easier to preserve, but this is not necessary for a squirrel or other small mammal.

The skinning process is now complete. You have removed the body with attached head, and you have also completely skinned the tail. The skin of the squirrel now contains only the leg bones, with the meat left on the bones.

Tracings, Sketches and Measurements. If you are a beginning taxidermist, you should make the artificial body as soon as you have completed the skinning. With the natural body on hand, you'll have an easier time constructing an accurate artificial body. However, it is not always practical to construct the body at this time, so it is a good practice to make tracings and sketches and to take measurements on all of the small mammals you skin. These drawings provide an accurate record of the various animals, and they help you develop an understanding of animal anatomy.

Lay the body on a piece of paper, and position it in the pose that you have already selected. Then trace an accurate outline of the body and head. Set the body aside and draw in additional body features, such as the shape of the skull, and the shape and position

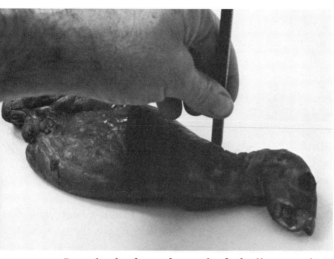

Lay the body and attached skull on a piece of paper and draw an outline of the carcass. You will need this outline and additional measurements to make the artificial body.

of the rib cage. Make note of the position at which each of the legs was attached. Also make notes on the size and color of the eyes. Some taxidermists also list the sex and the date of kill. All of this information may be useful later.

Now, setting the body aside, lay the skin on the paper and draw the outline of each of the legs. As you shape the legs in the position to be mounted, you will see that the thickness and length of each muscle changes as the position is changed. It is also helpful to note the thickness of the legs in various positions. Since the meat will be stripped from the bones, your only reference material will be your own notes. Better that your notes are too complete than too brief. Also draw an outline of the tail.

Two measurements should be recorded on the paper with your sketches. These are:

1. Length of the body from the tip of the nose to the base of the tail

2. Girth at largest circumference of body.

You will need the above measurements to obtain an accurate artificial body, whether you produce your own or purchase one from a supply company.

Fleshing and Cleaning the Skin. After you have made all of the sketches and measurements, strip the muscles and tendons off the leg bones. Leave sufficient ligaments in each joint so that the bones remain connected to one another. Open up the ear by slowly working the top end of an artist's brush between the ear cartilage and the skin on the back of the ear. Remove any attached muscle around the eyes and the base of the ears and nose. Split the lips by separating the skin inside the mouth from the outer lip skin Then lay the skin over a small bench-fleshing beam and cut away any other muscle or fat that adheres to the skin. Remove any remaining muscle from the leg bones.

Now cut the head away from the body so you can clean the skull. Using a sharp knife or scalpel, cut the jaw muscles away from the back of the skull. Cutting inside the lower jaw, you will be able to remove the throat muscles and tongue. Remove the eyes and any muscle in the socket. With snips or wire cutters, enlarge the opening at the back of the skull where the neck was attached. Then scoop out the brains with a brain spoon or forceps, both of which can be obtained from taxidermy suppliers. Or you can make an effective brain spoon by flattening the larger end of a crocheting needle; this leaves the hook for additional scraping.

The skin and skull are now ready for cleaning. In a wash basin or bowl, mix several quarts of cold water with a mild detergent,

Draw outlines of the legs in the position of the final mount. Make notes of the sizes and shapes of the upper and lower legs, front and rear. Since you will remove the muscle from the leg bones before mounting, these drawings will be your only references.

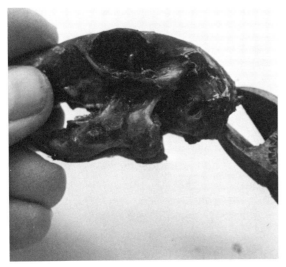

Clean the skull of all flesh. Most of the muscle is attached to the jaws, throat, and tongue. Also remove the eyes after you have recorded the diameter, in millimeters, and the color. The back of the skull can be opened with snips, allowing you to scrape the brains out of the skull cavity.

and wash the skin and the skull. This will remove any dirt or remaining blood, as well as any grease on the skin. Do not use warm water because this will set the blood and create a permanent stain. When the skin is clean, rinse it thoroughly to remove any soap. Then gently squeeze the skin to remove the bulk of the water.

PRESERVING AND MOTHPROOFING THE SKIN

In Chapter 2, I explained the importance of tanning a deer cape. Tanning not only preserves the cape; tanning also oils the skin, keeping it soft and preventing shrinkage. However, since the skin of a squirrel is quite thin in relation to that of a deer, there is much less need to tan or oil the skin. In fact, most taxidermists find that the time and expense of tanning small skins is not

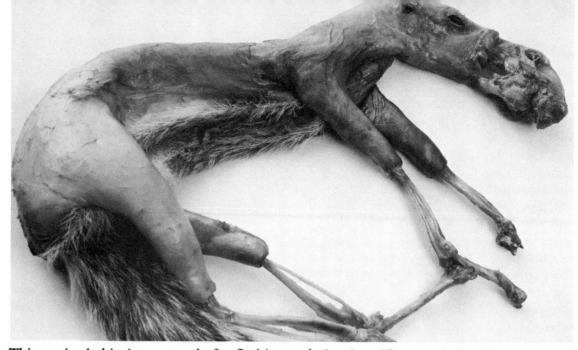

This squirrel skin is now ready for fleshing and cleaning. The muscle has been removed from the legs, but the bones remain attached at the foot. The skull has also been cleaned. Note that the bone from the left upper foreleg was destroyed when the squirrel was bagged. Such a missing bone can be replaced with a sliver of wood or a short length of wire. In this case, use the opposite bone as a guide for size. For taxidermists, missing or damaged leg bones are a common challenge.

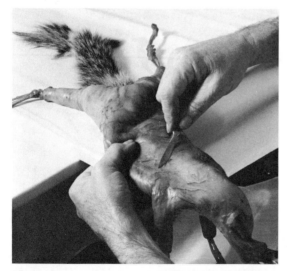

Here I'm using a small fleshing beam to scrape the skin before preserving it. All fat and tissue remaining on the skin must be removed at this time. The ears should be turned and the lips and nose fleshed.

justified, except in special cases. Nevertheless, it is important to preserve and mothproof the skin in order to produce a long-lasting mount.

Degreasing the Skin. Some species of small mammals are almost always very fat and greasy. These include raccoons, opossums, beavers, and skunks, just to mention a few. To ensure that the preservatives penetrate the actual skin, you must degrease the skin as soon as you complete the skinning.

First, split the tail skin by making an incision the length of it. Now turn the rest of the skin inside out, including the legs all the way to the toes. Place the skin on a piece of newspaper and thoroughly rub the skin with powdered borax. Rub the borax into the fat and over the entire skin. Also be sure to work it into the ears, nose, and lips. Treat the skull in the same manner. Now put the skin and skull in a plastic bag and store them in a freezer for a couple of days.

After a minimum of 48 hours, remove the skin and skull from the freezer and allow them to thaw. When the skin is soft, you will find that the fat on the skin has "set" and that the skin is no longer as greasy as when it was fresh. Using a small fleshing beam, scrape all of the fat from the skin. Go over the entire skin thoroughly, including the tail, and be sure that you have removed all of the fat. Pour about a quart of white gasoline, Coleman fuel, or commercial degreasing agent into a plastic container and soak the skin for an hour or two. (Since degreasing agents are usually flammable, be sure that you perform this operation outside and away from open flame.) Then remove the skin, squeeze out the extra solvent, and wash the skin in cool, soapy water. The skin is now ready to be mothproofed and preserved.

Preserving the Skin. Regardless of whether you have gone through the degreasing process, you have now washed and rinsed the skin and squeezed excess moisture from it. Now turn the skin inside out, being sure that the leg bones are exposed all the way to the toes. Salt the skin with non-iodized pickling or curing salt. This salt is slightly coarser than regular table salt. It can be purchased at the supermarket in 5-pound bags at a much lower cost than table salt. Be sure that you work the salt into the tail, ears, nose, and toes. Next turn the skin right-side out.

Salt is one of the best preservatives known. The damp, salted skin can be sealed in a plastic bag and stored in a freezer, or the salted skin can be allowed to thoroughly dry for a week or more in the air, then stored in a sealed plastic bag.

A salted skin can last indefinitely, except that it is not mothproofed, and it may be

Left: After you have fleshed the skin, salt it and allow it to cure. Work non-iodized salt into all parts of the skin, paying particular attention to the head and face, the feet, and the tail. Pickling and canning salt can be obtained at a small cost from a supermarket. Yet, even though salt is one of the oldest and best preservatives, it will not protect the skin against insects. *Right:* After being cured with salt, the skin and skull must be preserved in a formalin-borax solution. Mix these ingredients with lukewarm water in a plastic or ceramic container. This solution will not weaken with use. You can reuse it until it gets dirty.

attacked by bugs. So in most cases, you should continue to the next step in preserving the skin.

The borax-formalin solution is a safe, inexpensive method of preserving the skin— beyond the use of salt. Although 20 Mule Team Borax can be obtained at the supermarket, it is not as fine-grained as the borax sold by taxidermy supply companies. Borax should be one of the first items that you purchase. You can obtain formalin from a taxidermy supply company, but many druggists carry it too. Formalin is the commercial name for a formaldehyde solution. In most cases this will be 37 to 45 percent formaldehyde. Since this is a very strong preserving agent, the actual percentage is not important because only a small amount is needed.

Your druggist can also supply hypodermic syringes in various sizes. These are very useful in measuring small quantities of solutions, such as formalin. Syringes are graduated in cubic centimeters (cc), and 30cc equals 1 ounce. Another readily available measuring device is the standard shot glass which holds 1½ ounces.

To mix the borax-formalin solution, pour 2 quarts of lukewarm water into a plastic or glass bowl. Then sprinkle in a handful or more of borax and stir. When the borax will no longer dissolve, the solution is saturated. Then add 1 ounce of formalin and stir the solution. When the solution has cooled to the touch, put the squirrel skin in the solution. Be sure that you cover the entire skin. Although the skin will be thoroughly preserved in an hour or two, you can leave the skin in the solution overnight if you like.

Some taxidermists prefer the extra step of preserving the skin in alcohol. This is done after the skin has soaked in the borax-formalin solution. Although grain alcohol is preferred, denatured alcohol sold as shellac thinner is less expensive and works well. Simply rinse off the borax-formalin solution, squeeze the skin to remove extra solution, and soak the skin in the alcohol for an hour or two. Then remove the skin and rinse it thoroughly.

Mothproofing and Tanning Creams. Edolan U is a strong, safe mothproofing agent. It is available from most taxidermy supply companies, but it may be marketed under a trade name such as Moth Magic. Pour about 2 quarts of water into a plastic or glass container and add about 10cc of Edolan U. Ideally the amount of Edolan U should be based on the weight of the skin. Follow the directions obtained with the Edolan U. Using too much will result in a coating on the hair and skin making the hair impossible to fluff. If this happens, add more water to dilute the solution.

The Edolan U bonds to the skin and fur of the skin. Consequently this solution will gradually become depleted and must be replaced. However, the borax-formalin solution and alcohol retain their strength and may be used repeatedly.

The use of tanning creams is optional on small animal skins. Although called "tanning" creams, they do not actually tan the skin. Rather they are oil-based preservatives that can be worked into the skin, which then remains relatively soft and will not shrink as much as a dry skin. These creams are usually applied warm to the flesh side of the skin. After the skin has set for a few hours, you should massage and knead it with your hands, working the oils well into the fiber of the skin.

Now that you have degreased, preserved,

and mothproofed the skin, it is ready for mounting. However, if you prefer to delay the actual mounting, put the skin into a sealed plastic bag and store until later. If the skin is to be mounted within the next day or two, store it in the refrigerator. But if you anticipate more than a couple days of delay, freeze the skin.

PREPARING SKULL AND FEET

After skinning, only the leg bones were still attached to the skin at the feet. The skull was cut from the carcass and cleaned of all muscle, brains, and tongue. Since the leg bones and skull were included in all of the processes that preserved the skin, these bones are now preserved. Nevertheless, you must go over the skull carefully again, scraping away any remaining flesh. Double-check the brain cavity and the eye sockets for muscle that can be removed. When you are satisfied that you have scraped all of the meat from the skull, dust the skull thoroughly with borax.

Now you should attach a wire to the skull so that the skull can be anchored to an artificial body. Purchase a small can of any auto-body putty from your local automotive supply store. A pint container will last a long time. Cut a piece of wire 6 to 8 inches long, and bend a tight loop at one end. (Galvanized, annealed wire is best, but coathanger wire will work too.) The loop should be small enough to fit into the brain cavity. Cut a sharp point on the other end of the wire with snips; then file it sharp. Mix about 1 tablespoon of auto-body putty with hardener, according to the instructions on the container, and use a scrap of wood to force

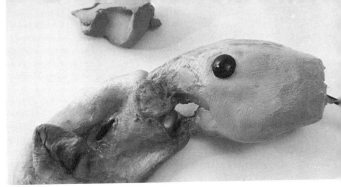

To prepare the skull for attachment to the artificial body, anchor a wire in the skull cavity with auto-body putty, as described in accompanying text. Then use potter's clay to sculpt simulated skull muscles. When modeling these muscles, use your sketches and measurements made on the original head after skinning. At this point, you can set the glass eyes. On the head skin itself, at left, notice that the ears have been skinned and turned in the same way that the ears of a big-game head are turned. An earliner of soft lead sheeting, aluminum, or cardboard can then be glued into place.

This skin is ready for mounting. The skull has been sculpted with clay, and the skin has been fleshed and preserved. A final dusting of borax readies the skin for mounting. At this time the skin can be frozen for mounting at a later date. Yet when possible with a fresh skin, it is best to continue through the complete mounting process.

the bondo into the brain cavity. After you have filled the brain cavity, insert the wire loop. Then prop up the pointed end of the wire so that it extends straight out from the back of the skull.

When the bondo has set, in about 15 or 20 minutes, double-check the leg bones to be certain that they have been thoroughly cleaned of all extra muscle. Be careful not to remove the cartilage in the joints. The bones of the legs should remain connected to each other but free of any remaining muscle. Also scrape away any fat that remains inside the skin on the pads of the feet.

THE ARTIFICIAL BODY

When mounting a small mammal such as a squirrel, you have several artificial-body options. The most commonly used body is that created by the taxidermist himself—of excelsior, sometimes called "wood wool." This is the same material used by upholsterers for the stuffing of furniture. As a second option, some taxidermists actually stuff the skin with sawdust or other materials. Third, many taxidermists prefer to buy precast bodies.

Although each body option has advantages and disadvantages, if you are a beginner, you should probably start with excelsior. Yet, in time, you should eventually experiment with the precast bodies before deciding which option you ultimately prefer.

The taxidermist creates the wrapped excelsior body, while referring to tracings, sketches, and measurements made while using the actual body of the animal whose skin will be mounted. Thus, in skilled hands, the wrapped body can closely match, like hand and glove, the skin you prepared. The excelsior body is practical for any size animal

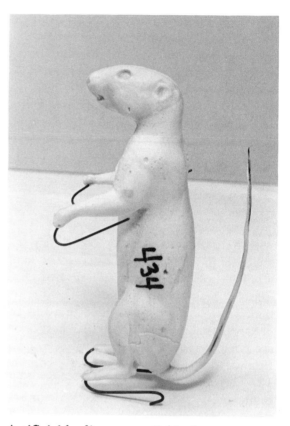

Artificial bodies are available for most common North American animals. Shown here is a "flexiform" squirrel body modeled by Leroy Martinez. The head is rigid foam, whereas the body is flexible, within certain limits. This body could be inserted through a cased incision along the back legs. Commercial bodies may save time, but they limit you to available poses and sizes.

up to and including bobcat or fox. In fact, during the early part of the 20th century, big-game animals such as deer and buffalo were mounted on bodies fabricated with excelsior. However, for animals of coyote size or larger, the excelsior body is not practical or cost effective because strong, lightweight precast forms are available at moderate cost.

Most taxidermists prefer to create their own artificial bodies by wrapping excelsior, the "wood wool" used by upholsterers. These bodies are inexpensive and strong. And they can be made to exact dimensions of the specimen, provided you earlier made good tracing sketches and took careful measurements. Excelsior bodies can also be wrapped in any pose you prefer. Use nylon string for wrapping so that the body can be wrapped very tightly. This tight wrapping ensures that the leg wires anchor firmly.

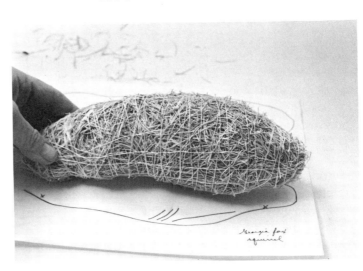

These precast forms are anatomically accurate, and they are easy to use.

Precast forms are also available for small mammals, such as squirrels. In this case, a rigid polyurethane form will cost only about $5. Flexiforms, in which body and limbs can be repositioned within limits, cost about $15. In these forms, anatomical accuracy varies with manufacturer. But in general, quality is reflected in price.

Do-it-yourself wrapped excelsior will remain popular because body forms can be made from it in a matter of minutes for only a few cents and because it allows unlimited poses. Nevertheless, after you have mastered excelsior-wrap techniques, I recommend that you eventually try mounting a squirrel or other small mammal over a precast commercial form just to see which of the methods you prefer.

The Wrapped Excelsior Body. Excelsior, the "wood wool" used by upholsterers for stuffing furniture, can be obtained from most taxidermy supply companies if you can't obtain it locally. Many taxidermists obtain their excelsior from discarded chairs and sofas. You will also need a small amount of tow, or jute, and either synthetic cotton batting or fiberglass insulation. A ball of nylon kite string and a supply of wire will round out the supplies. (Although a tremendous number of small mammals and birds have been mounted with coat-hanger wire, galvanized annealed wire works better. Avoid using copper, brass, or aluminum wire because it is too soft and will produce a wobbly mount.)

Lay your tracings and sketches of the squirrel on your workbench to serve as guides while you wrap the body. Then take up a small amount of excelsior, wrapping it tightly with nylon string to form a ball that will serve as the core of the artificial body. Gradually add small amounts of excelsior and wrap them until the body begins to take the shape of your tracings and sketches.

There are several important points to remember here: (1) Since the body will anchor the leg wires, you must wrap it very tightly. By gradually building up with small wads, you will create a firmer body than if large wads were used. (2) Don't use cotton string.

It is too weak and cannot be wrapped tight enough to make a good body. (3) If necessary, use calipers to determine the correct body dimensions. If the artificial body is too small, the skin will fit too loosely; if the body is too large, you won't be able to close the incision. (4) If the body is the wrong size or shape, take it apart and start over. You can reuse the excelsior and string. (5) Mark the points on the body where legs should be attached.

When you are satisfied with the size and shape of the body, prepare the wires needed to anchor and serve as framework for the legs and tail. A squirrel should be mounted with size Number 13 or 14 wire. Since coat hangers are painted or coated steel wire of this size, you can begin by straightening about three hangers and cutting them to needed lengths.

Each leg wire should be approximately twice the length of the leg and foot bones. Stretch the leg bones out and note the length from the sole of the foot to the hip or shoulder socket. Then double this length and cut the wire. The tail wire should be the length of the tail, plus about one-third. (So if the tail skin is 12 inches long, make the tail wire 16 inches long.) Remember, it is better to cut the wire too long than too short. With wire cutters, trim each end of the wire to a point and file the point smooth on a file or grinding stone.

Wrap the tail using the same technique you used when wrapping the artificial body. Using tow, cotton, or fiberglass, build up the tail wire to nearly the same size as the natural tail. Note: Make the artificial tail slightly smaller in diameter because the tail skin always shrinks quickly, and the artificial tail will certainly be difficult to insert into the skin if it is too large.

Now insert the leg wire into the skin. With the skin right-side out, slip a wire into the skin of the front leg and push the wire out through the palm of the foot. Then repeat the process for the other three legs. With beginners, there is a mistaken tendency to have the wire too far to the back of the paw. Avoid this so that the wire will not show in the finished mount. In general, it is better to have the wire too far forward, near the toes, than to have it emerge at the back of the palm. Also, the exit point for the leg wires will depend on the pose of the mount. For example, a squirrel sitting on its haunches will have the entire hind foot flat on the limb or ground. But when a squirrel walks on all fours, it walks up on its toes.

After you have inserted the leg wires into the skin, use a piece of nylon string to tightly tie the upper and lower leg bones to the wire. This will hold the wire in place while you are wrapping the legs.

MOUNTING A SMALL ANIMAL

Wrapping the Legs and Tail. Using the sketches as a guide, wrap each leg with tow, cotton, or fiberglass. Wrap the upper leg separately from the lower leg in order to avoid an unnatural buildup of wrapping material over the knee and elbow joints. Since these joints are directly beneath the skin on a living animal, the buildup of material will produce an unnatural joint and misshapen leg. As you did with the artificial body, wrap the legs to the shape and dimensions of the natural legs. After wrapping each of the legs to your satisfaction, you can slip the skin over the wrapped legs by pulling the toes

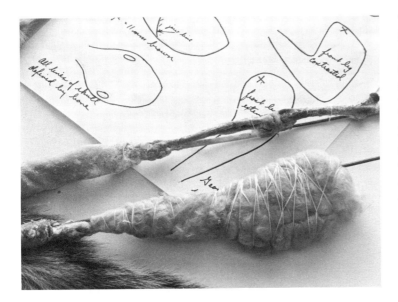

This photo shows one leg that has been finished and the exposed bones of the other leg ready to be wrapped. After inserting the leg wires, tie them to the bones with nylon string. Then wrap each section of the leg with tow, cotton, or fiberglass. If you use fiberglass, wear a pair of thin plastic food-handler's gloves because broken glass filaments can be itchy.

gently. Now examine the legs carefully, comparing the mounted legs with the sketches you made. Beginners tend to make the legs too round. While the lower legs are somewhat rounded, the upper legs generally are elliptically shaped or flat-sided. If the leg skin is baggy, indicating that you wrapped the legs too small, either rewrap the legs or stuff additional tow or cotton into the skin to fill it out properly. Then add any final shape by working the legs with your fingers to distribute the stuffing properly.

Now insert the artificial tail into the skin. When properly wrapped, the artificial tail should slip into the skin easily. Sometimes it helps to wet the tail—the water acting as a lubricant as you slip the tail into place. If you earlier made an incision in the tail skin, you should sew it up next.

Preparing the Skull or Artificial Head.
Now turn your attention to the skull. The natural skull has already been scraped and

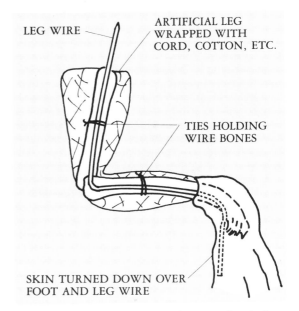

LEG WIRE

ARTIFICIAL LEG WRAPPED WITH CORD, COTTON, ETC.

TIES HOLDING WIRE BONES

SKIN TURNED DOWN OVER FOOT AND LEG WIRE

The leg wire is tied to the bones after it has been extended through the foot. Then each section of the leg is wrapped separately until it matches the size and shape of the original leg. If you pack the leg-wrapping material on the joint, the leg will not bend properly when you attempt to pose the mount.

preserved, and you have anchored a wire into the skull with auto-body paste. Using potter's clay and referring to your earlier tracings and sketches, model the muscles back onto the skull. Avoid using too much clay, and allow the natural shape of the skull to be your guide. As a general rule, the skin of the head is in direct contact with the base of the lower jaw, the top of the skull, and the cheekbone, or zygomatic arch. When you are satisfied with the shape, slip it into the skin and again examine the fit. If the head is too large, you will have difficulty fitting the head into place, requiring that you remove some of the clay. If it is too small, you will notice that the eyes and ears are too far back on the skull, so you'll need to add clay to the skull. When you are satisfied that the skull fills the skin properly, mark the position of the eyes in the clay, and then remove the skin.

Set the artificial eyes in the clay. (Earlier, when skinning, you should have made note of the eye size and color. For example, a fox squirrel requires 11mm brown eyes, but the smaller red squirrel needs 9mm hazel. The eye size will vary somewhat with the size of the squirrel and the region of the country.) Press the glass eye into the soft clay, making sure that they are directly opposite one another when viewed from the top and from the front. Also, be careful not to press the glass eye into the clay too deeply. Once the skin is mounted, you can always set the eyes more deeply, but it is difficult to pull them out further.

The built-up skull with eyes set can now be attached to the artificial body. Push the wire from the skull into the end of the artificial body at the point where the skull would naturally join the neck. The head wire should extend out through the neck or shoul-

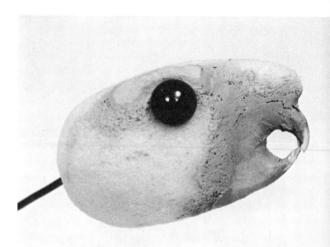

If the skull has been severely damaged or destroyed, as is often the case with squirrels, you must create an artificial head. Carve the head from balsa wood or polyurethane foam using measurements or another skull as a guide. If the skull is for a rodent, you may want to use the natural teeth, which can be attached with potter's clay. Anchor the head wire with hot glue or other cement.

ders of the artificial body. Bend a loop in the end of the wire and force it back into the body. You will probably need pliers to achieve a firm anchor. The skull is now firmly attached to the artificial body, and the wire is concealed in the excelsior.

It is not uncommon for the skull of a small animal to be badly damaged or destroyed by a bullet. In this case, you must replace the damaged skull with a skull carved from hard foam, balsa wood, or some other material. Since the natural skull is not available for measurements, you can carve the initial skull form somewhat smaller than what you estimate to be the natural skull size. Then build up the skull with potter's clay. If you are fortunate enough to have two of the same species to mount, the two can be mounted at the same time and the undamaged skull can serve as a carving guide. Carpenter's glue or a hot glue can be used to anchor a wire in the artificial head, permitting you to attach the head to the excelsior body.

The Final Mounting. Insert the artificial body and head into the skin and check for a proper fit. The head, tail, and legs have already been mounted and checked for size. Now examine the skin carefully to be sure that the body is the proper size for the skin. Pull the edges of the incision together and make certain that they will meet. The fit should be snug without being tight. When you are satisfied that everything fits properly, you are ready for the final wiring and assembly.

When the artificial body was wrapped, you should have marked the points where the shoulders and hips attach to the body. These marks are your guides for attaching the leg wires in correct places. Slide the leg wire back into the front leg until the end of the wire is even with the end of the upper leg bone. Then put the end of the leg bone and wire against the shoulder mark on the excelsior body and push the wire into the body and out the opposite side. Bend a shepherd's-crook hook on the end of the wire exiting the body. Then, holding the leg bone against the body, pull the remaining leg wire back out through the foot until the loop is firmly anchored on the far side of the body. Anchor the other front leg and the hind legs the same way. Then anchor the tail wire. All wires are now attached.

Next, holding the squirrel firmly in one hand, use your other hand to bend the legs into the approximate position of the final mount. This will produce a very tight bend

in each leg wire at the point of attachment to the body.

Double-check to ensure that the incision will still close. There may be some slack in the skin at the base of the skull and at the shoulders and hips. If so, use needle-nose pliers or forceps to stuff additional tow or cotton into those areas.

Lay the mount on its back and move the tail and legs enough to sew the skin. Most taxidermists prefer to use waxed nylon thread for sewing small animals. Waxed dental floss is excellent sewing material. Also, use a leatherwork needle if possible. This is a three-cornered needle that does not tear the skin as easily as a conventional round sewing needle. Begin at the chest and sew toward the anus. (It is almost always better to sew in the direction that the hair lies.)

Before beginning to wire the mount, make one last check of the skin to be certain that the body fits properly. It should be snug but not tight. If you haven't inserted the earliners yet, do so now. The earliners shown in this photo were cut from a lead wrapper that covered a wine bottle cork. If you haven't set the eyes yet, do so now.

WIRING DETAILS

Left: The leg wires are inserted at the points where the leg bone would attach to the natural body. The wire is pushed through the excelsior body and a hook is bent at the end exiting the body; the wire is then pulled back into the body and anchored. From here on, move the wire as little as possible; otherwise it could loosen in the excelsior. *Right:* Leg wires extend through the body and out the opposite side. A hook is then bent in the end and pulled back into the wrapped body. Regardless of the final pose of the mount, the legs remain straight during the wiring. Bend them to the desired shape after sewing.

To begin sewing, knot the end of the thread. Bring the needle through from the inside of the skin. Then cross over and come through from the inside again. This will produce a "baseball" stitch that is strong and does not pull hair into the stitching.

Many skins will tear easily when being sewn, including a tough squirrel skin. You can reduce the chance of tearing if you draw several stitches together at a time—slowly, with a needle-nose pliers or forceps. Also, pull the skin together with your fingers before tightening up a set of stitches. In this way the thread will not be putting undue strain on the skin at one point. Another tip: Tie off the thread midway down the incision. That way, if the thread breaks farther down, you will not have to resew the entire inci-

Left: I skinned this skunk with a dorsal incision to reduce the possibility I would be sprayed during the skinning. In this photo, the legs have been wrapped and await installation of the artificial body. *Right:* The leg wires have been anchored into the body, and the skunk skin is now ready to be sewn. The long fur on the back will adequately conceal the stitching. So this dorsal incision is most suitable for long-haired specimens.

sion. Also, tying off midway enables you to work with a shorter thread, which is less likely to become entangled in the leg wires and claws.

When you have completed the incision, go back and check the entire incision to be sure the stitches are tight. If there is any slack, tighten it up all the way to the end of the incision. Also, be sure that none of the belly hair is caught in the stitches. You can now knot the thread and clip off excess.

Posing and Finishing the Mounts. Preparation of the base was described earlier in this chapter on page 54. Since the mount's body and toe positions cannot be altered after drying, you should place the mount on the permanent base at this time. Besides, a new base might even adversely affect the balance of the mount.

Assuming that the squirrel is going to be mounted on a limb, hold the mount up to the limb and note where the foot wires must be attached. Then bend the legs, head, and tail of the mount into their final positions. Be sure that the bones of the legs are supported and that all of the bending is limited to the joints. Also, be sure that the shoulder and hip joints are bent close to the artificial body. Do not bend the wires any more than necessary. A lot of bending and pushing of the wires might tear the skin. Too much bending, with the wires being worked against the excelsior body, can also cause the mount to become wobbly.

After you have posed the mount properly, bend the extra leg wire extending from the foot to the proper angle so that it can be anchored into the limb. Cut off the extra wire, leaving only about 1 inch extending from the foot. Now drill a hole in the limb for each of the leg wires. Put a small amount of carpenter's glue on the leg wires, then force them into the drilled holes. The mount is now attached to the permanent base.

You can now begin preliminary grooming. Use a damp rag to wipe off any extra clay that may be left on the face. Next, using

Left: After placing the mount on the base, and before the mount begins to dry, pin the toes and facial features in place. Pin each toe separately. Here, be certain that the claws grip the base realistically. *Right:* The puffiness in the lips and toes can be restored by injecting them with a mixture of formalin and water. The formalin "sets" the lips and reduces shrinkage of the lip skin. Use only enough pins around the nose and eyes to hold the skin in place while drying. Adjust the eyelids and eye lashes to the proper angle.

a comb or brush, go over the entire specimen, and then comb the hair into place. Comb the tail carefully. Be sure that the hair on the body is combed or brushed in the natural direction. Don't ignore the feet. Pay special attention to the ventral incision. If the specimen is still rather wet, a hair drier may speed up the grooming process. Caution: Use reduced heat levels; otherwise the mount could dry too rapidly, causing excessive shrinkage.

There may be a few places where the hair refuses to lie properly, particularly along the incision. To remedy that, apply a small amount of hair spray and comb the hair into place. The hair spray can be brushed out later, and it will produce a better-groomed mount.

After completing the preliminary grooming, pin the mount to hold the details into place. Run a pin through each toe and into the base. Make sure the toes are evenly spaced

and that they properly grip the limb. You may need a pin in the corner of each eye. Reference photos of live animals will show you that the eyes are oval, almost almond-shaped. To set the eyelids, place a small amount of carpenter's glue on a toothpick and apply it to the inside of each eyelid before doing the pinning. Pin the lips into place if needed. One or two pins in each ear will help to mold the ears upright. Then stuff a small wad of paper towel or aluminum foil into each nostril.

As the skin dries, it will shrink to the shape of the artificial body. You will also notice shrinkage in the toes and feet. This shrinkage can be reduced by injecting a formalin solution. The formalin will add fullness to the skin and reduce the amount of final shrinkage. With a little experimenting, you will learn how much formalin to inject in order to obtain the desired effect in the final dried mount.

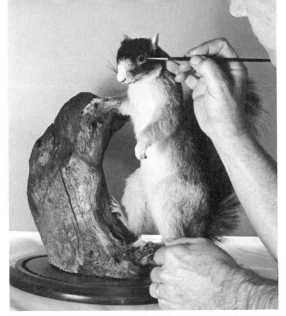

After the mount has dried for a week or 10 days, remove the pins and paint the nose and eyelids. Use the proper color for the species. As explained in the text, the nose should be glossy without looking shiny.

day or two, paint the nose and eyelids with a tiny No. 1 artist's brush using black artist's paint—either oil or acrylic. In most cases, a squirrel's nose is glossy rather than shiny. You can achieve this desired glossy look by giving the painted areas a coat of spar varnish.

Groom the mount again if needed. If the base or limb is to be hung on the wall, screw a hanger or hook into place. If the base is intended to rest on a table, you may want to screw a finished panel to the base of the limb, as shown at left, to obtain a more finished effect. This completes the mount.

The mount is now finished except for final grooming and touch-up. Some of the hair may have been disturbed during the pinning and injection process. Go over the entire mount again and do whatever additional grooming is needed. Grooming is difficult with the pins in place, so you will have to work carefully around the pinned areas.

When you are satisfied that the mount is in its final form, set it aside, allowing a minimum of a week or 10 days to thoroughly dry. The drying time may vary with the season and the geographic area. This is something you can learn only from experience. During the first couple of days, check the mount as frequently as possible to ensure that the pins are holding and that the mount is drying in the proper position. Add pins as needed.

After the mount is thoroughly dry, remove all of the pins and fill the pinholes as needed with potter's clay. After the clay has dried a

Taxidermist Roger Martin of Albemarle, North Carolina, sculpted the artificial body for this juvenile raccoon in clay, then cast a form from polyurethane foam. The form is now sold by McKenzie Supply Company of Granite Quarry, North Carolina. The unusual mount depicts a young coon struggling to keep its balance on a limb. For a small mammal, the number of poses are infinite, but they should also be natural. This mount won Martin an award in a National Taxidermist Association competition.

MOUNTING BIG-GAME ANIMALS

The steps required to mount big-game animals are a combination of the techniques described for mounting game heads and small mammals. Once you have mastered these techniques, mounting even the largest animal is not difficult. It just requires a little extra planning. As is the case with game heads, the beginner should not mount a once-in-a-lifetime trophy on the first attempt at big-game taxidermy. A coyote is a good choice for the beginner. These predators are widespread and the hides are relatively easy to obtain. Also, the supplies are not excessively expensive, compared with those needed for mounting a life-size bear or cougar. Just remember that your first couple of attempts are for practice, and practice will result in a quality mount when the once-in-a-lifetime trophy comes along.

We'll assume that you have a coyote to mount. Begin by making and recording these four measurements:

1. Tip of nose to front corner of eye
2. Tip of nose to back of skull
3. Length of body from tip of nose to base of tail, along the curvature of the body
4. Belly circumference measured at the largest circumference.

Now the coyote should be skinned using the three belly incisions described in Chapter 1 for field care of big-game animals. The leg incisions begin at one foot, following the inside of the leg to the belly, then extend down the opposite leg to the other foot. The ventral incision begins at the base of the neck and extends to the anus. The skin is then removed using the same techniques I described earlier in this chapter for a squirrel.

Skin the feet to the last toe joint. Split the tail skin along the bottom and remove the bone. Then skin the head in the same way that the squirrel was skinned. The skin around the eyes, nose, and lips should be split. Turn the ears inside out in the same manner as I described for game heads in Chapter 2. After you have thoroughly fleshed the skin, lay it flat and salt it. When the hide has drained and partially dried, you can ship it to the tannery, also explained in Chapter 2. Or, if you prefer, you can tan the hide yourself using the methods I describe in Chapter 4.

Tanning Cream. One other hide preparation option is to use tanning cream. Tanning creams can be purchased from most supply dealers. As mentioned in an earlier section of this chapter, tanning creams do not actually tan the skin in the same way that the complete tanning process does. Rather these creams consist of preservatives mixed with tanning oils which soften the skin. Thus the skin remains soft and pliable for mounting, but it is not actually tanned as the commercial name suggests.

After you have thoroughly fleshed and salted the hide, you should wash it, rinse it, and allow it to drain. Apply the tanning cream according to the directions on the container. In most cases the cream is heated in a double boiler until lukewarm and then applied to the flesh side of the hide. Use only enough to coat the skin. Work it into the skin with your hands, then fold the hide—flesh side together—and allow it to stand overnight. The next day, work the skin with your hands and pull the skin back and forth over the edge of a table or your bench. Gradually the oils will be worked into the skin and it will remain pliable.

Tanning creams are ideally suited to animals the size of coyote, bobcat, and fox. The skins are thick enough that oils are needed to prevent excessive shrinkage in the mount. Skins of small animals such as squirrel do not require oils, and the larger hides of deer and bear are difficult to adequately treat with tanning creams.

Preparation of the Big-Game Form. Although you could construct an artificial body for a coyote from excelsior or other material, that would not be very practical. Because a coyote is a relatively large animal, a do-it-yourself body would need an armature of ¼-inch threaded rod as the core. Then large amounts of clay are required to sculpt the artificial skull, and the whole structure becomes rather heavy and wobbly. On the other hand, an expertly sculptured artificial body can be purchased for $60 to $90, and it will allow you to produce a strong, lightweight, quality mount. In fact many of these commercial forms are so good that they can help make a beginner look like an expert.

At this point you should review the supply catalogs and determine the size of the form that you need to order. The size of the form will depend on the measurements that you made on the carcass, particularly the body length and circumference. Select a form that is as close to the actual body measurements as possible. When in doubt, order a form one size smaller than the body measurements. Although an inch or two in the size of the finished mount will not be noticeable, it makes a lot of difference in the mounting process. It is much easier to build up a small form than to cut down a large one.

If you are unable to obtain a fresh coyote, you can obtain a tanned skin through one of the trade journals. Since the artificial body

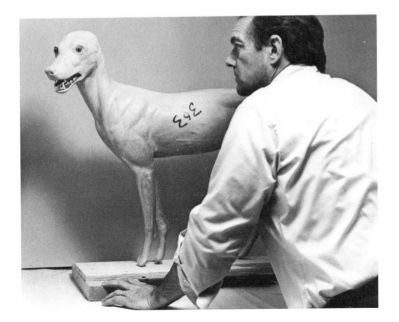

Although you can construct an artificial body for a big-game animal, it is usually more practical to purchase a commercial form. Here I'm examining an L-303 polyurethane coyote form from Research Mannikins of Lebanon, Oregon, after I modified it to show an open-mouth pose. The form should be ordered to fit the size of the skin and the pose can then be changed, within limits.

is anatomically accurate and the *stretched* skin is not, you should always order a body that is a few inches shorter and few inches wider than the skin. This way you can always stretch the skin in width, and this stretching tends to shorten the skin, making it fit the form well.

For example, a coyote skin, from nose to base of tail, might be 39 inches long, and it might be 18 inches wide, totaling 57 inches. The proper artificial body for a 39 × 18 skin would be 36 inches by 21 inches, totaling 57 inches also. In other words, the combined dimension of length and width (circumference) should be close.

After the form arrives, attach it to a sturdy wooden base. This base will later become the core of your final base. Be sure that the legs are properly spaced and that the form does not wobble. Then prepare the form in much the same manner as I described for

prepping the headform for a big-game mount.

Sand the form with a coarse-grit sandpaper to remove any chemicals that may remain on the surface of the form. Then give the sanded form a coat of orange shellac. Now wrap the tail with cotton or tow as I described for the squirrel earlier in this chapter. Cut the lip slot with a knife or saw, and open up the eye sockets and nostrils with an electric hand grinder, such as made by Dremel. The form is now ready for mounting.

Set the glass eye in a bed of soft potter's clay. The eye of a coyote and most predators has a considerably different angle than that of a deer. A coyote's eyes are located much farther forward, at an angle of about 67 degrees from the axis of the skull. Also, the upper edge of the eye tilts back toward the top of the skull at an angle of about 15 degrees, as shown in the drawing.

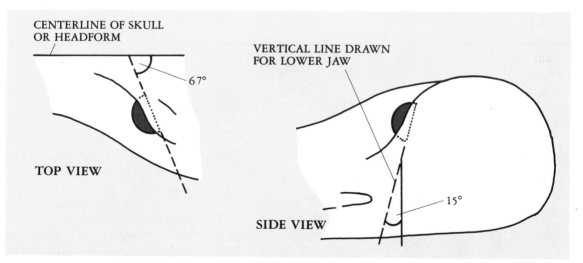

The eye position and angle are much different for predators, such as coyotes, than for horned and antlered game. The angle of the eye, from the centerline of the head or face, is about 67 degrees. This gives the predator more frontal and less peripheral vision. Also, the top of the eye slants backward at about 15 degrees. Proper eye setting is one of the more difficult tasks when mounting a predator.

Preparation of the Hide. The skin of a big-game animal is prepared for mounting in the same manner I described earlier in this chapter for small animals and in Chapter 2 for game heads. At this point, you have either tanned the hide or treated it with tanning cream. And you have washed it and rinsed it out. Lay the skin on the workbench, flesh-side up, and examine it for cuts or other holes. Repair any cuts or holes with nylon thread. A circular hole will tend to pucker around the sides when sewn unless you extend the hole a short distance on each side. See page 128 for an illustration of this.

Put the hide in a small fleshing beam and remove any extra tissue on the nose, lips, and the base of the ears. Double-check the ears to make certain that they have been completely turned to the tip. Be sure to leave enough lip and nose skin so that it can be tucked under the clay when mounting, as I described in Chapter 2 on game-head mounting. Be certain that you have skinned the feet all the way to the last bone in the toe. When you are satisfied that you have repaired all of the damage and that you have properly fleshed and thinned the skin, you are ready to mount it.

Mounting the Big-Game Skin. Slip the skin over the form and check for a proper fit. It is quite likely that the skin will be too long from nose to tail and too narrow around the body. With your hands gripping either side of the body skin, stretch the width of the skin around the form. Make sure that the eyelids line up with the glass eyes in the form. You will probably need to stretch the skin of the muzzle and the lower jaw also. In general, it is far easier to stretch the skin at this time than to do the stretching while you are sewing up the skin. Do not proceed

Fleshing beams can be various sizes and shapes. I carved this one from a piece of 1 × 4-inch pine for attachment to a bench with a C-clamp. For fleshing the features of a small mammal, a pointed 1-inch dowel works well; as does a hammer handle.

until you are satisfied that you have stretched the skin to fit the form properly.

Now mix up a batch of hide paste from a supply company. About 1 cup of hide paste should be adequate for a coyote mount. Using an inexpensive 3- to 4-inch paint brush, apply a liberal coat of paste over the entire form. Paint hide paste on the inside of the skin of the head, particularly around the eyes, nose, and lips. Also work some paste up into the ears.

Slip the earliners into place. Commercial earliners cost only a couple of dollars from a supply dealer, or you can make your own using hardware cloth. With the ear right-side-out, check to see if the skin of the inner ear is drumming. Drumming occurs when

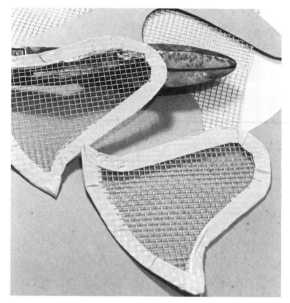

You can make earliners from hardware cloth, as shown. Or you can purchase earliners. For these earliners, I cut a cardboard pattern to the shape of the natural ear cartilage, and then cut the earliners from ¼-inch hardware cloth and taped the edges.

Test-fit the skin on the form. The skin should be snug but not tight. If the skin does not fit, the form must be trimmed down, built up with clay, or replaced. After you are satisfied that the skin will fit the form, apply a coat of hide paste to the entire form.

the earliner is too big, causing skin of the inside of the ear to draw tight across the concave surface of the earliner. When this happens, remove the earliner and trim the edges until the skin of the inside of the ear fits against the liner. Then make a roll of potter's clay and press it around the base of the earliner to replace the muscle that was removed. It is better to use too much clay than not enough. So use plenty of clay, as long as you don't create an unnatural bulge in the skin.

Mount the skin on the form, being careful to avoid getting hide paste on the pelt. First pull the skin over the head and adjust the position of the eyes, nose, and mouth. Then line up the skin at the base of the tail in the

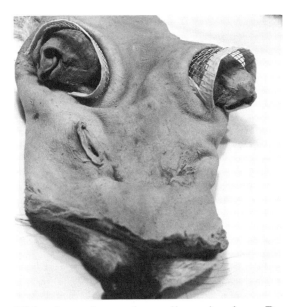

This photo shows the earliners in place. Before slipping the earliners into place, I put a heavy coat of hide paste in the ear. I then built up the ear butt with potter's clay. The final modeling of the ear butt is postponed until the skin is on the form.

correct position on the form. Check the color pattern of the pelt and make sure that the center of the back is aligned properly. Now drive a couple of nails or large pins through the skin of the back and into the form. Put one on the top of the head and one at the base of the neck. Insert another nail or pin at the base of the tail. Don't drive these all the way to the head. Since you will remove them later, they should penetrate just far enough to hold the skin in place. Then pull the skin down around the sides of the form and put a nail or two on each side of the belly incision.

Next comes the coyote's face. Line up the skin of the nose on the form and then use a small pin to hold the skin in place. Push

After placing the skin over the form, anchor it in place with a couple of nails along the head, neck and back. Then pin the facial features into place. The skin can then be sewn. Begin by sewing the ventral incision. Then sew the legs.

The toes should be pinned to the base. Be sure there is plenty of hide paste on the skin around the mouth and eyes. Use whatever pins are necessary on the face, particularly around the eyes, nose, and mouth. Groom the mount with comb, brush, and a hairblower while the skin and fur are still damp.

the extra skin into the nostrils of the form, and then stuff a wad of foil or paper towel into the nostril to hold the skin until it is dry. Also put one or two pins into the corner of each eye. Tuck the lip skin into the slot that you cut in the form, as shown on page 38. Tuck in the skin of the upper lip first, beginning with the nose and working toward the corner of the mouth. Be sure that there is plenty of hide paste on the lower jaw and skin. Then tuck the edges of the skin from the lower jaw into the slot. Add a pin or two along the mouth to hold the skin in place. Put a nail at the base of each ear.

At this point the facial work is not finished, but you have glued and pinned the major features in place. Dampen a rag and wrap it around the face of the mount and hold the rag in place with a nail. This will keep the facial features moist while you do the sewing.

The sewing technique is the same as I explained for the squirrel, beginning on page 72. Begin at the base of the neck and sew toward the anus. Take three or four stitches at one time; then pull them tight. If you find that the skin fits tightly around the belly of the form, put a few pins along the sewn incision for additional strength while the hide paste is bonding. This will prevent the skin from shrinking away from the incision and tearing open the stitching. While you are sewing along the belly, occasionally check to be certain that the color patterns of the pelt align properly with the legs and flanks.

The leg incisions are sewn after the belly incision is closed. Begin sewing at the foot and work up to the belly. Although this requires sewing against the hair, contrary to my earlier advice, I've always found it easier to close the leg incisions in this way. How-

Allow the mount to dry for 10 days or more before removing the pins and painting the bare skin. During this time, check the mount daily and make whatever changes are needed. Pay particular attention to the stitching, and don't let the skin around the eyes and mouth draw away from the form.

ever, the particular pose of the mount could make sewing from belly to foot easier. A little experience will teach you which sewing methods work best with a given pose.

After the sewing is complete, examine all incisions to be certain they have all remained closed and tight. Then with a damp rag, wipe off any hide paste that might have been picked up by the hair along the incisions. Now, using a brush and comb, groom the entire mount. A hair drier with low heat setting will help to fluff the hair. Comb any knots out of the tail, along the flanks, and under the neck and brisket. If you do not have a suitable brush and comb—or if your mate refuses to make the donation—purchase a set from a pet shop. These combs and brushes work as well for coyotes and bear as they do for poodles and bassets.

Next comes the final touch-up on the face. Remove the damp rag and examine the eyes.

Using a modeling tool or the top end of an artist's brush, shape the eyelids and push them close to the glass eyes. Insert a pin or two if needed. Check the nose and mouth. The hide paste will actually hold the skin in place, but some shrinkage may occur before the paste bonds the skin to the form. So a few pins may help, particularly around the mouth. If the ear butts are not symmetrical, work the clay around the earliner and the form to model the proper shape.

The mount is now finished and can be set aside to dry. Allow a week or 10 days at the minimum. During this time, check the mount daily and make any adjustments needed. This includes grooming, repinning as needed, and perhaps the repair of some

Few taxidermists are as knowledgeable about the caribou as taxidermist-sculptor Forest Hart (standing) of Hampden, Maine. The large bull shown carries a Boone and Crockett record-book-size rack and is in the final stages of completion by Hart and Peter Summers, Chief Taxidermist for the Royal Scottish Museum in Edinburgh, Scotland. Stapled strips of tape and cardboard hold the hide against the form while the paste sets.

stitching. When the mount is totally dry, remove all of the nails and pins, and save these for use on your next mount. In some cases you may want to leave the pins in place, so simply push them all the way into the form. The heads can then be covered with clay. Also use clay to fill any places around the nose or eyes that have pulled away from the form. When the clay has dried, in another 24 hours or more, you can paint the nose and eyelids. Use black or brownish black on the nose and eyelids, and finish with a coat of satin spar varnish.

Preparation of a realistic artificial base for a big-game animal can be very involved, depending on the environment that you want to duplicate. Therefore your first mounts can be left attached to the temporary base for the time being. I offer a detailed description of construction of bases in Chapter 9.

Your first life-size mount is now finished. Examine it closely and compare your mount with reference photos of coyotes. By comparing your work with your reference photos, you will probably see the problem areas that you'll want to remedy on your next mount. Typically, the eyes and the mouth are the problem areas. Even the best professional taxidermist has trouble setting the eyes so that they are focused on a particular spot. Setting the eyes properly is a skill that can only be acquired with study and practice. Also, it is not uncommon to have the lip skin shrink away from the form. The only solution is more hide paste and pins. Don't become discouraged if your first couple of mounts have imperfections. Each successive mount you do will show improvement. Perhaps someday you will be producing life-size mounts that win ribbons in competition.

GALLERY OF OUTSTANDING MOUNTS

With this coyote mount, I earned second place in the mammals category in a recent annual National Taxidermist Association competition. Coyotes are widespread and so are readily available.

(Continued)

(Outstanding Mounts continued)

Right: Tim Hages of Beloit, Kansas, mounted this whitetail, which won the People's Choice award at an annual Kansas taxidermist competition. Antlered game animals mounted full body require an incision along the back of the neck during skinning. This allows you to slip the skin over the head and antlers.

This half life-size muskox shows an interesting and practical way to mount and display a large animal. The trophy muskox was bagged and mounted by taxidermist Toby Johnson of Sheridan, Wyoming. This style of mount gives maximum display when you have limited display space. The mounting techniques for half life-size are the same as for life-size, except that you can order a special form from a supply company, at about 40 percent cost savings relative to the cost of a full life-size form. In this case the key measurements would be on the face and head and not on the body dimensions.

(Outstanding Mounts continued)

This life-size caribou was mounted by Ron Reynolds of Bath, Ontario, on a form that was sculpted by Forest Hart of Hampton, Maine. The mount won a blue ribbon in a national taxidermy competition. For mid-size to large game, using quality commercial forms is much more practical than attempting to create forms in the workshop. Only the larger commercial studios sculpt and manufacture their own life-size forms.

Black-maned lions such as this require the same mounting techniques that I described for coyotes. The job just takes more time. This mount won Best of Show at a National Taxidermist Association competition. It was mounted by Vince Tanko and Calvin Farner in the Jonas Brothers Studio, Denver, Colorado.

Here while giving a seminar, Harry Paulson is putting the finishing touches on a javelina mount. The same techniques are used for any big-game mount. Whether the specimen is a fox squirrel or a javelina, each requires practice and skill. Harry Paulson is the President of the Mountain Valley School of Taxidermy in Phoenix, Arizona. (Tom Masamori photo)

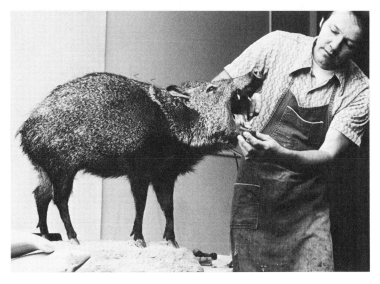

4 TANNING AND LEATHER MAKING

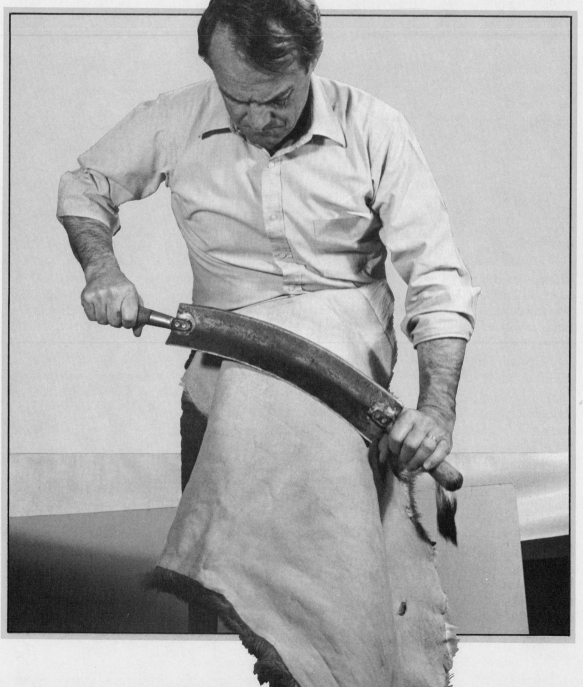

Just what is leather? Leather is a hide or skin that has been physically and chemically processed to a stable and less destructible form. In this processing, tanning chemically renders the skin resistant to decomposition and bacterial decay. Tanning also improves certain physical properties of the skin, such as tensile strength, flexibility, and resilience. In addition, tanning allows the taxidermist to work with a more durable material than raw skin.

Taxidermy and tanning are very closely related professions. Yet today, very few taxidermists do their own tanning, and few tanners find time for taxidermy. Each is a profession in itself requiring special talent and equipment. In addition, there are many tanneries that cater to the taxidermist. Since they offer fast, quality service at a very reasonable cost, it often is impractical for the taxidermist to do his own tanning. Most professional taxidermists have their tanning done by a commercial tannery and pass the tanning costs on to the customer. In this way, the taxidermist is able to put his own talents to full use, while depending on the tanner for his skills.

Although taxidermy can be practiced in the kitchen, garage, or basement, those settings aren't usually adequate for tanning and leather making. The vats, kickers, and drums required for tanning require a considerable amount of room. Also, tanning has its own public relations problems. Through the ages

Here I am using a fleshing knife to thin out a tanned deer hide. The knife also serves in removing fat from the raw skin.

tanners have been prized for their almost magical ability to turn rough, raw animal hide into supple, wearable materials. But a tanner's good works have not necessarily made him popular locally. Strong chemicals and unpleasant odors are frequently associated with the tanning process. And the tanning industry was among the first slapped with water-pollution regulations by the Environmental Protection Agency in the early 1970s.

The antagonisms toward tanneries are age-old. In ancient Palestine, the law required tanneries to be situated east of town so that residents would generally be upwind from them. In fact, tanners were excused from pilgrimages because they weren't welcome in crowds. And a tanner's wife could get a divorce at any time simply by declaring her distaste for her husband's profession. In India, tanners have been classed as the lowest of the "untouchables." Even in colonial America tanners were forced to live and work outside the city walls of New Amsterdam. According to the *Talmud*, the code of Jewish law, "The world can exist neither without a perfume maker nor without a tanner. Happy is he whose craft is that of a perfume maker, and woe to him who is a tanner by trade."

Today many of the historic problems have been remedied. For example, modern chemicals such as lye have replaced dog dung as a tanning ingredient. Nevertheless the dehairing process in leather making is still a controlled decaying of the skin that enables the tanner to scrape the hair from the skin. But how do you get rid of a strong lye solution mixed with decayed skin and hair?

Even though you may not become deeply involved in tanning, it is important to understand the tanning and leathermaking processes. In this way you will be able to provide better skins to the tannery, and this will result in better mounts. Also, you can save time and money by doing some of your own small tanning. This chapter is intended to teach the fundamentals of tanning and leather making. In the end, even if you don't find tanning to be a tremendously challenging hobby, you will find that your knowledge of tanning will help you obtain better skins for taxidermy.

Origins of Tanning. The process of tanning gets its name from the use of tannin or tannic acid, common in the bark of oaks and other trees. Modern technology has developed a large number of chemical agents and processes to produce leather, although vegetable tanning (with barks) is still used for certain kinds of leather.

The use of hides and skins for clothing and shelter has been known since earliest times. Prehistoric man used the skins of the animals he killed; the American Indians were very adept at leather making and developed a unique type of leather called "buckskin." Egyptian carvings dating to 3000 B.C. depict leather dressers at work. The literature and history of classic Greece contain abundant evidence of tanning as a flourishing art and trade. In the Roman era, Pliny refers to tanning with bark and to the usefulness of certain woods and berries.

During the medieval period, tanning flourished in the Near East and a great variety of leathers were introduced in Europe by the Moors of North Africa. Moroccan leather became widely known throughout Europe for its fine quality and beautiful color. By the 15th century the art of leather making was once more widespread in Europe,

and there were leather-making guilds in the principal cities where leather was in demand.

In the 18th century, the principles of vegetable tanning and the use of crude machines for the process were well known. Although the scientific basis for the action of tannic acid was not understood, the value of materials such as oak bark, sumac, valonia, hemlock and other vegetable materials was well established. Tanning with chrome salts, introduced at the end of the 19th century, was probably the first change in the chemistry of leather manufacture in at least 2,000 years. Chrome tanning shortened the process from weeks to days, and it provided more uniform products.

It is important to understand the difference between fur dressing and leather making. In both processes, the skin is tanned to leather. However, fur dressing is a tanning process in which fur is left on the skin during the tanning process. Leather making is a tanning process in which the hair is removed from the skin. Both processes are useful. While the taxidermist will be primarily interested in fur dressing, the outdoorsman may wish to make a coonskin cap, buckskin, or leather garments.

A word of caution about different types of skins—not all skins are identical in makeup. For example, there is a considerable difference between a deer hide and a snake skin. Shark and ostrich can be tanned to durable leather also, but they require different techniques which are beyond the scope of this book. Sheepskins are also unique because they are high in lanolin and the dense wool is difficult to comb out. Since these are specialty skins, their tanning should be left to the professional tanner.

Since the purpose of this chapter is to introduce the processes of tanning, I will explain the methods of fur dressing for capes, rugs, and small pelts. I also describe the fundamentals of leather making, including the methods of making buckskin and rawhide. And I will introduce snakeskin tanning. You'll need to invest additional study if you want to engage in leather making or large-scale tanning.

Skin Structure. An animal skin is composed of three layers: (1) the outer layer or epidermis; (2) the corium, or derma; and (3) the adipose tissue that holds the corium to the muscle beneath, as shown in the accompanying drawing.

The epidermis is the outer layer of skin in which the hair roots are anchored. It is

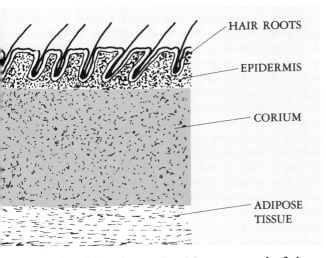

HAIR ROOTS

EPIDERMIS

CORIUM

ADIPOSE TISSUE

The skin of an animal is composed of three layers: the epidermis, the corium, and the adipose tissue. The adipose tissue holds the outer layers to the underlying muscle, and it is removed during the fleshing process, leaving the tanned hide of epidermis and corium. When the skin is not properly fleshed and salted, the epidermis deteriorates and the hair slips—falls out. (Reprinted from *American Taxidermist***)**

thin and relatively dry. This layer also contains the pigment that gives the skin its color. If the skin is white, there is little or no pigment, as in the case of deerskin. However, pigment is commonly found in the skin of thin-haired species, such as pigs and African animals of which the Cape buffalo is a good example.

The corium, or derma, consists largely of connective tissue, of which 85 to 88 percent is the protein collagen. Collagen is arranged throughout the corium as interlacing fiber bundles and fat cells. There are also small quantities of other proteins along with small amounts of lipids, carbohydrates, and mineral salts. The tanning process removes the nonfibrous proteins, lipids, carbohydrates, and mineral salts from the interlaced fiber structure of the skin. These are then replaced by oils that are worked into the skin structure. The result is a soft, flexible hide that will not shrink or deteriorate.

The proportion of collagen to fat cells may vary according to the kind of animal, as well as the age, sex, and general health of the animal. Also, the corium within a particular hide may vary according to the location on the hide. For example, in humans corium is thickest on the back and thinnest on the eyelids.

The adipose tissue is the connecting fibers that hold the corium to the underlying muscle. This is removed during the fleshing process and before the skin is tanned.

Skin Preparation for Tanning. I covered the techniques for skinning a cape or full hide in chapters 2 and 3. According to Mario Panattoni, Chief Tanner for New Method Fur Dressing in South San Francisco, pretanning care is essential for quality tanning and fur dressing. Reprinted from *American*

Taxidermist, Panattoni's recommendations are as follows:

"First, the skin must be thoroughly fleshed to remove all attached fat, tissue, and muscle from the skin. This can be done using a manual fleshing knife and fleshing beam or one of the electric fleshing machines that are on the market. Whichever technique you use, it is essential to thoroughly flesh the hide while it is still fresh." The amount of fleshing will depend on the animal and its condition, but some animals require a great deal more work than others. For example, bear skins are almost always very fat, unless it happens to be a spring kill. Panattoni adds, "Skin out the feet all the way to the end of each toe, and don't forget to skin the tail. The ears, lips, and eyes must be turned and fleshed down properly.

"When the skinning and fleshing is completed, lay the trophy down, flesh-side up, on a tilted surface and apply a heavy coat of salt. Be sure that all spots are salted, and work the salt into the lips and ears, around the eyes, and into the toes. Watch for wrinkles in the skin that may not have been salted. Leave the salt on the skin for about two days. During this time the salt will draw moisture out of the skin. When salted on a tilted surface, the body fluids will drain away from the skin or cape."

Panattoni concludes, "After about two days, scrape the salt off the skin, and the salt can be discarded. Check the skin to be sure that salt has gotten into all areas of the skin, then resalt the hide a second time. As soon as the hide begins to stiffen up, it is ready for tanning—or for shipment to a commercial tannery."

Up to this point in hide care, all skins are

FLESHING THE SKIN

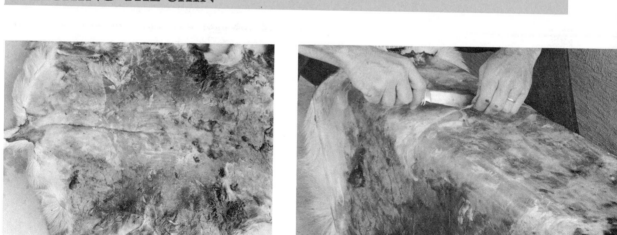

Left: Most raw hides retain a considerable amount of flesh, blood, and tissue. You must remove all of this as soon as possible and before you salt the hide. If tissue is left on the skin, the salt cannot penetrate properly, and the hair will slip (fall out), ruining the hide for anything but leather. *Right:* Begin the fleshing with a skinning knife at the rear of the hide. I am using a fleshing beam here. But a picnic table bench works well too.

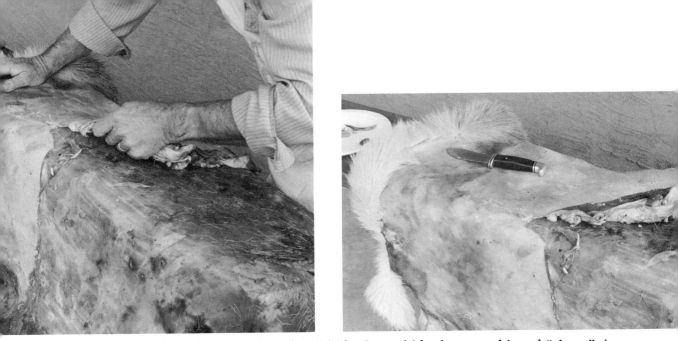

Left: Frequently it is easier to flesh a "dirty" hide than a hide that was skinned "clean." A dirty hide contains a great deal of flesh and fat that is all held together by tissue. Once you get under the tissue, you can pull the flesh and fat free by hand. *Right:* Note the difference between the "clean" and "dirty" ends of the deer hide. Once you have all of the flesh and tissue moving in a single piece, the fleshing job becomes much easier.

treated the same. This is called the curing process. The salt is a preservative that will protect any kind of skin from spoilage, whether it is a snakeskin or buffalo hide. Once the hide is salt cured, it will last for many months or even years when kept cool and dry. However, if possible, tan the skin before storing it, for a tanned hide is also mothproofed and a cured hide is not.

If you plan to tan the hide of a hoofed animal, you must skin the legs all the way to the hoof. Also, there is a small bone in the dew claws that should be removed.

(Fleshing continued)

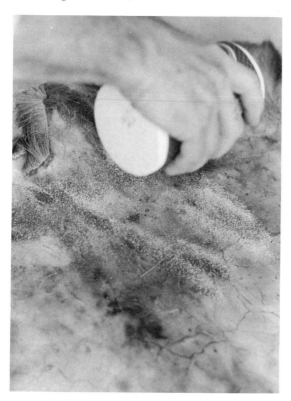

Left: Common table salt can be used, but non-iodized pickling salt is best. Don't spare the salt. Put a large amount in the center of the hide and then spread it toward the edges. Since the edges may have curled up, work around the edges with additional salt so that every part of the skin is salted. *Above:* After salting the hide, fold the flesh sides together and allow the skin to drain for 24 hours. Then open up the hide and resalt it. A sloping surface is best for draining the hide, and it should be away from any direct sunlight.

Gerard Terrier of Gatineau, Quebec, developed the Quebec Fleshing Machine. Although too expensive for the beginning tanner or taxidermist, a fleshing machine is invaluable if you have many hides to flesh. Not only does the machine remove attached flesh and fat; it can also be used to thin very heavy hides for quality leather.

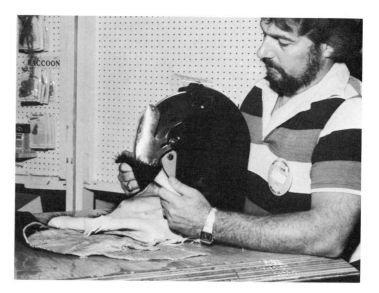

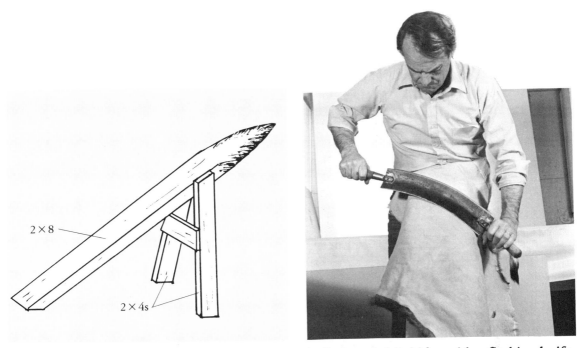

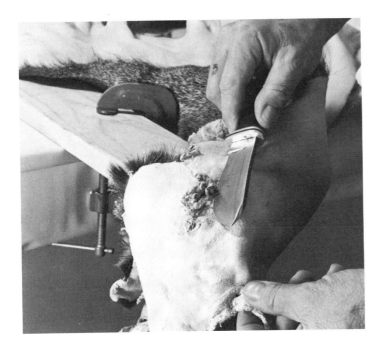

Left: A large fleshing beam is essential to properly flesh and thin hides with a fleshing knife. The beam itself can be made from 2 × 8 pine about 5 feet long. The supporting legs should be 2 × 4s. The upper end is carved and sanded to a smooth, rounded point. *Right:* I am using a fleshing knife with hide draped over a fleshing beam. If kept sharp, these knives greatly simplify the fleshing process. They also thin heavier hides so salt penetrates.

Smaller fleshing beams can be clamped to a workbench.

PRINCIPLES OF FUR DRESSING AND LEATHER MAKING

Any tanning process requires the use of chemicals. Some of these are the same products found in automobile batteries or in kitchen drain cleaners. They are safe when properly used—but they should always be used with caution. Whenever possible, all tanning operations should be performed in areas that are well ventilated and where there is plenty of running water. It is also best to work on a concrete or dirt floor. In addition, the work area should have a drain available for disposing of the tanning liquids when they are no longer needed.

Most of the solutions used in tanning are either acidic or basic. The chemical symbol "pH" is used to designate the amount of acid in a solution. On the pH scale of 1 to 14, a pH of 7 is neutral, with acids being less than 7 and bases being more than 7. For example, drinking water and human blood are about neutral with a pH of 7; battery acid has pH of about 2 and a lye solution is strongly basic at about 13. This fundamental of chemistry is important to understand for both quality tanning and personal safety. The pH of a tanning solution must be controlled so that the pelts are not destroyed by the acid or allowed to rot in a solution that is too weak. Likewise, any solution can be neutralized from acidic or basic in order to make it safe. For example, an old tanning solution may have a pH of 3 or 4 and would destroy your plumbing if poured down a drain. However, by adding salt, you can raise the pH to 7 (neutral) and then safely dispose of the solution. Or, since water has a pH of 7, sufficient water can be added to an acidic solution to dilute it back to a pH of 6 or 7, which is safe to handle.

All tanning should be done in large, plastic containers. Both acids and bases react strongly with metals and would destroy containers as well as any skins in the solution. Purchase some old-fashioned wooden spoons for stirring the tanning solutions, or else carve your own wooden spatulas for this purpose. A wooden or plastic canoe paddle works well. Do not use metal spoons. Glass or

Use plastic containers for all tanning and pickling solutions because they do not react with the chemicals. The size will depend on the amount of solution you need and the number of hides being tanned. Avoid making more than about 20 gallons of solution at one time; otherwise the solution becomes too heavy to manage safely.

earthenware containers can also be used for tanning solutions, but these may break and create a sizable cleanup problem. Try to avoid mixing more than about 20 gallons of solution at one time. Since 1 gallon of solution weighs about 7½ pounds, the weight of more than 20 gallons would be unmanageable.

Always add acid to water, never water to concentrated acid. Never break this basic rule of chemistry. The best way to avoid this error

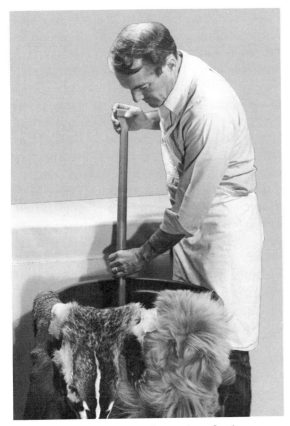

A plastic trash can makes a handy, inexpensive tanning barrel. Use a large wooden spatula or even a canoe paddle for stirring the solutions and turning the skins. Be careful to keep the solutions off skin and clothes.

is to begin with water and then add to it. After you have put the proper amount of water in the vat or tub, add the other ingredients, including acid, as required.

It is always a good idea to wear rubber or plastic gloves when working with tanning solutions. This is not essential, but it is a wise habit to begin early.

Fur Dressing. There are six basic steps to the complete fur-dressing operation. They are as follows:

1. Rehydration of the skin. The skin is soaked in a solution to return it to its original flexibility.

2. Scouring. This is the process of washing and degreasing the skin.

3. Pickling and shaving. When the skin is pickled, it is acidized and the nonfibrous proteins, liquids, and carbohydrates are flushed from the corium (fibrous skin tissue). Shaving is the process of thinning the hide in order to make it softer and more workable.

4. Dressing. This is the actual tanning process.

5. Oiling the hide.

6. Finishing the hide. The oils are worked into the fabric of the skin so that it remains soft and flexible.

As I will describe in upcoming sections of this chapter, all six of the above steps are necessary for a properly dressed skin or fur. Yet there are cases when one or more of these steps can be eliminated for a hide or cape that is going to be mounted. In all other cases the six steps are necessary.

Commercial Tanning Kits. Most taxidermy supply companies sell tanning kits that are complete and ready for use. It is a good idea for the beginner to purchase one of these kits, which contain all of the chemicals and oils needed for tanning a coyote skin or deer cape. The kits are inexpensive and handy, and they give the beginner a "feel" for the tanning process. The Trapline Tanning Kit by Rittel and sold by McKenzie Taxidermy Supply is available for less than $10 and is designed for small animal skins. The Van Dyke Supply kits are slightly more expensive, but they will tan considerably more material. J. W. Elwood Supply also markets a complete tanning kit. When using any of these commercial kits, simply follow the directions supplied with the kit.

Commercial tanning kits also enable the beginner to work with a small number of skins. Because of the amount of ingredients required, most tanning solutions are for 10 coyote skins or a single deer skin. The commercial kits are designed to be used for one or two hides so they can save you money in the long run.

The Formic-Alum Process. At this point, the skins and capes are "flint dry" after having been fleshed, salted, and dried. Mix a rehydration solution in a plastic container large enough to submerge the dried skins and/or capes. Use the following ingredients for each 5 gallons; for 10 gallons of solution, simply double the amount of each ingredient.

  5 gallons of water
  1 cup of deiodized salt
  ¼ cup of laundry detergent
  2 tablespoons of Lysol

Soak the skins in this solution until they are soft and flexible. A deer cape will require about four hours to rehydrate but small, thinner pelts of furbearers need a much shorter time. The skins do not have to be completely soft before you proceed, and you will find that the forehead area and ear butts will be the last parts to completely soften. These areas will continue to soften as you proceed with the next steps.

The skins must now be scoured. Remove the skins from the rehydrating solution and rinse them thoroughly in fresh water. Gently squeeze out as much water as possible and hang the skins so that they will drain. Pour about 1 gallon of white gasoline or kerosene into a plastic tub and stir in the skins that have been drained. Even though you have already thoroughly fleshed the skins and removed all fat, the white gasoline will remove any grease or oil that is still on the fleshed skin or in the hair. This step can be eliminated when scouring most big-game capes, since they contain very little grease or oil. It is especially important to use a cleaning agent on the pelts of animals that are commonly very fat. Most greasy skins will require at least an hour in the solvent bath; in some cases you may need to leave the item in the bath overnight. After you remove the skins from the solvent bath, squeeze out the solvent and wash the skins in a soapy solution using laundry detergent. This final scouring process will remove any dirt, blood, and remaining solvent from the skin and the fur.

During all of these steps, be sure that you frequently stir and agitate the brew. This is necessary so the various solutions contact all parts of each skin. Otherwise the skins or capes will be tanned unevenly, and this will result in hair slip, greasy spots, or hard areas on the final product.

The pickling process prepares the skin to accept the tanning solution. Pickling opens the skin fibers, making them soft and pliable; the process also flushes out any remaining proteins in the skin structure. This allows the skin to "take the tan." Here are the ingredients for 5 gallons of pickle bath:

    5   gallons of water
    5   pounds of deiodized salt
    3½ oz. (100cc) of 85 percent technical-grade formic acid

Increase the proportions equally in order to mix a larger volume of pickle bath. It is important that the pickle have a pH of 2.5 to 3.5. If, after mixing your pickle solution, the pH is less than 2.5, the solution is too acidic and you should add more salt; add more formic acid if the pH is higher than 3.5. (When measuring the pH, be sure that you thoroughly stir the solution. It is possible that the pH might vary within the container.) The pH will vary for a number of reasons. The water in the skins from the preceding steps will tend to dilute the pickle and raise the pH; some formic acids are slightly stronger than others, so the same volume of acid may be stronger, resulting in a lower pH. The pH must be controlled with a salinometer or hydrometer that can be obtained from J. W. Elwood Supply. You may also use litmus paper from your local druggist or taxidermy supply house. But you should be aware that litmus paper is sometimes difficult to read and is not as accurate as a salinometer and hydrometer. In summary, the ingredients given above are intended for a general guide to mixing the pickle bath—the critical factor is that the pH be maintained at about 3.0.

A pickling solution can be used indefinitely, as long as the pH is maintained. As the solution becomes diluted from use, simply add more acid to lower the pH to the desired level. The solution will gradually become dirty and should be discarded after it has been neutralized to a pH of 7 by adding salt.

Immerse the skins in the pickle bath. Agitate them often so that the pickle will reach all parts of the skin. After the skins have been in the pickle for a day or two, remove them and shave down the skins as needed. This must be done on a fleshing beam, unless you use a fleshing machine. For small pelts such as squirrel, fox, or coyote, very little fleshing is required. Deer capes should be fleshed along the back of the neck, or on the forehead, and around the ear butts. The purpose of the fleshing is to thin the hide to a more workable thickness. For example, the cape of a moose is much thicker than is required for mounting, and the fleshing process thins the skin and produces a softer, more manageable cape to mount.

After you have fleshed the skins and capes, return them to the pickle bath for several more days. A deer cape needs three to four days to be completely pickled; smaller pelts require less time. Large skins may require a week or more. A skin is completely pickled when the skin is white throughout its thickness. Check this by cutting a sliver of skin from the edge of the cape or hide. The unpickled skin in the center will be semitransparent, but the pickled skin will be opaque or white. During this period continue to stir the skins and keep a constant check on the pH of the solution. The pickle will not hurt the skin. So long as you maintain the pH at the proper level and stir the skins and solution frequently, the skins can remain in the pickle bath indefinitely.

The tanning solution, or liquor, contains the following ingredients:

    5   gallons of water
    2½ pounds of deiodized salt

1¼ pounds of alum

1½ oz. phenol U.S.P. 88 percent (carbolic acid)

Dissolve the phenol in a solution of warm water and mix well. Then add the other ingredients. After you have removed the skins from the pickle bath and rinsed them thoroughly, stir them into the tanning liquor. This tanning solution works slowly, so the skins should be left in the solution for a week or longer. However, this is a safe and effective tanning solution.

Edolan U mothproofing treatment is an optional step that can be performed after the skins are tanned. After removing the skins from the tanning solution and thoroughly rinsing them in clear water, mix a solution of Edolan U according to the manufacturer's instructions.

The skins are now ready to be oiled. Always use neat's-foot oil for tanning and fur dressing. Neat's-foot oil is a natural oil made from the hoofs and bones of cattle. The more common types of oil, such as motor or gun oils, are hydrocarbons containing many additives that are detrimental to the skin structure over a long period of time. Neat's-foot oil can be obtained from many taxidermy supply companies. When it is available, purchase sulfonated oil because it will mix readily with warm water; whereas unsulfonated oil will not mix.

The skins should be moist or slightly damp, but not dripping. Remove as much water as possible from the skins before laying them flesh-side up on a workbench and removing any additional moisture with a scraper and rags. Mix equal parts of sulfonated neat's-foot oil and warm water and paint a thin coat of the mixture on the flesh side of the skins and capes. If you use unsulfonated oil, warm a small amount of oil in a microwave oven or a double boiler and paint this on the flesh side. Avoid getting excess oil on the hair. Work the oil into the skin with your hands, and be sure that the skin has received a uniform application of the oil-water mixture. Obviously, more oil will be needed on a deer cape than on a coyote or fox skin, but only experience will teach how much. In general, it is better to

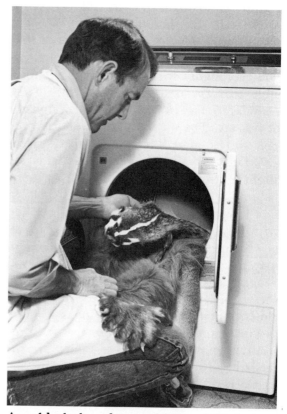

An old clothes dryer with heating element removed makes an excellent tumbler for hides. Simply operate it at low speed. Air holes in the drum must be plugged so that sawdust can be used during the process.

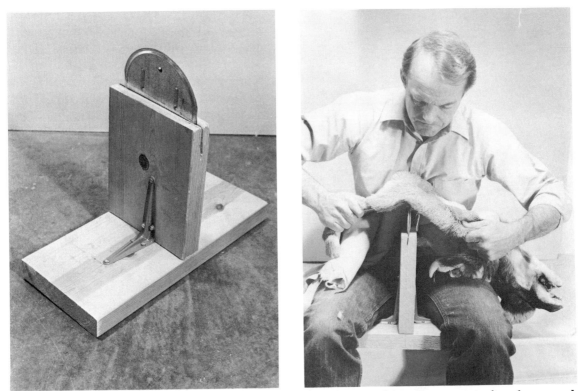

Left: A benchtop staking tool can be made from scrap 2 × 6 lumber, corner brackets, and a piece of rounded steel. The cost is minimal, and the tool is essential for working the skins properly. This type of staking tool is most useful for working smaller skins and capes. *Right:* Here I am staking an pronghorn cape using a benchtop staking tool. The tool works the oils into the skin and at the same time breaks up the fibers in the epidermis and corium. Staking is essential for a quality job. The amount of staking time necessary will depend on the size of the skin or cape.

add coats than to apply too much and need to wipe it off.

Allow the skin to lie for a couple of hours until the oil has had a chance to soak into the fibers of the skin. Then roll the skin up, flesh-side in, and let it stand overnight. After about 24 hours, unroll the skin and hang it over a pole—flesh-side out—until the skin is only slightly damp. The skin is now ready for finishing.

The quality of the tanned skin will depend on the amount of time and effort you put into the finishing. Although the skins have been tanned and oiled, they will remain rather stiff unless the oil is worked into the skin fibers by the finishing process. This process will also break down the skin fibers so they remain flexible. Most commercial tanneries "drum" the oiled skin in large, revolving drums that tumble the skins until they are soft. (A clothes drier, from which the heating element has been removed, makes

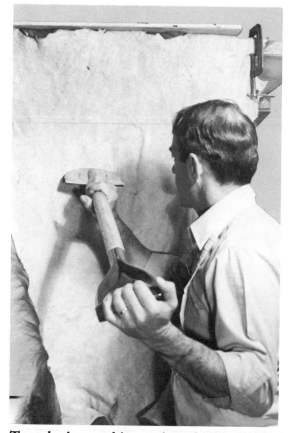

To stake larger skins such as deer and bear, clamp the skin between two 2 × 4s with C-clamps and suspend the hide from the ceiling at the desired height. Then make a staking tool by grinding down the head of a spade. While staking requires a great deal of effort, the results are worth it.

an effective and inexpensive tumbler for the beginning tanner.) If you don't have a tumbler available, you'll need to make a staking tool in order to finish the skins. The skins must be worked over the staking tool by hand, or in some cases it may be necessary to hold larger hides in a beam rack in order

to stake them properly. Although the staking process requires a considerable amount of hand labor, the results can be excellent.

When you have achieved the proper amount of softness by staking, treat the fur with sawdust or cornmeal. Put a cup of cornmeal or sawdust into a large plastic bag with the finished skin. Shake the bag until the cornmeal or sawdust has worked into the hair. Then remove the skin and shake the cornmeal or sawdust out. Use a switch to beat out any remaining cornmeal or sawdust, and give the fur a final brushing.

That completes the tanning and fur-dressing process.

Fur-Dressing Shortcuts. Any pelt that has gone through the complete formic-alum process will remain soft and luxurious for many years. This is the process used by furriers or by fur dressers catering to the taxidermist. Any pelt that must remain soft, whether it is for a coonskin hat or a bearskin rug, should go through all of the steps I described above. However, when the skin will be mounted, you can take several shortcuts. When the pelt will be mounted on a rigid form, as I described in chapters 2 and 3, the need for flexibility is eliminated. So you can eliminate the dressing (tanning) and greatly reduce the finishing steps of the formic-alum process. The final product is not tanned, as taxidermists frequently claim, but the pelt or cape has been pickled and oiled. Although this product is inferior to a completely dressed pelt or cape, it can still produce a long-lasting mount of excellent quality.

When the dressing or tanning process is eliminated, the pelt or cape is taken from the pickling solution and neutralized in a solution of 2 ounces of baking soda in 5 gallons of water. The pH should be about 6 for this solution. Soak the skins for about 15 minutes, stirring frequently, then remove the skins and thoroughly rinse them. A second rinsing will assure that the soda and extra pickle have been removed from skins. The skins should now be mothproofed with Edolan U.

The finishing process can also be shortened when the skin or cape is to be mounted. The oils must be added, as described above, because they reduce shrinkage and add to the longevity of the mount. But the amount of finishing can be reduced after you have applied the oil to the flesh side of the skin. Fold the skin double, flesh sides together, and leave the skin overnight or for six to eight hours. Then open the skin and wipe any extra oil from it. Shake or tumble the skin in sawdust to remove any extra oil; then tumble or work the skin over a staker. The skin is then ready for mounting. It can be kept in a plastic bag and refrigerated for a few days, or it can be frozen for longer storage. In either case, the skin can be mounted using the techniques I described in chapters 2 and 3. But the initial soaking process can be eliminated, since the skins are already moist and oiled.

LEATHER MAKING

Chrome-Tan for Heavy Hides. Home tanning of large hides into heavy harness leather requires a great deal of experience and effort. In fact it is very difficult for an amateur to produce quality leather with the appearance and strength of the commercial product. Still the average do-it-yourselfer can make serviceable leather that will have many uses.

One of the keys to quality leather is beginning with a good hide. For best results, obtain a fresh hide from your local locker plant or butcher shop. The hide should come from a steer or large calf so that the skin is large and strong enough to make good leather. Animals the size of deer or smaller are not large enough to make harness leather; however, these smaller skins can be tanned as buckskin for garments.

Whereas fur dressing requires six basic steps, several additional steps are required for the making of leather. These include removing the hair and dyeing the skin. The finishing process also is modified. Here are the steps in leather making:

1. Rehydration of the skin.
2. Scouring.
3. Dehairing and bating. This includes removal of the hair and neutralization of the lime or acids.
4. Pickling and shaving.
5. Dressing. The tanning process for leather is different from that used in fur dressing.
6. Dyeing the hide.
7. Oiling the leather.
8. Finishing the leather. This is somewhat different from the process used in fur dressing.

There are no shortcuts to leather making. All of the above steps must be followed in order to produce a serviceable leather.

First the steer hide should be fleshed, salted, and dried using the techniques described in the preceding section. Most leather manufacturers split the hide down the center of the back, dividing the hide into two "sides" for easier handling. Since the hide of a steer may weigh as much as 50 pounds and "square" 10 feet or more, a split hide is easier to handle and can be tanned in smaller containers.

While the hide is still reasonably soft but thoroughly drained, follow the rehydration process using the solution I mentioned on page 100. When the hide is soft, it is ready for dehairing. Mix a dehairing solution as follows:

20 gallons of water
10 pounds hydrated lime (calcium hydroxide or builder's lime)

After you have thoroughly mixed the solution, place the hide in the container and agitate it frequently. Leave the hide in this solution until the hair begins to loosen. Remove the hide occasionally and place it over your fleshing beam to scrape the hair free as the hair begins to "slip." This may require a couple of days to a week or longer depending on the temperature of the solution; the warmer the temperature, the faster the dehairing is accomplished. The lime solution will eventually weaken the structure of the hide, so it is important to check the condition of the hair frequently once it begins to loosen. As soon as you have removed all of the hair from the hide, you should remove it from the dehairing solution.

The dehairing process is actually a controlled decomposition of the epidermis in which the hair is anchored. In earlier chapters, I described the problem of hair slip as a result of improper fleshing. Hair slip occurs when salt does not penetrate through the corium to the epidermis. The epidermis then sluffs off, carrying the hair with it. In the dehairing process, lime is used to decompose the epidermis so that it can be scraped away with the hair. Then, in the finished leather, the smooth or pebbly grain is actually the upper surface of the corium

from which the epidermis has been removed.

After you have scraped all of the hair from the hide, use a deliming agent to "kill" the lime in the hide. First, rinse the hide thoroughly with plenty of fresh water; you may even want to soak the hide in clear water for five or six hours. Then mix 9 ounces of lactic acid in 20 gallons of water and put the hide in this solution. (You may substitute vinegar for lactic acid by mixing 1 pint of vinegar with each 5 gallons of water, but lactic acid is more effective. Boric acid is also a good deliming agent.) Allow the hide to soak in this solution for about 24 hours. Then remove the hide and rinse it thoroughly.

The deliming process removes enzymes from the hide that should be replaced before the hide is tanned. Dog dung was originally used for this process, but fortunately modern chemistry has produced better products. Bating (neutralizing) agents, which replace these enzymes, can be obtained from various supply dealers. Simply follow the directions provided with the bating agent. In some cases the deliming agent and a bating agent have been mixed so that both steps can be performed in a single process. *Warning*: Do not ignore the bating process. If you fail to restore the enzymes to a hide, it will not tan properly and all of your effort will be wasted.

The hide is now ready to be tanned.

Most of the early leathers were produced after many months of soaking the hides in vats filled with oak bark. Fortunately bark tans have been replaced by chromium salts that are much faster and produce a good quality of leather. The chemical used in chrome tanning is chromium potassium sulfate. This can be purchased from supply dealers under different brand names such as Krome Tan (Elwood Supply) or Tannium (Van Dyke Supply). Follow the directions

These robes at my cabin are both functional and decorative. The elk robe on the floor serves as a rug, and the deer hides are used as cushions. The deer hides are also exceptionally warm when anyone wants to wrap his feet in them after a day in the woods.

given by the supplier, but in general the directions for chrome tan are as follows:

Mix: 10   gallons of water
          5   pounds of salt
         1½   pounds of chrome salts

Put the water into a large vat or plastic tub and dissolve the ordinary salt in the water. Then heat about 2 quarts of water and dissolve the chrome salts in it. Boil the solution for 7 to 10 minutes. Allow it to cool, then stir about one-third of the chrome solution into the water-salt mixture. (Increase all of the proportions equally to make a larger amount of chrome tan.) The skins should now be placed in the tanning solution and stirred well. After 24 hours add another one-third of the chrome solution and again stir the hides. The last of the chrome stock should be added on the third day.

To ensure that the skins tan evenly, stir the tanning solution several times a day. Wrinkles or untanned spots may result if a skin is folded so that the solution cannot reach all parts of the hide.

The amount of time required for tanning will depend on the thickness of the hide and the temperature of the tanning solution. Calf skins will normally require from four to six days; heavy steer hides may require as much as two to three weeks. Check the depth of penetration by cutting a sliver of hide from the edge of the skin and then examine the color. Chrome tan gives a bluish-green color to the skin as it penetrates toward the middle of the skin. When the color reaches the center of the skin, the hide is completely tanned. However since the thickness of the skin varies, the final check should be made along the middle of the back or on the upper neck where the skin is thickest. (Another check can be made this way: Cut a small piece from the hide; measure it carefully, then put it in boiling water for a minute or two. Remeasure the piece. A tanned skin will show very little shrinkage; whereas the untanned hide will shrink considerably.) Also, chrome tan will not damage the skin, so it can be left in the solution indefinitely. It is better to leave the hide in the solution for a few extra days than to remove it too early.

When tanning is complete, remove the hide from the solution and rinse it thoroughly in fresh water. Then soak the hide in a mixture of ½ pound borax and 10 gallons of water for about eight hours. Remove the hide and wash it thoroughly in five or six changes of clean water before the skin hung up to drain.

The hide is now ready to be dyed, oiled, and finished.

Dyeing the hide is an optional process. Many tanners prefer the natural pale greenish-gray color of a chrome-tanned skin, so if you do not want to dye the hide just omit this step. In order to dye the hide a rich brown color, mix a solution of quebracho, also called bark tan, according to the directions obtained from the supplier. Quebracho is a leather dye made from the root of a South American hardwood. One or two pounds of quebracho dissolved in a half gallon of boiling water is adequate for dyeing a calf skin. The strength of the dye and the intensity of the color will depend on the amount of water used. The dye should be applied with a brush to both sides of the moist hide. Or for total penetration of the hide, soak the skin in the quebracho solution. After the hide is dyed to your satisfaction, rinse it in clear water to remove any remaining dye on the surface.

The uniformity of the dyeing job frequently depends on the quality of the hide, and this is a factor that is difficult to de-

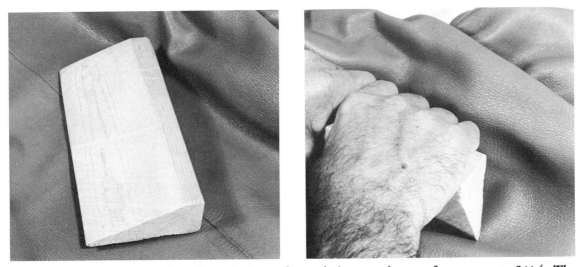

A sleeker is simply a wedge-shaped piece of wood that can be cut from a scrap 2 × 4. The edge of the sleeker helps pull the fluids off the leather. Do not use a metal sleeker because metal edges can scar the finished surface of the leather.

termine in advance. For example, scars and brands on a hide will not dye to the same intensity as adjoining tissue because the texture of the corium is different. Unfortunately there is little that can be done other than to select the best quality hides for leather making, then hope that the animal had not been seriously injured while alive.

Follow the same oiling instructions I provided for fur dressing, beginning on page 102. The only difference is that the thicker hides used for leather making will require more oil. Mix sulfonated neat's-foot oil with warm water and apply it to the flesh side of the hide. Allow it to soak for about 12 hours, then make a second application. Stretch the hide out flat on a floor or large workbench and rub the hide with a "sleeker" made from wood. This begins the finishing process, but you should also work the oil into the skin. You can apply oil to the dehaired side of the leather, but you should be careful not to let the sleeker scratch the leather.

The finishing process for leather goods is similar to that for fur dressing except that the size and thickness of the hides are not conducive to tumbling and drumming. Therefore, the hide should be stretched on a frame or beam rack and staked. *ALWAYS* stake the leather on the flesh side so that the finished side of the leather is not scratched or marred during the finishing process. The final step in the finishing process is called "stuffing." Lay the leather on a smooth surface, "grain" or hair-side up, and roll the surface with a large bottle or rolling pin. This will press the grain down uniformly and produce a smooth, slick-looking surface on the leather.

This completes the leather-making process, which requires a lot of effort. And it is time consuming, but the results can be very satisfying. Two of the most common errors in leather making result in a cracked surface on the grain of the leather. These errors are: (1) failure to neutralize the hides after the dehairing (lime) process and (2) failure to work sufficient oil into the leather. Remember, there are no shortcuts in leather making. Each step must be followed completely.

SPECIALTY LEATHERS

Buckskin Tanning Techniques. The buckskin leather made by the American Indians was renowned for its durability and toughness. However, considering the methods that were used, it is surprising that Christopher Columbus was not able to locate the New World by his nose. I'll describe the Indian method of making buckskin for your interest only. I do not recommend the Indian method if you intend to wear your buckskin in public.

Deer skins were fleshed, then soaked in a stream overnight in order to remove all dirt and blood. The skins were then draped over a log and the hair was scraped from the hide. Occasionally the hides were soaked in a mixture of water and ashes from the fire pit; the ash contained lime that helped to release the hair. The skin was then rinsed and was ready for tanning.

The brains of the deer were put in a pot of water and boiled for an hour or two. After the mixture had cooled to the touch, the brains were ground and stirred in the water until a paste was made. The skin was then coated with the mixture and kneaded periodically throughout the day; it was occasionally stretched and more of the mixture was rubbed into the surface, and again the hide was kneaded. After about 24 hours, the skin was stretched to its maximum size and allowed to completely dry. It was then rolled up and allowed to stand for about two weeks. A slow fire was then built with a tentlike structure of branches constructed over the fire pit. The skin was then unfolded and draped over the branches while the fire was maintained with decayed wood and green willow twigs. The purpose was to smoke the skin but not to cook it. After one side of the hide was smoked to a light yellow to yellowish-brown, the skin was turned and smoked on the other side. The skin was then rinsed and allowed to drain, after which it was "worked" over a stake or limb until soft. In some tribes the squaws chewed the skin to increase the softness.

A more "sociable" type of buckskin can be made from the skins of deer, elk, caribou, or calf. First, the skins must be thoroughly fleshed, then washed in a laundry detergent to remove any dirt, grease, or blood. Then mix ¼ cup of lime in 10 gallons of water and allow the skins to soak for a day or two until the hair is loose. After the hair has been scraped from the skin, rinse it thoroughly in clear water to remove the lime from the hide.

Purchase two bars of naphtha soap at the supermarket and shave them into a small amount of warm water. After the soap has dissolved, add 1 pint of sulfonated neat's-foot oil and stir until it is smooth. Add enough water to make about 4 gallons of solution, then immerse the hide in the liquid for about three days, stirring frequently. Remove the hide after three days and squeeze out as much liquid as possible. Hang the skin up on a clothesline and watch it until slight spots begin to appear. The skin should now be staked and worked over a fleshing beam until completely dry. Now return it

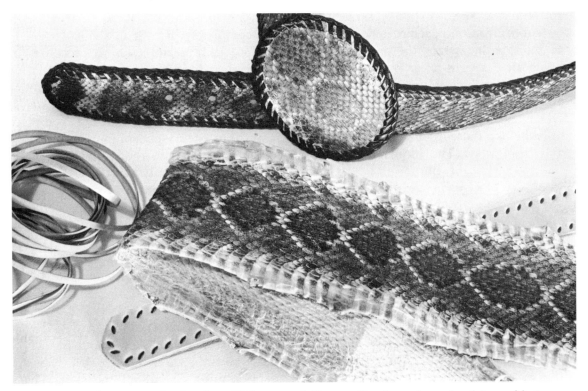

Snakeskin makes attractive leather. This tanned diamondback rattlesnake skin and belt were processed by Ben Haden of Cleburne, Texas. Haden tans nearly 50,000 rattlesnake skins annually. The skins are used for the making of Larry Mayhan boots. The belt is made by gluing the skin to heavy leather and then finishing the edges with a double-loop stitch.

to the soap-oil mixture for another three days of soaking. Then remove the skin from the solution and repeat the drying, staking process until the skin is smooth and soft.

The staking process probably will produce some baggy and uneven spots on the skin. Lay the skin flat, flesh-side up, and wet the skin with a sponge. Roll the skin up for a couple of hours until it is uniformly damp, then stretch it out on a board or workbench and tack down the edges until it is dry. It can then be drummed or tumbled until soft. The buckskin is now finished. However if you wish to add color, you can dye the skin

with a thin solution of quebracho or you can smoke the skin Indian fashion, as I described a few paragraphs earlier.

Rawhide Tanning. The name "rawhide" is appropriate. It is simply an untanned skin from which the hair has been removed. But rawhide is strong and durable, and it has many practical uses since it will mold to virtually any shape. Deer, elk, and calf make the best rawhide, but smaller animals such as coyote and woodchuck can also be used.

Wash and flesh the skin as described above; then soak the skin in a dehairing solution of lime and water used for buckskin. When the hair begins to slip, remove the skin from the solution and scrape the hair off. Wash the dehaired skin in clear water to remove any remaining lime solution. Then stretching the skin to its maximum dimensions, tack it flat onto a sheet of plywood. After the skin has thoroughly dried, remove it from the plywood. The skin will now be stiff and hard as a board, but it can be stored in a cool, dry place until ready for use.

When you are ready to use the rawhide, soak it in water until soft and pliable. Then cut it to size with a sharp hunting knife, linoleum knife, tin snips, or shears, and use as needed. If you want the rawhide to be flexible, such as needed for boot laces, oil the softened rawhide with neat's-foot oil.

Snakeskin Tanning. Snakeskins make attractive leather trim and novelties, but tanning snakeskin is an uncertain proposition at best. The problem arises from the snake's periodic shedding of its skin. If a snake has recently shed its skin, the "new" skin may be soft and very fragile; an "old" skin may be starting to dry out and will crack or split when tanned. You need to start with a skin that isn't too "new" or too "old," something you don't really know. So when you obtain a handsome snakeskin, you have no way of knowing how good the final leather will be. Although there is no guarantee of success, tanning is usually worth a try.

If you are beginning with a fresh kill, remove the head. Then split the snake from stem to stern along the midline of the belly. Scissors or shears work well for this. You may want to hang the snake with hook and chain and then carefully peel the skin off from head to tail, mindful that snakeskin tears easily. Flesh the skin, then lay it flat,

flesh-side up, and salt the skin. It will curl and completely dry out in about 24 hours.

The pickling and tanning processes for snakeskins are the same as those used in fur dressing. First, soak the skin in the formic-alum pickle solution. After about three days, rinse the skin in a salt brine and then place it in the salt-alum-phenol tanning solution. When the skin is thoroughly tanned, drain it until the skin is only moist. Mix a solution of one part sulfonated neat's-foot oil and three parts of water and soak the skin overnight or for 8 to 10 hours. Then remove it from the oil-water solution, blot off the remaining solution from the skin, and tack the skin—flesh-side up—on a board until it is dry. The skin can then be drummed or worked over a staker until soft and flexible. A warm electric iron (not hot) can be used to flatten the skin after it has been drummed.

By this time you will notice that the scales are beginning to fall off the skin. That's good. Snake scales are a chitinous material, similar to fingernails, which protect the skin. Since they are transparent, the color of the skin is not lost when the scales are removed. Lay the skin on your workbench, flesh-side down, and gently rub the skin with a large, gum-type eraser, working from tail to head. An eraser is used because it has a good holding surface that will pull the scales out of their sockets without damaging the skin. Remember, work from the tail to the head with the lay of the scales—*not* against the scales.

Snakeskin has very little inherent strength, so you will need to sew the tanned snakeskin to another piece of leather in order to give the skin support. If you are making a snakeskin belt, simply purchase a leather belt of the proper size and have it stitched to the belt. First apply a small amount of rubber cement from an office supply store to the back of the snakeskin and press the skin to the belt. Trim the edges with a scalpel or razor blade; then have your local shoe repairman sew the edges. A smaller snakeskin can be sewn to a strip of buckskin and used for a hat band. If you simply wish to hang the skin up on the wall for decoration, sew the skin to a piece of felt. To attach a piece of snakeskin to a solid surface, such as a belt buckle, use superglue.

PRESERVING CREAMS AND POWDERS

A number of speciality products offered by taxidermy suppliers are supposed to simplify or eliminate the need for tanning. In fact, many of these products are called "tanning cream." As I've shown earlier in this chapter, tanning is a very involved process requiring many different steps. Proteins, lipids, and carbohydrates are flushed from the structure of the skin, and these are replaced by enzymes, salts, and oils. Clearly, no one-step application of a so-called tanning cream can do all of this. As the old saying goes, "You can't make a silk purse out of a sow's ear," and you can't make tanned leather by applying a one-step cream. It would be more appropriate to call these "preserving creams" rather than tanning creams because they certainly do not tan the skin.

Even though these creams are not what their name implies, they are useful to the taxidermist. If you are not interested in going to the time, effort, and expense of tanning a skin for mounting, a cream will improve the quality of the mount. Most of these products contain a mixture of preservatives and sulfonated neat's-foot oil. Generally the creams are applied to the flesh side of the skin after it has been salted and dried, then rehydrated. The cream is then worked into the skin or hide. Since the hides have already been cured by salt, the oils will reduce shrinkage and add longevity to a mount.

Usually, the creams work most effectively on small mammal skins and capes for game heads. Since the skin is wrapped around a form and remains immobile, the cream will produce a long-lasting mount. But under no circumstances should creams be used for making rugs because they just cannot achieve the flexibility and luxuriousness of the fur-dressing process.

A few supply companies market a dry tanning powder. Chemical analysis of most powders shows that they are little more than borax and/or salt. They have no tanning capability whatsoever and should be avoided.

In summary, tanning and leather making add a totally different dimension to taxidermy. Though the two are generally unrelated, you should understand the tanning process so that you can better prepare your capes and skins for mounting. Even if you choose to use a commercial fur dresser, a knowledge of tanning will enable you to properly flesh, cure, and ship the trophies so that the fur dresser can return them in top condition. On the other hand, leather making requires a great deal of time and manual labor, and the do-it-yourself conversion of a raw hide into workable finished leather is a true accomplishment.

5 RUG MAKING

A trophy rug is one of the most popular means of displaying an animal. And there are good reasons for this popularity. First, a rug is functional—whether displayed on the floor, on a sofa, or on a wall—or whether it is used as a robe. Second, it allows you to display a near life-size big-game animal without blocking traffic in the display room. Third, it costs less than a life-size mount if you have a pro make it for you, and it takes less effort than a life-size mount if you make it yourself.

Rug making requires most of the traditional skills of a taxidermist, as well as those of a tailor. And it enables you to produce a useful product from a skin that might otherwise be wasted.

The popularity of bear rugs is well known, yet nearly all other big-game animals and furbearers can be displayed as rugs or wall hangings too. Today most homes lack the space to display a life-size bear or cougar mount. And the mere head and shoulders of a large bear or cougar is rather unimpressive, but a rug stretched to its full dimensions is an eye-catching trophy on a wall. And it doesn't block traffic on a floor.

The skins of predators are most commonly mounted as rugs. By nature, their fur is able to withstand the stress of being walked upon and it will take a moderate amount of abuse. For medium-size game you are not limited

to predators when making rugs. Several years ago I was asked to make a rug from a large beaver. While somewhat hesitant, I later admitted that the finished rug was unusual, to say the least, complete with big, yellow teeth and round, flat, naked tail. My client was thrilled with his beaver rug, and that was gratifying to me.

Members of the sheep and deer families are seldom used for rugs, yet they can make attractive wall decorations or rugs. In the early West, trappers and Indians frequently wrapped themselves in buffalo robes to keep warm. A robe was a full hide of any large animal tanned with the hair on. Even today the Eskimos use caribou robes for blankets. Taxidermists refer to these as "flat" rugs rather than robes, but they serve as robes.

Strictly speaking, only the head of a big-game rug is mounted. The rest of the rug-making process can be performed by anyone who can use a needle and thread. Since use of needle and thread is essential in rug making, you are about to become a tailor too, unless you have a willing spouse.

In most cases you will want a full-head mount as part of the rug, complete with open mouth. A typical bearskin rug is a good example for rug mounts of all types on animals, so I use that for illustration in this chapter. The half-head rug was common in the past but is rarely mounted today. This is a mount in which only the upper part of the head is mounted after the lower jaw is removed. A half-head rug resembles Fido swimming in a pond, and it lacks the impact and appeal of a full-head rug. It was used 50 years ago when the natural skull was not available, and consisted of a half-head rug

Rugs are functional displays that don't disrupt normal room traffic. Here, after mounting a bear head, I've spread the skin over a stretching board for grooming. Next come finishing touches on the face.

form made from excelsior. A full-head rug can be mounted with the mouth closed to give a more relaxed appearance. Bears are occasionally mounted in this way, but the closed mouth doesn't usually appeal to hunters. I have also seen mountain goats, Barbary sheep, and even deer mounted as closed-mouth wall hangings, but this is not common. In summary, virtually any skin can be mounted as a rug or wall hanging, and there is a wide range of styles you can use.

As in the previous chapters, you should practice on a skin that is not of trophy quality. Begin with a small animal such as a fox or raccoon. They are easier to handle and less expensive to mount. Also, for the purposes of making your first rug, it is not necessary that the raw hide be in perfect condition. A missing foot or damaged skin is not important as long as the face and head of the skin are in repairable condition. You can purchase an imperfect skin for a fraction of the cost of a perfect one. The important thing is having a mountable head; even a damaged skin can be stretched and lined. The resultant rug might not be the prettiest in the world, but offers excellent practice, helping you become experienced enough in rug making so that you can create that perfect trophy skin when it arrives.

SKIN CARE

When a trophy has been bagged, it must be skinned, cured, and tanned before you can begin to make the rug. I have explained the various skin-care processes for preparing a rug in the earlier chapters, but I'll reiterate the highlights here for your convenience. Remember, a quality rug requires a quality tanning job on the pelt. So whether you

follow all of the techniques described in Chapter 4 or send the pelt to a custom fur dresser, you must follow certain steps, as follows:

As I explained in more detail in Chapter 1, regardless of the animal's size or specie, three incisions are made on the underside: (1) the length of the body from the vent or anus to the middle of the throat; (2) from one front foot, down the inside of the leg and across the chest to the other front foot; (3) across the inside of the hind legs from foot to foot through the vent. As well, there are several important points to remember when making these incisions. First, if you always work the skinning knife under the skin and cut upward, you will do virtually no damage to the hair. But if you cut downward against the skin, you will damage the hair, and the edges of the rug will show this. Second, make the incisions symmetrical and properly centered on the legs and belly. If the incision on one leg follows a different angle than the incision opposite, the rug will look crooked or twisted. Likewise, if the belly incision is off to one side of the animal, the finished rug will either have to be trimmed on the "wide side" or else it will look lopsided. By contrast, on a life-size mount, the same three incisions are sewn closed, so crooked incisions there are not obvious. Not so with a rug. So remember, when skinning for a rug, make the incisions straight and symmetrical.

Once you have removed the hide, you must follow the same fleshing techniques that I described for gameheads (in Chapter 2) and for tanning (Chapter 4). A fleshing beam is essential for removal of all membrane and fat from the hide before it is salted and allowed to cure. Also you must flesh the face, split the lips, and turn the ears. Skin the feet all the way to the last joint in the toes. Then lay the hide flat and thoroughly salt the skin. For best results, salt the head, lips, ears, and eyes first. Then pour about 2 pounds of salt into the center of the hide and work it to the edges. Repeat this process 24 hours later, allowing the skin to drain during the interim.

After you have salted the skin twice and allowed it to cure, you can ship it to a fur dresser or tan it yourself. As I described in Chapter 4, the complete fur-dressing process is long and involved, but the process is also essential in order to produce a quality hide that will become the rug. Most professional taxidermists prefer to have pelts commercially tanned for rug making because tanning requires much added time and effort. If you are a beginning taxidermist, it would be advantageous for you to use the services of a commercial tanner, or fur dresser. You will then be assured of a quality tanning job for your first attempts in rug making. As your ability in both tanning and rug making improves, you may then decide to do both processes and thereby have the satisfaction from having done the whole job.

BUILDING A STRETCHING BOARD

To mount a rug, you'll need a stretching board. This is essential to properly shape and stretch the rug after you have mounted the head. I advise that you build a stretching board that can be used for rugs of most sizes. For example, any board that will fit a respectable black bear will be suitable for cougar, wolf, coyote, and smaller animals. Such a board will be large enough to do the job and yet small enough to store or conveniently handle. If you should ever need to stretch an Alaskan brown bear, you could

BUILDING A STRETCHING BOARD

You can make a stretching board assembly from inexpensive lumber. For materials you will need a pair of sawhorses, two 6-foot horizontal members, and two 4 × 8-foot panels of ½-inch plywood. I recommend using sawhorse brackets so you can disassemble and fold the horses for storage.

(Building a Stretching Board continued)

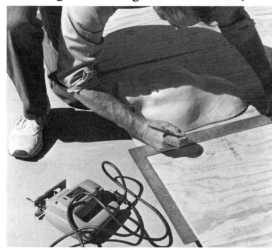

Left: After building the sawhorses and nailing the ½-inch panels to the horizontal members, divide one of the panels lengthwise so you have a 2×8-foot piece to broaden the 4×8-footer. This will produce a surface area of 6×8 feet, which will be adequate for black bear and anything smaller. You can then use the rug shell (headform) as a guide for locating the head opening, which you will saw out. *Right:* After marking the opening for the headform and making the parallel cuts, cut the curve of the opening with a saber saw at a 40° bevel.

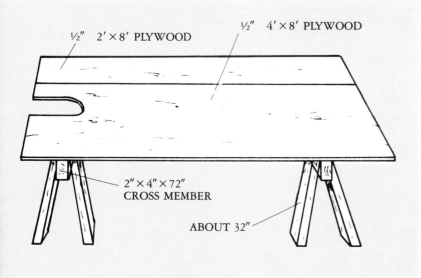

½″ 2′ × 8′ PLYWOOD

½″ 4′ × 8′ PLYWOOD

2″ × 4″ × 72″
CROSS MEMBER

ABOUT 32″

Here are stretching board dimensions. The finished board is also useful for sewing the rugs and for other tasks in the taxidermy shop. Again, a takedown model, employing sawhorse brackets, can easily be stored against a wall.

Center the head opening at one end of the stretching board. Then bevel-cut the back of the opening so the rug will fit comfortably. Dimensions shown are adequate for a black bear and smaller animals.

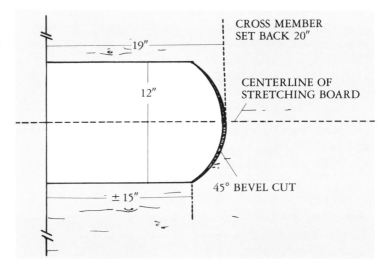

The finished stretching board is reasonably lightweight and easy to move, yet it is strong enough to support your stretching and stapling labors. Paneling thinner than ½-inch would be too weak. Thicker paneling would be too heavy to move about.

always build a larger stretching board.

A very serviceable stretching board can be made from the following supplies:

    2 pair of sawhorse brackets
    2 sheets of ½-inch plywood sheeting
    6 standard framing studs (2 × 4s)

These materials will cost a moderate amount, yet they are one-time expenses on a device that will last for years—and many rugs. Also these materials will yield a small amount of waste lumber from which you can make artificial bases or other things.

I recommend using sawhorse brackets because they are more versatile than a standard, one-piece sawhorse. Begin by cutting four of the 2 × 4s into legs of equal length. The sawhorse should be about 32 inches high, so cut the legs accordingly. Then cut the remaining two studs to 72 inches. These serve as the cross members for the sawhorses.

Now lay one of the pieces of sheeting across the sawhorses and split it in half lengthwise to obtain a piece that is 2 × 8-feet long. The uncut piece of sheeting should now be put on the sawhorses, producing a stretching board that is 6 feet wide and 8 feet long. Then adjust the sawhorses so that one of them is 12 inches from one end and the other is 20 inches from the other end. The sheeting can now be nailed to the sawhorse cross members.

Next you must cut an opening for the head in the stretching board at the end on which the cross member is set back 20 inches. Mark the stretching board in the middle—3 feet from either side. Then mark the board 6 inches on either side of the middle, and with a framing square draw 10-inch lines from the end. Connect these two lines with a half circle having its apex 19 inches from the centerline of the board, as shown in the

drawing on page 118. Now saw this piece out of the board with a saber saw. The half circle portion should be beveled toward the skin side at about 45 degrees. Sand the boards down as needed. That finishes the job.

If you have used sawhorse brackets, you can now lift the cross members and entire stretching board out of the brackets and store the assembly against a wall until needed. The legs and brackets can also be set aside.

MOUNTING OPEN-MOUTH RUGS

While the hide is being tanned, order a skull form (shell) and jaw assembly from a supplier. In some cases these items can be purchased assembled. Other suppliers send the parts separately, requiring that you assemble the jaws and rug shell. You should also purchase an artificial tongue and the glass eyes. As I will explain later, since you can make earliners from hardware cloth, commercial earliners are not needed for a rug.

Most hunters and beginning taxidermists ask, "Why not use the natural teeth?" The answer is simple: Plastic teeth last longer than natural teeth. For many years taxidermists used the natural skull, and this required that the taxidermist spend a great deal of time and effort modeling a rug shell over the natural skull. Not only was the rug form heavy, the natural teeth had a tendency to crack, split, and fall out. This is because the natural skull gradually dehydrates and shrinks, and because the tooth sockets loosen. Thus, in the old days, the owner of a rug of a few years found himself in possession of a beautiful rug with no teeth. Invariably the hunter blames the taxidermist, but the loss of natural teeth is nearly impossible to pre-

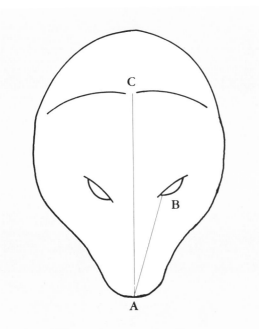

Jaw sets, which usually include the upper and lower jaws and the artificial tongue, are manufactured to fit most rug shells. Order the rug shell that most nearly matches the measurements from your trophy, and order the jaw set to fit the shell. In other words, the measurement for a large black bear may be 5½ inches (nose to eye) and 14 inches (nose to back of skull). For such a skull, you would order a rug shell to these measurements and a "large" jaw set. For the same bear you probably would order a set of size 15mm eyes. Most supply catalogs explain their own methods of measuring.

While you are preparing the rug shell for

When ordering a rug shell (headform) from a supply company, you'll need two measurements: nose to eye *(A–B)*; nose to back of skull *(A–C)*. You won't need neck measurements, as are needed for game-head mounts. Because brown bear and grizzly are technically one species, you can use one form for either. Unless there is a significant difference in jaw size, such as between a cub and large adult, one size is made for each species.

vent. If the hunter demands the natural teeth, most taxidermists offer the additional service of a separate bleached-skull mount. Here the natural skull is bleached and mounted with closed mouth that keeps the teeth from falling out.

The rug skull form, or shell, as it is usually called, should be ordered according to the measurements made from the original trophy. Two measurements are needed:

Nose to eye

Nose to back of skull

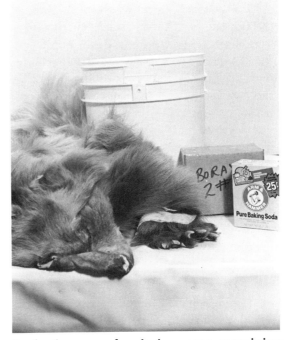

Soak the tanned pelt in water containing ½ cup of baking soda or borax to neutralize any acid that might remain in the skin. A few drops of liquid detergent will help to remove any dirt left in the fur. Allow the pelt to drain while you prepare the shell.

mounting, the tanned hide should be soaked in water to prepare it for mounting. A medium-size black bear hide will require about 2 gallons of water in a plastic bucket. Into the water, stir ½ cup of baking soda (sodium bicarbonate) and 1 teaspoon of liquid dishwashing detergent. The baking soda will neutralize any acid in the hide that was not flushed out following the tanning process. (The same amount of powdered borax may be used instead of baking soda.) The detergent gives the pelt a final cleansing. You will be amazed at the amount of dirt that remains after the pelt has been tanned. Leave the pelt in the solution for about two hours, then remove the skin and squeeze out the excess water.

Most of the skin will be soft by now, although the ears, nose, and feet will still be somewhat stiff. Fold the head and feet to the inside. Then roll up the skin and allow it to set for several hours or longer. When the ears, nose, and feet are soft, the hide is ready for repair and mounting. I frequently put a damp hide in a plastic bag and store it in the refrigerator overnight. If you encounter delays in preparing the rug shell, freeze the damp hide until you are ready to mount it.

SETTING ARTIFICIAL JAWS AND EYES

In many cases, the jaw sets are already assembled in the rug shell. This is a time saver. But this is not essential and in many instances you may find that you can do a better job of setting the jaws than is done by the supplier. First examine the artificial jaws. You will see that the upper jaw and palate are wider than the lower jaw. Also note that the lower canine teeth close in front of the upper canines when the jaws close. With this in mind, you can set the jaws properly. If the upper and lower jaws are separated when you receive them from the supplier, join them at the back of the jaw set with a spot of superglue and then anchor them with a wire or two. For this, common straight pins serve well when punched through the back and twisted.

Most rug shells are molded from polyurethane with varying amounts of recess in the mouth area for the artificial jaws. Put the jaws into the mouth area and check for proper fit. In most cases you will need to cut away some of the form to set the jaws properly. This can be done with a knife, a hand rasp, or a rasp head mounted on a power drill. Whatever tool you use, cut away enough of the rug shell to fit the jaws into place. In some cases it may be necessary to trim the edges from the jaw assembly with heavy-duty scissors or shears. This is particularly true of the lower jaw. If the mouth area is too large, set the jaws in a bed of papier-mâché in order to fill the extra space.

Before you begin to set the jaws, refer to photos showing live animals with an open mouth. You can even benefit by examining the teeth of a pet dog. On a dog you will see that few of the teeth would be exposed, even in the most intense snarl. Also, most lip movement is in the upper jaw. If you lack good reference material, you are likely to commit any one of the three common errors in setting the artificial jaws: (1) the jaws are set too shallowly; (2) the jaws are set too far back in the mouth; (3) the jaws are set at the wrong angle.

Too Shallow. The jaws are set too shallowly

JAW SETS

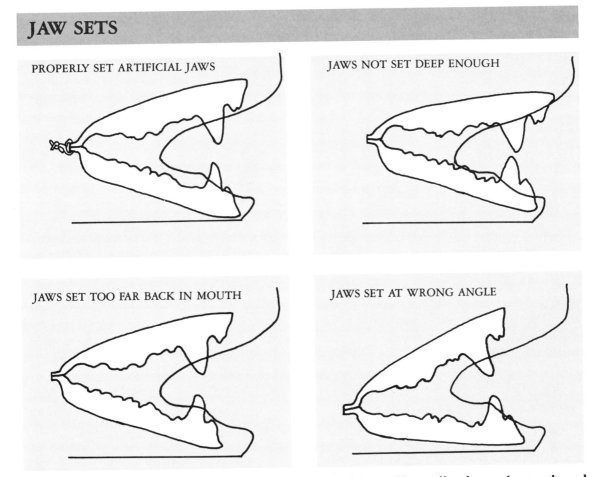

PROPERLY SET ARTIFICIAL JAWS

JAWS NOT SET DEEP ENOUGH

JAWS SET TOO FAR BACK IN MOUTH

JAWS SET AT WRONG ANGLE

Drawing A shows the proper setting for the artificial jaws. Normally, the canine teeth and the lower incisors should be visible. Note the small wire (or pin) at the back of the plastic jaws holds them firmly while they are being set. Study the remaining drawings for illustration of common mistakes. In *Drawing B*, the jaws look too shallow because the shell was not set deep enough. In *Drawing C*, the jaws are set too far back into the mouth, exposing too much lip area. In *Drawing D*, the jaws are set at the wrong angle, possibly because the shell was not properly prepared.

when insufficient material has been removed from the rug shell. This will produce a mouth with too much tooth-and-gum area showing. This is usually most noticeable along the lower jaw. You can easily remedy this problem by removing the jaws and cutting away more of the rug shell inside the mouth.

Remember, it is easy to build up the mouth if you remove too much material.

Too Far Back. When the jaws are set too far back in the mouth, too much lip area will remain at the front of the jaws. The rug may look all right when viewed from the front, but the side view will show too much lower lip and snout ahead of the teeth. In this case, simply remove the jaws and stuff a bed of papier-mâché or potter's clay behind the artificial jaws. This will force the jaws forward and into a better position.

Wrong Angle. Jaws set at the wrong angle will overexpose one jaw and underexpose the other. Commonly the lower jaw will be set too deep and this will pull the upper jaw back too far. The result is that the mount will have too much muzzle. This can be corrected by adding mâché or clay, or else by removing more material from the shell.

When you are satisfied that the artificial jaws fit the form properly, remove the jaws and put a small amount of superglue around the edge of the jaws to hold them in place. Then with a hot-glue gun, run a bead of glue around the edge for a more permanent anchor. You can also run a couple of pins through the outside of the jaws on the rug assembly and into the lower part of the artificial jaws. You now have a firm attachment of the jaws to the rug shell.

Using a coarse-grit sandpaper, sand the entire rug shell, removing the glossy finish and any remaining separator still on the form. Be particularly careful to sand any depression or recessed area; this will help ensure adhesion of hide to form there. Go over the lips, both inside and outside the shell and around the nose. Then grind out the eye sockets and nostrils with a small electric hand grinder or a knife. Most forms are designed to look good, but they leave insufficient room for setting the glass eyes and for tucking the skin into the nose. Also, if you are using one of the Van Dyke TPV series eyes with the white scleral band around the cornea,

you will have to remove additional material from the shell. Don't remove so much material that the shape of the form is lost. Still if you do remove too much from the eyes or nose, you can always restore as needed with potter's clay. This is the same technique I described for preparing a deer headform in Chapter 2.

Put a wad of potter's clay into the eye sockets and press the glass eyes into place. These should be set at the same angle shown for all predators on page 78. Again, on predators the back of the eye should be slanted so that the top of the eye is approximately 15 degrees behind the bottom of the eye. Also the eye should be approximately 67 degrees from the centerline of the rug shell.

Use potter's clay to model any additional features around the muzzle or the eyes. Also at this time, fill any imperfections in the rug shell with clay. The shell is now ready for mounting.

SEWING TECHNIQUES

All of the holes in the skin must be repaired in the presoaked hide. This is particularly important for rugs because holes will become enlarged when the hide is stretched. Scars, rubbed spots on bear hides, and other damaged areas can be removed to improve the quality of the rug.

Use nylon thread for sewing. In the past many taxidermists used cotton thread that had been waxed to add strength and reduce deterioration. However nylon thread is much stronger, fiber for fiber, and there is virtually no deterioration of nylon. Also, select a thread color that most nearly matches the color of the hair. In most cases this will be black or brown. Some taxidermists use clear

PREPARING THE HEADFORM

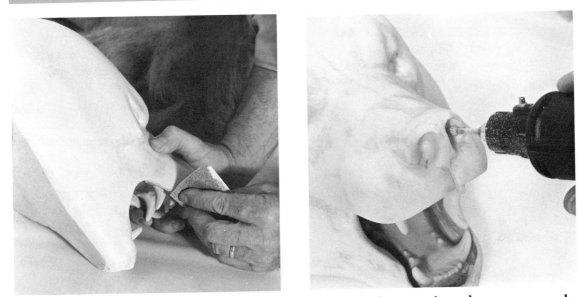

Left: Sand the outer surface of the shell with a coarse-grit paper in order to remove the hard, slick surface on the polyurethane so that hide paste will bond the skin to the form. Be sure to sand all of the depressions around the lips and the nose. *Right:* Most commercial forms are modeled to look good to the buyer. But these forms usually don't provide enough room for application of clay at the nose and eyes, and so they must be enlarged. A small portable electric grinder lets you hollow out the nostrils and remove material around the eyes. You could also use a scalpel or sharp knife and then sand the areas smooth.

After filling unwanted depressions with potter's clay, set the eyes in a bed of clay. The top of the glass eye should be slanted back at about 15 degrees from the base, and the back of the eye should be at an angle of about 67 degrees from the centerline of the form. You can here see a wad of clay in the nose. And a depression on the bridge of the nose has been filled with clay. This shell is ready for mounting.

nylon monofilament fishing line for all of their sewing because it is almost invisible. Unfortunately, clear monofilament lacks flexibility, making it more difficult to work with, and it is also difficult to knot. If you have a hide of unusual color, such as a blond bear, use unwaxed white nylon dental floss. When you have finished the rug, you can dye or paint the exposed thread to the approximate color of the pelt.

Sewing is an important part of rug making. In the earlier chapters of the book, I recommended the baseball stitch for the closing of the incision that was made during skinning. For those mounts incisions were made where the hair was quite long, and in positions on the mount where they would not be easily spotted. So for those mounts, the perfection of sewing technique is not as important. That's not the case with rugs.

You need to know several different stitches in order to make a quality rug. The baseball stitch is used for repairs where the hair is fairly long. The shoelace stitch is a modification of the baseball stitch. The casting stitch and the blind stitch are used where the hair is rather short, such as on the face. These produce a less detectable seam where appearance is important.

The **baseball stitch**, as I described in Chapter 2, gets its name from the standard stitching on the cover of a baseball. For the taxidermist, the baseball stitch has two advantages: (1) Since the needle is always brought through the skin from the underside of the skin, this stitch gathers very little hair or feathers. When it does gather hair, the hair is relatively easy to clean out. (2) It is fast and minimizes sewing time.

The disadvantage of the baseball stitch is that it has a tendency to pucker the skin along the seam. On the back of a deer head or on the heavier parts of a rug, this stitch works well, but it should not be used where the hair is thin or very short, such as on the flanks or face.

The **shoelace stitch** is essentially a double baseball stitch. It requires two needles, so you probably will stick yourself twice as often. The advantage of this stitch is that it is extremely strong where stretching of the skin will occur, and the double threads reduce the amount of puckering along the seam.

The amount of puckering can be reduced by carefully angling the needle from underneath to the hair-side edge of the incision. This is shown in the detail of the stitching drawing and will produce a smoother seam. In this case, most of the puckering will occur on the underside of the skin.

Unlike the baseball stitch and the shoelace stitch, the **blind stitch** is always begun on the hair-side of the skin. It has the advantage of making a clean, neat seam that is virtually invisible when the thread is drawn tightly. This stitch works well where the hair is very short, such as on the facial skin and where stretching is minimal. However the blind stitch has a tendency to entangle hair, so it is a time-consuming stitch to use. Also, this stitch will stand very little stretching without exposing the thread.

The **casting stitch** is a combination of the baseball stitch and a blind stitch. It is begun on the hair-side of the skin and therefore has a tendency to pull hair into the stitches. The casting stitch does not pucker the seam as badly as a baseball stitch, and it will stand a great deal more stretching than a blind stitch. This probably is the best all-around stitch for sewing game heads or rugs.

Most of the damage to a skin is the result of bullet wounds, poor skinning technique

TAXIDERMY STITCHES

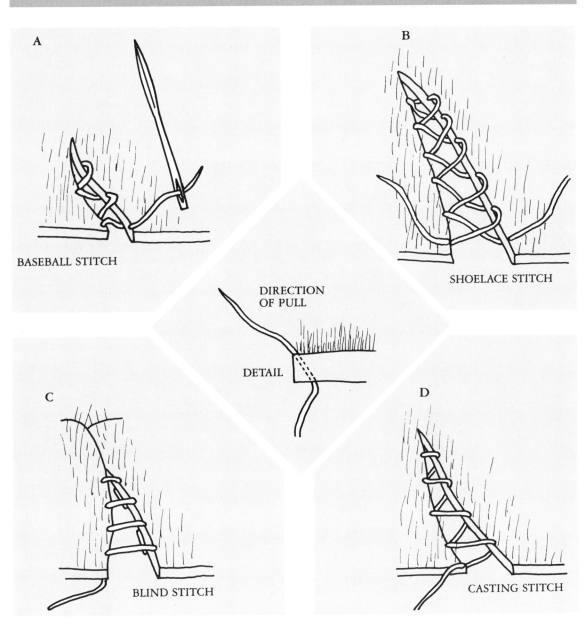

A
BASEBALL STITCH

B
SHOELACE STITCH

DIRECTION
OF PULL

DETAIL

C
BLIND STITCH

D
CASTING STITCH

The four most common stitches used by taxidermists are *A* the baseball stitch, *B* the shoelace stitch, *C* the blind stitch, and *D* the casting stitch. Each has its advantages and disadvantages. To reduce the amount of puckering along a seam and increase the strength of the seam, run the needle through the skin at an angle, as shown in the centered sewing drawing.

REPAIRING DAMAGE

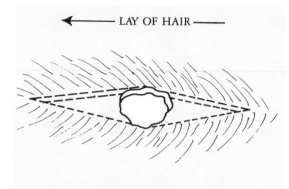

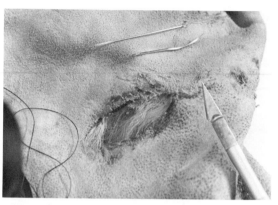

Left: A round hole will pucker badly if it is not properly trimmed before being sewn. With a sharp knife or scalpel, cut a wedge-shape piece out of the skin on opposite sides of the hole. When sewn with a baseball or casting stitch, the hole will close to a tight seam. Wedges cut parallel with the lay of the hair result in better-concealed stitching. *Right:* In order to close a large, irregular hole in the pelt, you will need hide needles, a scalpel, and strong thread. Two 3-sided hide needles are shown above the hole, one curved and one straight. Use nylon thread that matches the color of the hair.

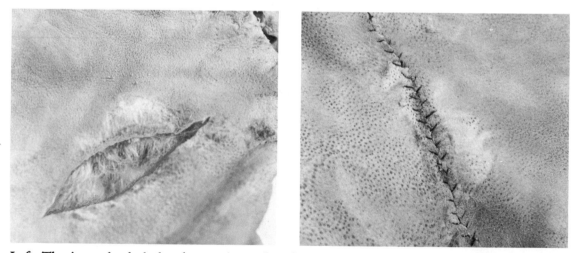

Left: The irregular hole has been trimmed and enlarged by cutting a wedge out of the skin on either side of the hole. A scalpel was used to trim and thin the skin along the edges of the opening so the edges of the skin would be uniform when sewn. *Right:* Note the lack of puckering when the locking baseball stitch is used. The light-colored area shows where thinning was done prior to sewing.

in the field, or (occasionally) damage at the tannery or during the fleshing process. In most cases round or oval holes are produced in the skin. If a round hole is sewn closed without trimming, the skin will pucker on each end and the stitches probably will be exposed in the center. When repairing a hole in the skin, cut out a wedge-shaped slice on both sides of the hole, making an elongated cut as shown in the accompanying drawing. Then sew the cut closed using the most appropriate stitch. This type of repair can be used to close any size circular hole, and it will eliminate any puckering.

MOUNTING THE HEAD

At this point you have rehydrated and repaired the skin and prepared the rug shell. Now the head is ready to be mounted. First you need to make a pair of earliners using the techniques shown in accompanying photos. The ears of the rug have been turned

EAR LINERS

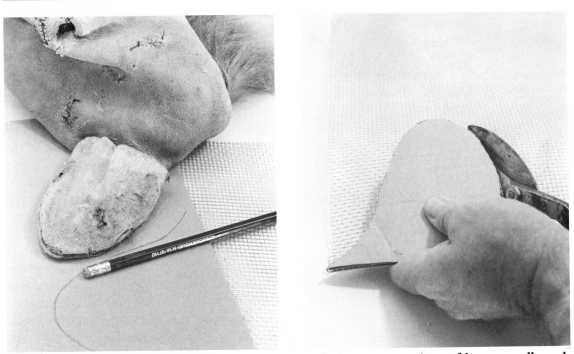

Left: After turning the ear inside-out, trace around the ear on a piece of heavy cardboard. Cut out the pattern with scissors and insert the cardboard into the ear skin to be sure that it fits properly. If it is too large, trim it down. You can then use this pattern for both ears. *Right:* Using the cardboard pattern as a guide, cut the earliners out of ⅛-inch wire cloth. These earliners will hold any shape and are particularly useful for ears of rug mounts.

An earliner is made in three steps. First, cut a cardboard pattern. Cut the actual earliner from wire cloth. Then tape the sharp edges, making the liner easier to insert and shape.

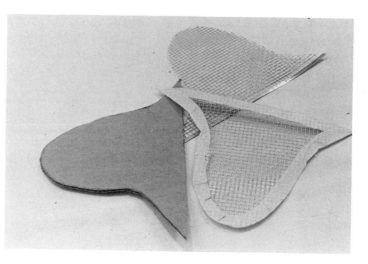

completely, so draw a pattern of the ear cartilage on a piece of cardboard. Cut the pattern out, then slip it into the ear skin to be sure that it fits properly. Using the cardboard as a pattern, snip the earliners from ⅛-inch wire hardware cloth. Trim the edges with a strip of masking tape.

Mix a small amount of hide paste—about 1 cup should be adequate for most black bear rugs. Paint some of the hide paste onto the ear skin and insert the earliners. Then with a brush, paint a coating of the paste on the rug shell. Now spread the bear skin flat, hair-side down, and paint some of the paste on the inside of the head skin, around the eyes and ear butts, and on the lip skin. Coating the lip skin is particularly important because you must have a good bond between the lip skin and the rug shell. Insert a small amount of potter's clay inside the nose skin, and place a roll of clay into the base of each ear so that it can be modeled into an ear butt later.

You can now slip the rug shell into the head skin. Work carefully and avoid as much as possible any contact between the rug shell and the body of the rug. After you have the rug shell inside the head skin, with the lips and nose properly fitted, use a damp cloth to wipe any hide paste off the skin of the rug. Until now you have been working with the rug upside down. Now turn it over and adjust the skin to the rug shell.

Using the same methods as I described for mounting a game head in Chapter 2, center the lip skin on the lower jaw and hold it in place with a pin or two. Also pull the jaw skin down under the rug shell and pin the skin to the bottom of the shell. Adjust the nose and pin it into place, then insert a pin or two into the corner of each eye. Wrap the lip skin around the lips of the rug shell and push it down inside the mouth between the rug shell and the artificial jaws. Put a sufficient number of pins in place to hold the lip skin. If you have too much lip skin, you may need to trim some of it away with scissors before pinning inside the mouth. It is better to have too much skin than not enough, but this is seldom the case.

MOUNTING THE HEAD

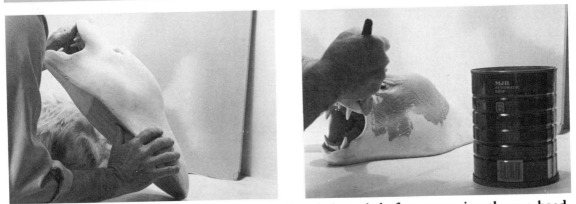

Left: Make a final inspection of both the shell and the pelt before mounting the rug head. Be certain that you have sewn holes in the skin and that you have trimmed and shaved the muzzle skin as necessary. Also inspect the shell for any areas that have not been adequately sandpapered or filled with potter's clay. *Right:* After test-fitting the head skin over the shell, paint the shell with a heavy coat of hide paste. You will need about 1 cup of paste; an empty coffee can makes a convenient container in which to mix the paste. Be sure you apply the paste to the entire shell, around the eyes and nose, and both inside and outside the lips. Avoid getting any more paste than necessary on the artificial teeth.

Left: Apply a coat of hide paste inside the ears, on the flesh side of the lips, nose and eyes. Applying paste inside the skin assures that the skin will be adequately affixed to the rug shell. *Right:* Insert the earliners into place and work the skin down evenly to the edge of the liner. Then press the skin against the earliner and shape the ear to its natural position. The wire cloth will hold its shape. Then to prevent drumming of the ear skin while the hide paste is bonding, staple several strips of heavy paper inside the ear and along the edge. Milk cartons are good for this purpose.

(Continued)

(Head Mounting continued)

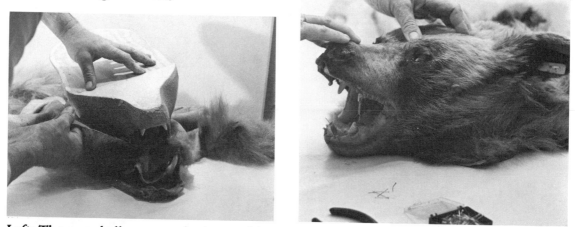

Left: The rug shell can now be inserted into the head skin. Turn the pelt upside down on the stretching board or a workbench; then work the shell into the skin of the head. Since the hide paste is primarily on the shell, by working upside down you help prevent the paste's running onto the main body of the rug. If the skin is too tight around the lower jaw, split the skin a little more under the chin. *Right:* Once you have the head skin in place, turn the rug right-side up and work on the facial features. Use pins and needle-nose pliers to hold the skin in place, using the techniques for the mounting of game heads in Chapter 2. Begin by centering the skin on the nose and lower jaw. Then work back to the eyes and ears.

Use plenty of pins to hold the lip skin in place. Wrap as much of the skin as possible inside the lips and rug shell. You will need to leave some pins in place, but you can pull out others after the hide paste has set.

Use pins to hold the skin in place around the nose, lips, and eyes. Staples serve better on the face. Use a staple gun with ½-inch staples, and align the staples parallel with the lay of the hair. Use staples wherever there is a chance that the shrinking skin will drum across depressions in the rug shell (that is, pull away from concave surfaces). This is vital along the nose, on the forehead between the eyes, and along the ridge of the skull.

Use No. 4 finishing nails to hold the skin against the shell along the back of the head and around the edges of the form. Drive a few nails through the skin and into the board that is molded into the bottom of the shell.

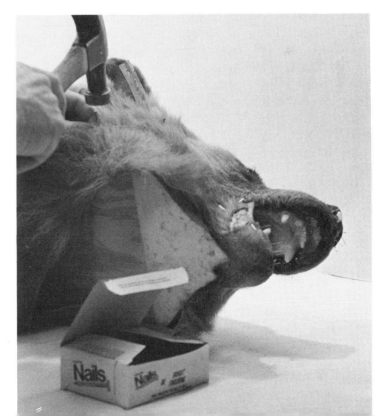

Now turn your attention to the facial features. Using a modeling tool, such as the wooden end of a small paintbrush, shape the nose properly by working the clay under the skin. If there is too much clay, you can dig it out of the nostrils; you can also add clay through the nostrils. Do the same for the eyes, and add the pins necessary to hold the skin in place until the hide paste bonds properly. Work the skin back to the base of the shell and use a few No. 4 finishing nails to anchor the skin around the base of the shell. (Most rug shells are manufactured with a wooden core at the base into which the nails will anchor, as shown on page 133.)

The last step is modeling the ear butts and shaping the ears. I recommend that the rug be mounted with the ears laid back. There are several advantages to this method rather than mounting the ears erect. First, it is easier to work on the rug if the ears are flat or laid back. Second, ears that stand erect are much more subject to damage after the rug is in use. Third, an angry bear's ears are laid back. So with this in mind, fold the ears back and down against the side of the head. Don't overdo it. Just create a smooth flow along the side of the head. The hardware cloth will hold the shape you give it, and then you can model the clay inside the ear skin to the shape of the ear butt.

STRETCHING THE RUG

When you are satisfied that you have mounted the head properly, examine the rest of the hide and rinse off any hide paste that may be exposed around the edge of the rug shell. The pelt should still be soft and moist. If it has started to dry out, turn it hair-side down and go over the skin with a moist

When the head is mounted, nail a spanning stick or dowel to the bottom of the rug shell. Then spread the skin over the stretching board and comb the fur. Since this is the first time that the pelt has been combed and brushed, comb slowly and gently, removing knots and gnarls.

sponge or rag. Then tack a small dowel or stick to the bottom of the shell. The rug can now be placed on the stretching board with the mounted head suspended in the cutout section and held in place by the dowel.

Using a staple gun, tack the skin down to the stretching board around the edge of the head. A ½-inch staple will anchor the skin tightly and yet be easy to pull later. Then go to the back of the board and stretch the skin as much as possible from the head to tail and staple the tail in place. With the

STRETCHING THE RUG

With the head of the rug slipped into the cutout portion of the stretching board, the spanning stick holds the head at the proper position. Fasten a string of staples along the edge of the head cutout so that the neck area is strongly anchored. Then go to the tail, as shown, and stretch the skin lengthwise as much as possible without damaging the skin. After fastening four or five staples at the base of the tail, fasten a line of staples along the middle of the back from head to tail.

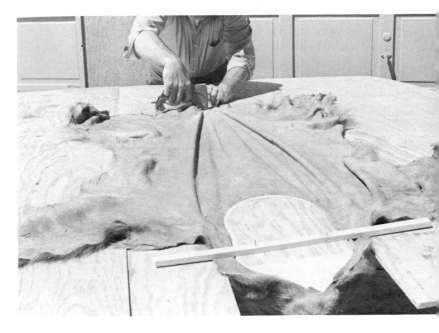

After stretching the rug lengthwise, begin stretching the side by starting at the narrowest part of the body. Then after stretching the legs lengthwise, aligning them and the feet properly, fasten a couple of staples in each foot. Then finish stapling around the skin perimeter.

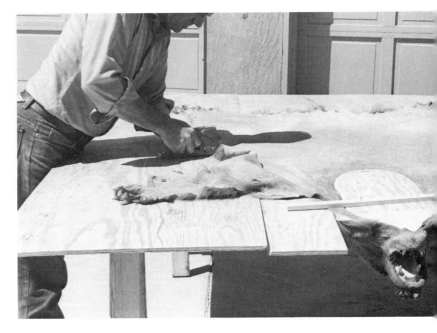

To align the skin so the rug will be symmetrical, make a few measurements after stretching the skin lengthwise. First, be sure the tail is aligned with the nose. Do this by measuring the distance from the nose (A) to the edge of the stretching board (C). The tip of the tail should be the same distance to the edge of the stretching board (B to Y). Now stretch the front leg to the desired position and anchor the foot with staples. Measure the distance from the middle toe (X) to the nose (A) and to the tip of the tail (B). Stretch the other front leg to the same position. Then stretch one back leg to the desired position and staple it. Measure the distance from the middle toe of that foot (Y) to the tip of the tail (B) and to the front foot (X). Then position the other back leg in like manner.

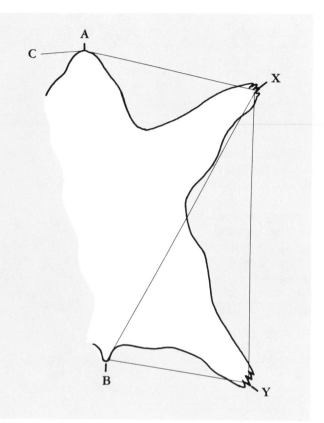

skin stretched to maximum length, place a line of staples—every 2 or 3 inches—along the centerline of the skin. Now go to each leg and stretch it out as much as possible; use a couple of staples to hold the foot and leg in position. Note: When stretching the legs, be careful to keep the rug symmetrical. You do not want one leg stretched at a different angle than the opposite leg.

You can check for symmetry by measuring from the middle toe of each foot to the tip of the lower jaw or the tail. The distances should be about the same for both front legs from foot to lower jaw, and both hind feet should be about the same distance from the tip of the tail.

Next, behind the front legs at the narrowest point of the body, begin stretching the skin out from the centerline, and tack it down with the staple gun. Continue to stretch and staple along the edge of the skin toward the feet. Finally, staple along the front legs to the head and along the back legs from tail to feet. Be sure that the tail is stapled flat. You will find that a fold of skin remains along the edge of the skin at the shoulder and behind the front legs. Simply stretch the skin tight leaving this fold of skin in place. After the skin has dried, you will cut out this extra skin.

Some supply companies sell hide stretchers to pull the skin while stapling, but pliers work just about as well. Remember, staples are cheap, and the more you use, the tighter and flatter your rug will be. A tight, flat rug is also easier to trim later.

The stretching technique that I describe above is generally used for bear. But the technique may vary with the type of skin. For example, bear hides are generally rather square, so I always gain some additional length by stretching from head to tail first. Whereas, a cougar skin is quite long—not to mention the tail—so I usually stretch the width first in order to broaden the rug. To stretch the width, simply lay the skin flat on the stretching board and put a row of staples along the centerline of the skin without a significant amount of stretching from head to tail. Then do the maximum amount of stretching away from the centerline to the edge of the skin and the legs. The goal is to stretch the skin into a symmetrical shape which is neither overly broad nor overly long and snaky. In fact the stretching technique may depend on the individual skin and not necessarily on the species. I have had some coyote rugs that looked better after I stretched them for length and others that looked better after I widened them.

The final step in stretching the skin involves the positioning of the claws. First put a staple into the skin of each toe and space the toes properly. It is easiest to begin with the middle toe and work to the sides. Then hold the claws upright by placing a nail on either side of each claw. No. 4 finishing nails work well for most big-game animals.

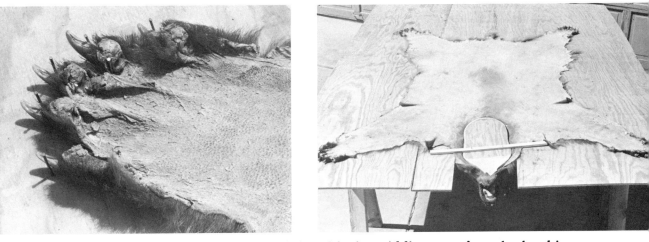

Left: The feet require special attention. Begin with the middle toe and staple the skin so that the toe is properly aligned with the leg and centered in the foot. Then drive a No. 4 finishing nail into the board on either side of the claw. This will hold the claw upright and straight. Now repeat the process on the other toes of that foot and the other feet of the rug. *Right:* When the rug is properly stretched, the skin is perfectly flat and the head, tail, and legs are all aligned symmetrically. A wedge of loose skin is always present in front of and behind the front legs at the shoulder. These wedges can be allowed to dry in place and removed later. The skin probably will dry more quickly than the mounted head, so it is a good idea to leave the rug on the board until the head has completely dried (3 to 4 days).

The rug is now fully stretched and ready to dry. You can leave the stretching board on the sawhorses, or to save space while the rug dries, you can lift the board and rug off the sawhorses and stand the assembly against a wall. In many commercial studios, as many as ten rugs and boards may be standing against the wall drying. In most cases, the rug will need three or four days to dry. In fact, the hide itself will dry much quicker than the head. So periodically check the head and facial features while the rug is on the stretching board.

FINISHING AND LINING THE RUG

As a result of the stretching process, the perimeter of the skin will be slightly irregular. In order to have a smoothly finished rug, go around the edge of the skin with a pencil to mark the areas that should be trimmed away. Then with a scalpel or razor blade, trim the edge of the skin to obtain a smooth contour along the edge, while being careful not to cut the hair.

Remove the rug from the stretching board by pulling all of the staples out and pulling the nails from the feet. Then thoroughly comb and brush the rug.

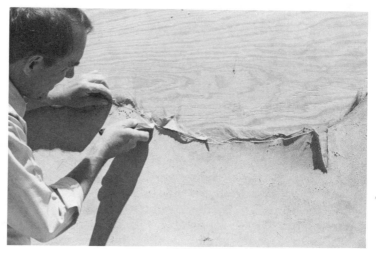

After using a pen or pencil to draw a uniform contour line along the edge of the skin, trim off the rough edges with a utility knife, as shown, or with a scalpel. Also, cut the skin wedges away at the shoulders.

Pull all of the staples out and turn the rug hair-side up on the stretching board. This is a good time to comb and brush the hair. Examine the face of the bear and finish it in the same way that I described for a deer head in Chapter 2. Clean the eyes, removing any clay or hide paste. Also clean the nose, lips, and mouth in the same way. Use a filler to repair any irregularities in the nose. Also, fill in the gum area between the artificial teeth and the lips. This should be modeled to a smooth contour so the lips blend smoothly with the jaws and teeth.

A variety of fillers can be used for this purpose. For many years taxidermists depended on colored wax for filling the mouth and for filling around the eyes and nose. However wax is soft and does not stand up as well as papier-mâché, potter's clay, or Sculpall. I recommend using Sculpall because it is an epoxy that can be worked in your hands and modeled. Once dry, it is very hard and durable. It also takes paint very well. However it is somewhat expensive. So for your first attempts at rug making, potter's clay or mâché can be used with good results.

When the filler has dried, carefully examine the head again and be sure that there are no unfilled damaged areas. Check along the jaws, gums, and teeth to be certain that no cracks are present. When you are satisfied that the head is finished, paint the eyes, nose, and mouth. For a black bear this is relatively simple. Using black or a very intense dark brown, paint the eyelids, nose,

FINISHING THE MOUTH

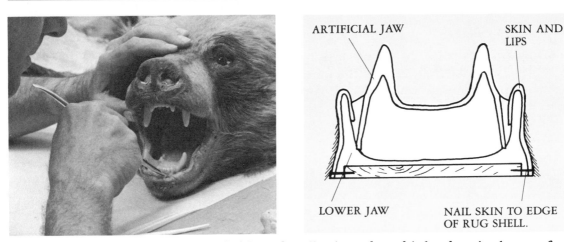

ARTIFICIAL JAW

SKIN AND LIPS

LOWER JAW

NAIL SKIN TO EDGE OF RUG SHELL.

Left: Sculpall is an epoxy. It is workable and easily cleaned, and it hardens in three to four hours. It is more durable than potter's clay or mâché, and most taxidermy supply companies sell it. Model it between the artificial jaws and rug shell—also around the nose and eyes as needed. *Right:* This is a cross section through the lower jaw after the head has been mounted and filled. The Sculpall or other filler acts as a permanent bond between the artificial jaws and the lip skin. You can leave some pins in the lip skin if you cover them with filler.

(Continued)

(Finishing the Mouth continued)

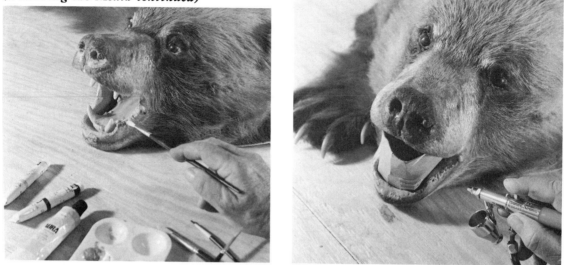

Left: After the Sculpall or other filler has thoroughly dried, restore the colors in the face and mouth. Some taxidermists prefer to use artist's colors and a brush while others swear by the airbrush. I prefer to use an artist's brush along the inside of the mouth and the hairline of the outer lips. Also an artist's brush is easier to use around the eyes. *Right:* When using an airbrush, place a piece of cardboard or paper inside the mouth to protect the artificial teeth. An airbrush blends paints very naturally but requires some practice. If you get paint on the teeth, remove it with a cotton-tipped swab and paint thinner.

and lips. Inside the mouth the black paint will blend with the flesh color of the inner lips and artificial jaws. This is not a sharp line. Rather it should be gradual and somewhat irregular. To get a good idea of the color change in the mouth, look at a dog's lips and mouth. The paint will require about a day to dry thoroughly. Then apply a coat of spar varnish as a sealer. Since the varnish gives a wet look, use it sparingly around the eyes. But you can use a glossy varnish inside the mouth if you wish. Finally, put the artificial tongue in place and check for size. In most cases it will fit, although I have had a few that required trimming at the back. When the tongue fits inside the mouth properly, put a bead of superglue along the un-

derside of the tongue and carefully put the tongue into place. Avoid allowing superglue to get on the teeth or exposed parts of the artificial jaws because it will show.

Now make the darts (wedge-shaped cuts) in the skin where the extra skin accumulated in front and back of the front legs. I recommend using a pencil to mark the wedge-shaped extra skin before cutting it out with a scalpel. Then using a casting or blind stitch, close the gap. Now the skin will lie flat.

No matter how prime a bear pelt is, it is always rather sparsely furred on the belly. This is usually apparent along the edge of the rug, particularly behind the front legs. Since the light-colored skin will show through the hair, these areas can be dyed

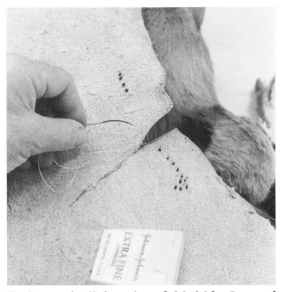

Owing to the light color of this hide, I sewed the skin wedge with white, unwaxed dental floss. I later dyed the floss to match the hair color. The small holes shown were created by the tanner's punch for identification of the hide. One or two stitches will close each of the punch marks.

with oil paints or liquid shoe dye of the appropriate color. I prefer to use shoe dye because it is easy to apply and is intense enough to cover easily. Dyes are available in gradations of brown and black that can be selected to match almost any bearskin. Skins from most other mammals do not have these bare spots and so do not need dyeing.

Most rugs are lined with a double-felt border, a pad, and a bottom lining. For species smaller than bear, such as raccoon, fox, or coyote, you can purchase felt locally in widths up to about 60 inches. The felt can then be cut to the desired size and shape with pinking shears. For larger animals, purchase precut felt borders from a taxidermy supply company. These borders are scalloped along one edge of a 3×72-inch felt strip. Contrasting colors are most attractive, and in most cases they should match the color of the skin. For example, a brown bear hide looks good with a brown and tan border. And a black skin is attractive when trimmed with a double border of black and gray. I have seen yellow, green, and even red felt borders, but my personal preference does not extend to pastel-colored trim on a rug. Nevertheless "beauty is in the eye of the beholder," and if a customer wants pink—give him pink. After all, the color may match the home decor.

Use the following formula to calculate the amount of felt border that you will need:

Square of rug $\times 6$ = *length of trim, in feet*

Example: 5 feet $\times 6$ = 30 feet of trim

In order to calculate the square of a skin, add the length and the width and divide by 2. The square is simply the average of the length and the width of the hide. A cougar skin that is 5 feet long and 4 feet wide will square 4.5 feet. (That is, $5 + 4 = 9 \div 2 = 4.5$.)

If the bearskin squares 5 feet, multiply this by 6, and the product equals 30 feet. So you will need five, 6-foot strips of felt to go completely around the skin. With a double border, you will want to purchase this amount of trim in two different colors. Felt border is not particularly expensive, so it is better to order too much than not enough.

When the felt border arrives, sew the two pieces of trim together, forming a single, double border of felt. For bear, I recommend about a 2-inch border. This means that the two pieces of felt trim should be sewn about 1 inch apart and will then extend out from

BORDERS, LINING, AND PAD

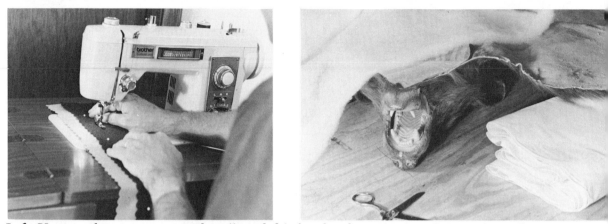

Left: You can buy a pre-cut and scalloped felt border from most supply companies. For a double-felt border, buy two matching colors and then sew the strips together. *Right:* Padding and lining can usually be purchased locally. The pad can be any soft material. But I recommend quilt padding, because it is not as spongy as foam rubber. Yet this is a matter of personal preference. The lining can be any inexpensive, but heavy, material that will take the abuse under the rug.

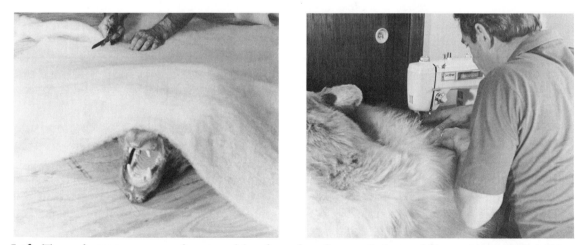

Left: Turn the rug over on the stretching board and spread the padding on top of the skin. Then cut the padding, using the edge of the skin as a guide. This will give you a pad that is the same size and dimensions as the rug. Use the same method to cut the lining, except that the liner should be cut about 1-inch larger than the skin. *Right:* Pin the double-felt lining to the edge of the skin. Using a leather needle, sew the felt border to the skin. Begin at the edge of the rug shell and sew toward the tail so that you will be sewing in the direction that the hair lies. Then turn the rug around and sew from head to tail on the other side.

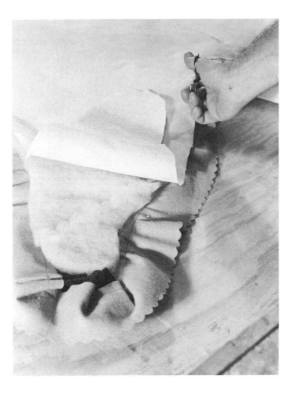

After sewing the felt border to the skin, stretch the rug out and lay the padding and the lining in place. Pinning the lining to the felt border will hold the padding in place. Then hand-stitch the lining to the border.

the edge a maximum of 2 inches. Sew the trim to the edge of the skin, beginning along the front leg. Always sew with the lay of the hair so that the stitching is easier to clean out. This means that you will want to start near the chin or lower jaw and sew toward the tail on *both* sides. Some taxidermists prefer to use a hot-glue gun to attach the felt border to the skin. However I consider this to be a quick-and-dirty way to line the rug. It gives a much less professional appearance. Most modern sewing machines will sew the lining to a bearskin provided that a leather needle is used, and the results are much more satisfactory and professional.

With the border attached to the rug, use a piece of quilt lining or foam rubber for the pad. I prefer to use quilt lining because it provides a cushion under the rug without

being springy. Although you can feel the pad beneath the rug when you walk on it, the pad won't create the rubbery feeling that foam creates. This, of course, is a matter of personal preference.

Whichever padding you use, turn the rug hair-side down and lay the piece of padding on top of the rug. Using scissors, trim around the padding in the shape of the *inside* of the felt lining. Then cover both the rug and padding with the piece of bottom lining that you have selected. This should be a heavy material that can take the wear and tear of the rug. If the lining will be on a hardwood floor, it should be of nonslip material. Trim the lining so that there is about 1 inch of overlap on the padding. Then turn the lining under and stitch it by hand to the felt border completely around the rug. If you cut everything properly, the hand stitching should just about follow the machine stitching of the two pieces of felt trim.

For rugs, there are a couple of finishing touches I recommend. You will already have found that it is impossible to sew the felt lining to the feet because the claws interfere. Thus each foot must be hand stitched to the felt trim. You may also find that it is easier to sew the tail to the felt by hand than by machine. The skin is nailed and pasted to the rug shell, but the felt border must be attached to the bottom of the rug shell with a hot-glue gun. Also, for additional strength, I recommend that a couple of upholsterer's tacks be used to hold the lining and trim to the bottom of the rug shell. These give a more finished appearance. They also hold the rug shell off the floor or wall so the lining stays cleaner. Now sew a D-ring on either side of the shell and one on each foot. These serve to hang the rug on a wall and eliminate the need to nail or staple the rug in place, so the D-rings are just a service to you if you keep the rug or to your customer. The rug is now finished and ready for use.

Glue or staple the felt border to the underside of the rug shell. A hot-glue gun works well for this purpose. Several upholsterer's tacks, as shown, can be added to increase the strength of the glue. It also is a good idea to staple a D-ring on either side of the head, driving the staples into the wooden baseboard. If you want to hang the rug on a wall, these D-rings will hold the weight of the head more easily than the felt lining would.

The finished bear rug! The time and effort to complete a quality rug are far less than required to mount the same skin as a life-size animal—and a rug can serve several functions. Although making a rug requires the skill of a taxidermist and the patience of a tailor, the result is well worth the effort.

A bearskin rug can be used as a floor rug or as a wall hanging. Wall hangings are not subject to as much wear and tear as a floor rug and therefore are likely to last longer.

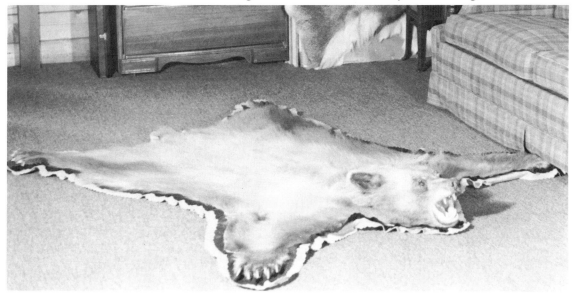

For Floor or Wall? The question of use is a debatable one. But I recommend that all rugs be used as a wall hanging rather than on the floor. The reason is that wall hangings sustain much less wear and tear. Household pets and mice will have a heyday with a rug because of the oils, salts, and sugars (in the paste) that have been added during the rug-making process. I once had a reasonably intelligent dog that ate the entire foot off a bearskin rug, and our family cat munched on more than one ear. While mice have never attacked my rugs, I've heard stories of mice that set up housekeeping between the lining and the hide. This is much less likely to happen if the "rug" is used as a wall hanging. Also it is amazing how many people want to pull on the artificial tongue. This is much less of a problem when the rug is on the wall, perhaps mounted over a sofa, out of reach of children and even out of convenient reach of adults.

MAKING FLAT RUGS

In the beginning of this chapter, I describe the differences among robes, flat rugs, and full-head rugs. A robe, such as those used by Eskimos and the early trappers, is not

Flat rugs, such as this zebra, are stretched hair-side up so that the color patterns are properly aligned. Made in Africa, this rug has a single felt border and no pad.

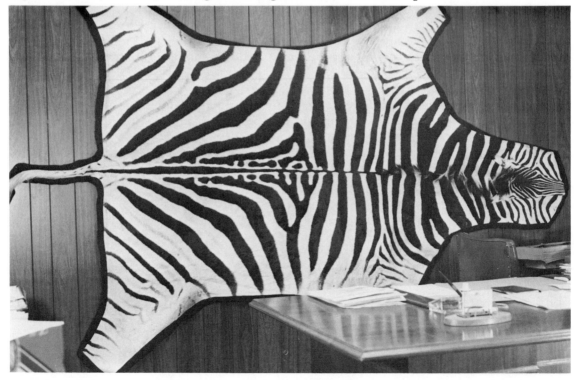

Flat rugs, such as this elk hide, should be stretched with the hair up. This allows you to see the color patterns in the hide and stretch the skin more symmetrically. Use the same stretching techniques that I described earlier for the bear hide.

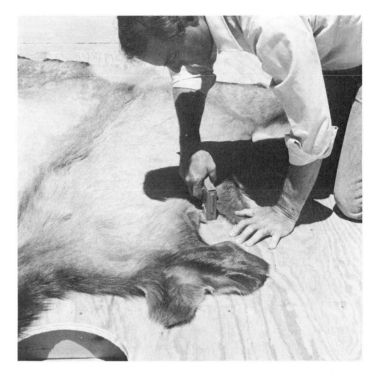

stretched. Rather, it is simply a tanned hide with the hair on. As you have already learned, the stretching process removes some of the flexibility from the skin, thus making it more of a decoration than a soft blanket or robe.

Incidentally, many African trophies are mounted as flat rugs. The process for the making of flat rugs is similar to that which I described for full-head rugs, with two exceptions: (1) the head is not mounted, and (2) the skin is stretched hair-side up so that the body markings can be properly aligned. North American species can also be mounted as flat rugs. In this case you lose flexibility for a robe but you can exaggerate the size.

After the hide has been tanned, moisten the hide using the same soda and soap mixture that I described on page 122. Now

repair any damage to the skin. Since African skins are usually very shorthaired, the stitches should be small and close together. Then laying the hide flat, hair-side up, staple around the upper jaw, neck, and head. Since skinning techniques vary in Africa, you will simply have to use whatever hide shape that arrives. But be sure to trim the head or neck so that you are beginning with a reasonably symmetrical hide. Once you have stapled the head to the stretching board, stretch the skin as necessary to get the proper distribution of skin and color pattern. Begin by lining up the mane with the back and tail, and keep this pattern straight. Then you should work to the sides and stretch the skin accordingly. When the skin is dry, you can line it and pad it using the same techniques described earlier for full-head rugs.

6 BIRD TAXIDERMY

Bird mounting is one of the more enjoyable kinds of taxidermy. You need very few supplies, and you can obtain most of them locally. Also, the abundance of birds enables the beginning taxidermist to practice on a number of birds before working on those once-in-a-lifetime trophies. In addition, in my view, the beauty of a well-mounted bird far exceeds that of a mounted squirrel or even a large rug. And since a bird is relatively small, it requires little display space. All of this makes bird taxidermy especially popular. In fact, in national competitions, bird entries often outnumber mammals two to one.

The keys to successful bird taxidermy are (1) understanding bird anatomy and (2) using good reference material. As a beginning taxidermist you will learn that although skinning and mounting a bird are not difficult, producing a quality mount can be. Fortunately, when you have mastered good bird-mounting techniques, you will be able to bring beauty into your home that is almost as good as in nature. And you will be able to enjoy colors, close up, that you usually can't in the field because the birds are far away or moving fast.

SELECTING A SPECIMEN

A bird taxidermist has the opportunity to be somewhat selective in choosing practice

Bird mounts should be balanced relative to bone and flesh structure, rather than to mere feather placement.

subjects. Since not all birds are created equal, the beginner should select a specimen that will give him the least number of problems. As I noted in Chapter 1, most birds in the United States are protected by migratory-bird treaties with Canada and Mexico. As a result, only the pigeon, starling, and English sparrow may be hunted throughout the year. Since both the starling and sparrow are relatively small and therefore difficult to handle, the common pigeon makes an ideal practice subject. Although crows are protected as a migratory bird, they are frequently considered to be predators that can be hunted throughout much of the year. Crows make excellent taxidermy subjects. But since hunting seasons on crows are seldom published, first check with your local conservation office.

Of the wild gamebirds, the upland game species are the best subjects for mounting. Most parts of the country are inhabited by some species of quail or grouse. Pheasant are also excellent subjects. Frequently these birds can be taken during the regular hunting season, then frozen and mounted later.

Avoid ducks and geese. The amount of fat on waterfowl presents a real headache to even the most experienced taxidermist; also they require a special incision on the head which should not be attempted until you become proficient with less difficult specimens. Doves lose feathers easily and so are also poor choices for the beginner.

Other sources of specimens are the ads in trade journals, such as *American Taxidermist*, or gamebird farms in your area. You can even practice on common barnyard fowl such as chickens. I recommend that you mount at least six pigeons before you consider purchasing specimens for practice.

FIELD CARE OF BIRDS

I cover proper field care in on pages 15 – 17. Still, there are a few factors that deserve further discussion here. First of all, most gamebirds are bagged with a shotgun. So if you are able to be selective, avoid practicing on specimens that have broken legs or wings, or that have been shot in the head. Since these bones are used in the mount, they would need to be repaired during the mounting process. As a beginner, you don't need bone-repair headaches.

As soon as the bird is killed, make good field notes on the colors on the feet, beak, or any fleshy parts of the bird and the size and color of eyes. All of the fleshy parts of a bird will fade with time, and the natural colors may have faded by the time that you begin to mount the specimen. If you can take close-up color photos, all the better.

Another task is to keep the bird clean. Stuff a piece of cotton into the mouth to absorb blood. Since you are likely to bag a number of quail or pheasant on a hunt, separate those that you plan to mount from the rest of the bag. I recommend that you carry some newspaper in your hunting vest. When you bag a particularly striking bird, wrap it in a piece of newspaper as soon as you retrieve it. You can then carry it in your game pouch without soiling it with blood or dirt from other birds.

Lastly, keep all of your birds cool, of course, but take special care to keep those you plan to mount cool.

PREPARATION OF THE BASE

It is important to have a base for the mount before you actually begin to skin the bird. This is because the skin will begin to dry even during the skinning process, requiring that you pose the bird on the base properly.

The base for a bird mount can be very

Take color photos and make color notations in the field as soon as you bag the bird you intend to mount because colors will begin to fade immediately. Record the color of the fleshy parts of birds, such as the feet and around the eyes. For many birds there is a variety of color in these areas. Note whether the color changes are blended or abrupt. Also take note of the colors of the beak.

simple. A pigeon or quail can be mounted on any stump or limb available. Many taxidermists make base-collecting trips, carrying a saw, obtaining a number of bases in a few hours. Most lakeshores will yield attractive driftwood. With permission, I have sawed the tops off a quarter mile of fence posts in less than an hour. Old fence posts are weathered and rugged-looking. Besides they are commonly used as perches by many birds.

Match the base with the specimen. Pheasant don't roost in trees, so don't mount a ringneck on a limb. On the other hand, quail frequent fence posts and low-lying trees, so for quail these perches are good choices. But for your practice on pigeon, just pose the birds standing flat-footed on a board. This is both easier than other poses and natural for a pigeon.

TOOLS AND SUPPLIES

Before you begin skinning, you will need only a few inexpensive items. First, an X-acto knife is an ideal skinning tool. These knives are razor sharp and come with replaceable blades. They are small enough to work on a small bird such as a quail. Or you can use a scalpel or sharp, small-bladed pocketknife.

Because a bird is small and can best be skinned when hanging up, a set of hooks and chains is also a must. The hooks resemble No. 1 barbless fishhooks joined to a ring by small chains. It is almost impossible to properly skin a bird without them.

During the skinning process, you will need either some powdered borax or cornmeal. And for mounting, you will also need some wire, a pair of glass eyes, a ball of string, and an artificial body made from either excelsior or styrene foam. You will also need a small amount of cotton or similar material.

With the above tools and supplies, as well as the base, you are ready to proceed.

THE STRUCTURE OF A BIRD

Most of the mammals I described in earlier chapters have bone structures similar to that of humans. Though of different shapes and sizes, mammal bones are directly comparable. This similarity helps in understanding the skinning and mounting techniques. This is not the case with birds. Therefore, I describe the bird skeletal system, and add some terminology.

The skeleton of a bird consists of a column of anywhere from 37 to more than 60 articulating vertebrae which form the tail, backbone, and neck. The bones of the skull are little more than plates and struts dominated by large eye orbits, or sockets. And the brain is restricted to the back of the skull behind the eyes. Ribs from the backbone join the breastbone, or sternum. This keeled sternum provides a broad attachment for the wing muscles. The wings themselves are attached to the pectoral girdle, which is composed of three bones that are held to the rest of the skeleton by strong ligaments. The bones of the wing are similar to those in a human: (1) the upper arm, or humerus; (2) the forearm, or radius and ulna; (3) the outer wing, composed of the thumb and fused bones of the first and second fingers. The third and the little fingers, found on humans, are missing.

The legs of a bird are joined in a socket in the pelvic girdle, which is actually en-

BONE STRUCTURE AND WEIGHT DISTRIBUTION

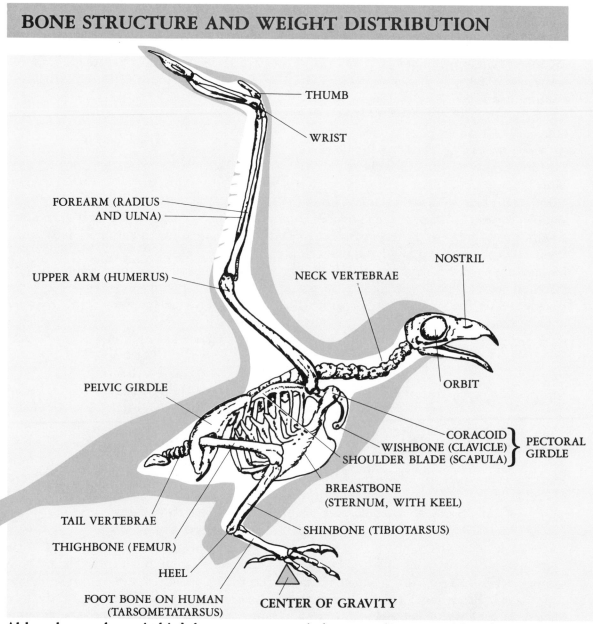

THUMB

WRIST

FOREARM (RADIUS AND ULNA)

UPPER ARM (HUMERUS)

NECK VERTEBRAE

NOSTRIL

ORBIT

PELVIC GIRDLE

CORACOID
WISHBONE (CLAVICLE)
SHOULDER BLADE (SCAPULA)
} PECTORAL GIRDLE

BREASTBONE (STERNUM, WITH KEEL)

TAIL VERTEBRAE

SHINBONE (TIBIOTARSUS)

THIGHBONE (FEMUR)

HEEL

FOOT BONE ON HUMAN (TARSOMETATARSUS)

CENTER OF GRAVITY

Although many bones in birds have counterparts in humans, they are positioned and shaped differently for flight. The unfeathered portion of the bird's leg is equivalent to the foot of a human. The shaded area shows the feathered portion of a bird, which adds very little weight and should be disregarded in considering the center of gravity when you position the bird for mounting. A long tail can be particularly deceiving, as to weight, when you are trying to balance a mount.

larged vertebrae. The point of attachment is the same as the human hip and it joins the thighbone or femur. The so-called drumstick in a bird is called the tibiotarsus.

The unfeathered portion of the bird's leg is called the tarsametatarsus and is equivalent to the foot bones in a human. Most birds have four toes, one of which points to the rear. The backward pointing toe is the "big" toe of a human, and the second, third, and fourth toes point forward. The so-called "little" toe, found on humans, is missing.

Most of a bird's bones are hollow. Although this gives the bird a lightweight skeleton strong enough to serve the bird well, the bones are more easily broken than in mammals. As a result, you need to treat the bones with care during skinning and mounting.

GENERAL SKINNING TECHNIQUES

Skinning the Bird. In the field, a wad of cotton or other absorbent material was stuffed into the throat of the bird to prevent blood drainage onto the feathers. Remove the cotton from the mouth of the specimen and replace it with a fresh wad. This will reduce the amount of staining on the neck feathers during the skinning process.

Now carefully examine the bird to identify its good and bad features. If the flight feathers of the wings are uneven or badly damaged, the bird probably should be mounted with wings closed. If one side is in good condition but there is damage to the other side, the bird can be posed as a flying mount with the damaged side against the wall. If leg bones are broken, the bird should be

Good reference material is essential when mounting a bird. Before you begin skinning, gather photos of the species and select the pose that you want. Also take the time to examine the anatomy of the bird. Note the position of the legs and that the wings fit into a pocket of feathers on the sides of the bird. The neck is quite flexible; when you pull the head in, the neck curls into the crop area. Begin by using simple poses for your early mounts. Save tricky poses for later.

posed in a squatting or a flying position. Consult plenty of reference material from books and hunting magazines that you have collected. Also, as a beginner, you should limit your poses to natural, relaxed positions. Exotic poses are difficult, but they will come gradually as your skinning and mounting techniques improve. Posing mounts is like skydiving—you become more daring as your confidence grows.

Skinning a bird requires a certain amount of finesse. Although the skin of most birds is quite elastic and will usually stretch before it tears, a stretched skin is just as difficult to mount as a skin that is badly torn. So you should strive to remove the skin slowly and as carefully as possible so you don't stretch it out of shape.

Begin skinning by laying the bird on its back with the legs and tail pointing toward you. Then, using the point of the knife, separate the feathers along the sternum in the middle of the breast. The breastbone of pigeons and quail is quite obvious. But in other species, and particularly waterfowl, you can locate the bone with your finger pressed against the body.

After separating the feathers along the sternum, begin an incision at the top, or front, of the bone and work toward the rear, stopping at the anus. Don't cut too deeply. You will notice that the skin is white, whereas the underlying muscle is very deep red. Once your incision is about an inch long, you will be able to lift the skin up and separate it from the muscle. This will show you the thickness of the skin so that you don't cut too deep. Avoid cutting through the intestinal wall after you leave the sternum and before you reach the anus.

As a right-handed taxidermist, I prefer to wield the knife with my right hand and manipulate the skin with my left. Working to the left (bird's right), the skin can be lifted away from the body. With care, you can work your fingers down along the side of the bird between the skin and the body. Now locate the femur joint (knee joint) between the femur and the tibiotarsus (drumstick). When you have found this joint, grasp the tarsametatarsus (lower part of the leg, or foot) and push upward, exposing the joint

more fully. With your knife, cut through this joint, being careful not to cut the skin behind the knee. After you have separated the two bones, you can push the foot still farther until the skin on the tibiotarsus (drumstick) is turned completely inside out. When the heel, or unfeathered part of the leg, is reached, use the knife to cut all of the muscle away from the bone and then discard the meat. Now repeat this procedure on the other leg.

At this point in the skinning process you might find that blood and body fluids are beginning to accumulate between the skin and the body. You can blot this up with a paper towel, or you can instead sprinkle some powdered borax on the skin to act as a preservative and drying agent. (However, if you plan to eat the bird after it is skinned, use cornmeal instead of borax. The cornmeal can later be rinsed off the meat and would not cause the ill effects that borax could.) Keep your fingers as dry as possible when skinning a bird. If you transfer blood from your hand to the feathers, this makes the skin more difficult to clean before mounting.

After the legs are separated from the thighs, the skin must be worked around the tail. Using a knife or scalpel, cut the tissue that joins the skin to the lower end of the body. Since you will cut through the intestine beneath the anus, it is helpful to stuff a wad of cotton into the exposed end of the intestine. Then, working slowly and carefully along the tail, you will be able to feel the joint between the tail vertebrae and the pygostyle, which is the large bone at the tip of the tail in which the tail quills are anchored. Using scissors or snips, cut through the tail vertebrae. Pick the bird up in one hand and fold the tail skin and feathers back along the spine. This will expose the remaining muscle of the tail so that you can cut it with the knife.

At this point the skin has been cut free from the body along the breast, the legs, and around the tail. Three bones, the pygostyle of the tail and the two tibiotarsi, remain attached to the skin.

For most beginning taxidermists, skinning around the tail is the most difficult step. This requires some finesse. Most of the difficulty arises simply because it is difficult to see where to make the cuts. Since there is usually fat in this area, the white skin is sometimes difficult to distinguish from the yellow fat. Work slowly and carefully. Also, never skin the tail out completely by removing the pygostyle. The quills of the tail feathers are anchored in this bone, and the feathers will fall out of the mounted bird if not still anchored to the pygostyle.

Once you have removed the skin from the body at the tail, hang the bird with a set of hooks and chains. Be sure that the hooks are secured in the bone of the pelvic girdle and not just in the abdominal skin. Then begin working the skin down the back, cutting the tissue whenever necessary. If you encounter shot holes in the body, stuff bits of cotton into the holes to restrict the flow of blood.

The wing attachment of the humerus (upper arm bone) to the body is set rather deeply in the chest. When the skin has been separated along the body and back to the wing, use your knife to cut into the base of the wing and locate the joint with the pectoral girdle. Then cut through this joint leaving the entire wing attached to the skin. A word of caution: when the wing is separated from the body, a large artery will be cut. Have a piece of cotton or absorbent paper available

(Text continues on page 159)

HOW TO SKIN A BIRD

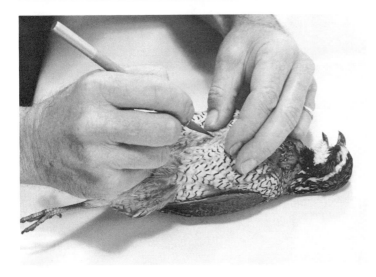

Lay the bird on its back, tail toward you, and separate the feathers along the breast with the point of a scalpel. Begin the incision near the top of the breastbone (sternum) and cut towards the tail. After you begin the incision, lift the skin and you will notice that the skin is quite thin but elastic. This will help you gauge the depth of your incision. Avoid opening the abdominal wall between the breastbone and the anus. You can avoid this mistake by working slowly and carefully.

(Continued)

(Skinning continued)

CUT THROUGH
KNEE JOINTS HERE.

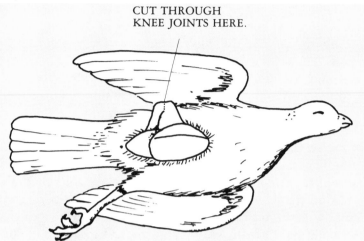

This illustrates the position of the leg when you are ready to cut through the joint between the upper and lower leg. By skinning down the side of the bird, you will expose the leg. If you push the foot forward, the knee will slip up into the position shown. Then cut the cartilage and separate the two bones.

After you have separated the bones of the leg, grasp the bone of the lower leg and slowly pull it out, simply turning the skin inside out to the bottom of the leg. Then cut the muscle off the bone. The bone remains attached to the skin. You can discard the meat.

After skinning and cleaning both legs, continue skinning toward the tail. When you reach the roots of the tail feathers, you are past the abdominal cavity and can cut through the tail at this point. By skinning around the sides of the bird near the tail, you will get a better "feel" for the position of the tail. Cut through the tail ahead of the feather roots. Cut the bones with a snips, or use a scalpel to cut between a tail-bone joint.

Left: A set of hooks and chains is invaluable. After severing the tail, hang the bird and gradually work the skin down the body. Very little cutting will be necessary except along the backbone. Sprinkle a small amount of powdered borax onto the body and skin to absorb body fluids and make the body and skin easier to handle. *Right:* In this photo, I have skinned the quail to the wings. Note that the feet and legs are hanging loose and that the skin is inverted over the body. When you reach the wings, make an incision into the base of the wing and feel the joint. It is deeper than you might imagine. When you find the joint, cut through the cartilage with a scalpel; then the wing will come free. *Caution:* There is a large artery in the wing that frequently bleeds a great deal when the wings are separated from the body. Use absorbent paper or cotton to keep blood off the feathers.

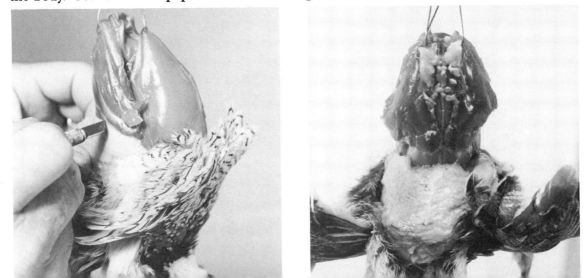

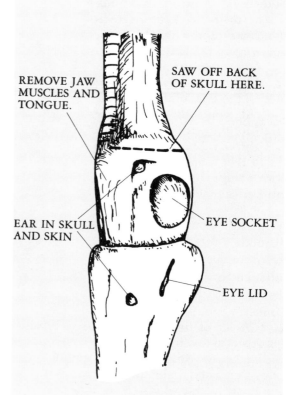

After you have separated the wings from the body, continue skinning down the neck to the head. The weight of the skin is usually adequate to facilitate skinning. There is usually some yellowish-colored fat in the neck that you should cut off.

Skin forward over the skull. The ear is the opening behind the eye. If you cut close to the skull with the point of your scalpel, the skin will come free. The eyeball itself is much larger than the pupil. Thus, lift the eyelid and cut close to the pupil so that you don't damage the eyelid. Work slowly and carefully. Then continue skinning forward until you reach the base of the beak. Use a hacksaw or coping saw to cut the back of the skull open and separate where shown. This will simultaneously expose the brains and separate the body from the skin. Use a brain spoon or some flat tool to scrape the brains out of the skull. For removal of brains, a forceps or needle-nose pliers will work.

to blot the blood that will be released. Now separate the other wing from the body.

On quail, pigeons, and most upland gamebirds, the neck skin can easily be inverted over the head. When the wings are free from the body, continue skinning by gently pulling the skin downward while the body is hanging with the hooks and chains. Occasionally a large cock pheasant may be difficult to skin over the head. In these cases and for virtually all waterfowl, an additional incision must be made on the head or throat. I discuss this more fully later in this chapter.

The ears are located behind and below the eyes. After you have turned the skin over the neck and reached the skull, cut the skin free from the skull at the ears. For best results, cut in against the bone of the skull so that the ear skin is not damaged or enlarged. Continue skinning forward, past the eyes to the base of the beak. Be careful not to damage the eyelids. Also, if you have not made any notations of eye color or size, do so now.

Remove the body and skin from the hooks and chains and lay it on the workbench. Then with tweezers or needle-nose pliers, grasp the back corner of the eyeball and cut it out of the socket. The eyeball contains a dark fluid, but it will not be spilled as long as you work carefully, cutting the eye muscles while pulling gently with the pliers. After you have removed both eyes, cut the body and neck free from the skull with a hacksaw or snips. Do not cut too much of the skull away, and be careful that it is not crushed in the process. You can then scoop the brains out of the skull with the tip of your knife or with a flat tweezers. Cut the jaw, muscles, and tongue away from the skull, but avoid separating the jawbone from the skull.

Rub a liberal amount of powdered borax into the skin of the head and neck. Also work borax into the eye sockets, the brain cavity, and around the jaw muscles. Finally, put a ball of potter's clay into each eye socket and shape it like the natural eyeball that you removed. The head and neck skin can then be turned right-side out. Refrigerate the neck and body until you are ready to make the artificial body.

The wings must now be skinned. I recommend that, whenever possible, the wings be hung using the hooks and chains. The hooks can be forced into the joint at the end of the humerus (upper arm bone). Then slowly work the skin down over the humerus to about the middle of the radius and ulna (forearm). Cut all of the flesh away from these bones and powder them with borax. After you have skinned and preserved the remaining wing (next page), turn both wings right-side out.

Some additional skinning of the wings may be necessary. There is very little muscle to remove in the outer part of the wing. For quail and pigeons, or birds of similar size, most taxidermists inject the outer parts of the wing with a liquid preservative. However for pheasant, most ducks, and any larger birds, it is necessary to make an incision on the underside of both the middle and outer section of the wing so that the muscle can be removed and the skin properly preserved. Simply make an incision along the unskinned portion of the wing and work the skin back from the bone. Cut away any tissue present and rub borax into the skin and onto the bone.

The skinning is now complete. The skin has been removed from the body and neck. But the skull, all of the wing bones, the tibiotarsi of the legs, and the pygostyle of the tail remain attached to the skin.

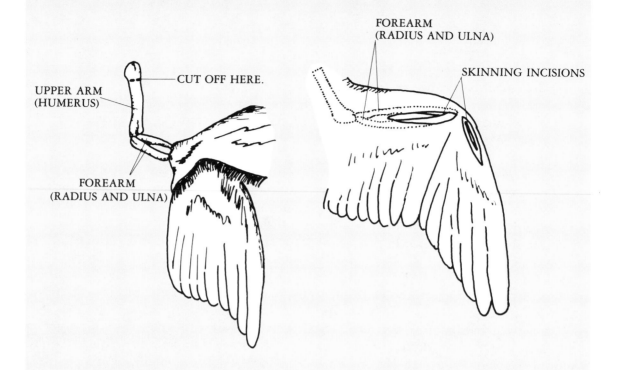

UPPER ARM
(HUMERUS)

CUT OFF HERE.

FOREARM
(RADIUS AND ULNA)

FOREARM
(RADIUS AND ULNA)

SKINNING INCISIONS

Skin the wings from both the inside and the outside. The upper arm (humerus) and the forearm bones (radius and ulna) are exposed and fleshed from the inside using the same technique I described for skinning the leg. Simply work the skin slowly down the wing, being careful not to cut the skin at the joint. Strip the flesh off the bones and saw the knob or knuckle off the end of the upper arm. The outer extension of the wing must be skinned through incisions made on the underside of the wing. Lift the feathers and make the incisions; then scrape away the muscle. Most taxidermists simply inject this portion of the wing with formaldehyde, which gives adequate preservation to most upland gamebirds. Geese and turkey wings should be skinned out.

After you have skinned the bird completely, apply a heavy coat of powdered borax to the entire skin. This will act both as a preservative and a mothproofing agent. Work the borax into all parts of the skin, legs and tail, as well as all of the bones and the skull. The skin is now ready for mounting.

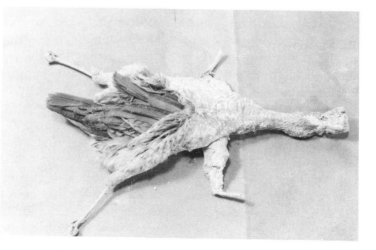

160

SPECIAL SKINNING TECHNIQUES

Waterfowl. Most waterfowl present a special skinning problem. All geese and most ducks have a neck that is too small in diameter for the skin to be inverted over the skull. There are also many exceptions, such as mergansers, some diving ducks, and some ringneck pheasants. In order to skin the head of a bird with a small neck, you need to make a special incision. Beginners should practice this special skinning technique so that they are prepared to deal with the problem when it arises.

Use conventional skinning techniques to skin the bird as far as possible. When you can no longer advance the skinning over the skull, cut the neck free from the skin and the remaining neck and head. This will usually be very close to the base of the skull. Then after applying borax to the neck skin, turn the neck and head right-side out and make another incision on the neck or skull where the neck was cut free, as shown in the accompanying drawing. This is commonly called a nape or throat incision, depending on whether it is made on the back of the head or the throat.

After making the incision, pull the skull-side end of the neck through the incision and hang the skin with the hooks and chains. The head can then be skinned, cleaned, and preserved as I described in the preceding section. This neck incision is the only possible means of skinning most waterfowl.

Birds of Prey. As I explained in Chapter 1, virtually all birds of prey are protected as migratory birds. Nevertheless, occasionally a taxidermist receives a bird of prey that is

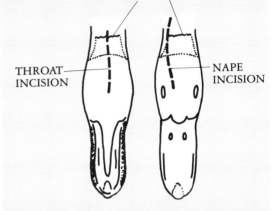

NECK AND BODY HAVE BEEN SEVERED HERE.

THROAT INCISION

NAPE INCISION

Most ducks, geese, and cranes have a skull that is too large to pass through the neck skin. So you need to make an additional incision on the head. Make this on the back of the head (nape) or on the throat. The incision should begin at the point where the neck was severed and then extend up onto the skull. Lift the skin and gradually work the skull out through the incision. Then continue skinning to the base of the beak. The skull should then be cleaned and preserved in the conventional manner. Sew up the incision as soon as you complete the skinning.

properly documented and thus legally mountable. These birds may offer special skinning problems. Most hawks and owls have an extended femur (thigh bone) and tibiotarsus (drumstick) so that the bird can more easily grasp its prey. This places the knee joint much farther forward on the body than for gamebirds. In some cases you may need to lengthen the breast incision to the base of the throat in order to skin this joint.

Hawks have a bony projection that extends out from the skull above the eye. This piece of bone should be left intact when

This shows the skin inverted over the skull through a nape incision. The skull has been scraped and preserved, and a ball of potter's clay has been placed in each eye socket. The next step is to pull the skin back over the skull and close the incision. Some diving ducks and mergansers have a large enough neck to make this head incision unnecessary. Although this incision is not needed for most upland gamebirds, an occasional ringneck pheasant must be skinned this way.

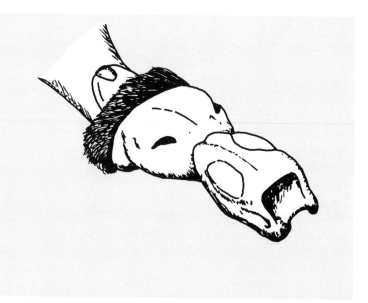

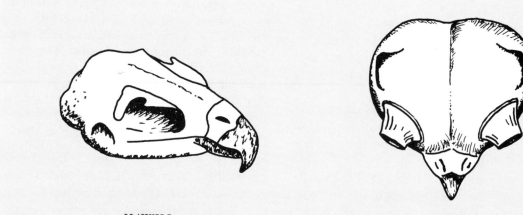

HAWKS   OWLS

All raptors are protected as migratory birds. But when a raptor is properly documented, it can be mounted. The eyes of raptors require special attention. Hawks have a thin bone over the eye that is not found in other birds. Leave this bone in place to retain the proper shape of the head; this bone gives the shaded appearance to the eyes of a hawk or eagle. The eyes of an owl are located in a cuplike bone attached to the skull. The pupil must be cut free from this bone, which is then left in place. Since an owl's eyes are fixed in the skull, an owl must turn its head to change its view.

skinning the head. It contributes to the shape of the head and gives the eyes a somewhat shaded and deep-set appearance. However, the eyes of an owl are firmly attached to a bony cup in the eye socket. This cup should not be removed. Instead you must cut the iris of the eye away from the bony cup and drain out the fluid, then preserve the cup with borax.

Cranes and Geese. The tendons should be stripped from the feet and lower legs of sandhill cranes and most geese. There is enough meat associated with these tendons that it may spoil. Also, removing the tendons opens the leg enough to facilitate inserting leg rods or heavy wire for mounting the bird. In order to remove these tendons, make an incision on the bottom of the foot and strip the tendons out with needle-nose pliers. An incision can also be made along the bottom of each toe so that you can pull out these tendons.

FLESHING AND CLEANING THE SKIN

So that the skin can be properly cleaned and preserved, all of the fat and tissue must be removed. The fat can be safely removed by snipping it off the skin with scissors. Avoid scraping the skin because this will stretch the skin out of its natural shape. If some scraping is necessary, always scrape *from tail toward head* with the lay of the feather roots. Also, snip away any tissue that has remained attached to the skin; most of this is likely to be in the lower neck area.

Waterfowl are particularly troublesome birds to clean because they invariably have a thick layer of fat on the breast. If this is not removed, the fat will gradually ooze out

of the skin and the mount will become very greasy and attract bugs. Much of the fat can be removed with scissors, but some scraping is required as well. Bird degreasers are available which greatly simplify the fat-cleaning process, but these are expensive and unnecessary for the beginner. The degreaser consists of a wire brush on an electric motor that lifts the fat and tissue off the skin without doing any damage to the skin itself.

After the skin has been fleshed, it must be washed and dried. Mix about a teaspoon of liquid detergent in a gallon of lukewarm

All bird skins must be washed before being mounted. This washing in a mild detergent and cold water will remove any dirt or blood as well as any fat or grease that is on the skin and feathers. Never use hot water because hot water will cook the skin and ruin it for mounting. Since warm water tends to set blood stains, rinse blood in cold water before washing the skin. Skins that are excessively fatty, particularly those of waterfowl, should be degreased before mounting.

water and allow the skin to soak for 10 to 15 minutes. Do not use hot water because it will cook the skin! You can stir the water from time to time, then remove the skin and rinse it thoroughly in cold water. Check any white feathers to make sure they are clean, and be sure that there is no dried mud clinging to the feet. Also ensure that you have washed all blood and grease away from the mouth area and along the incisions. When you are satisfied that the skin is clean, gently squeeze the skin to remove the water, working from the head toward the tail.

Waterfowl and particularly fatty skins should now be rinsed in a degreasing solution. These solutions not only remove any remaining grease from the skin and feathers, they also displace water from the earlier bath and simplify the drying and fluffing process. Degreasing solutions you can obtain locally include mineral spirits and white-gas camping fuel. Pour a small amount in a bowl and allow the skin to soak for about five minutes, then remove the skin and again squeeze out the extra solution.

The skin is now ready to be dried and fluffed. Put the skin in a large plastic bag and add two to three handfuls of hardwood sawdust, obtained from your local lumberyard. (Some supply companies sell ground corncobs that work equally as well.) After filling the bag with air and holding the top of the bag closed, shake the contents so that the sawdust will work into the feathers and absorb the moisture. Check the skin from time to time, and if the sawdust becomes

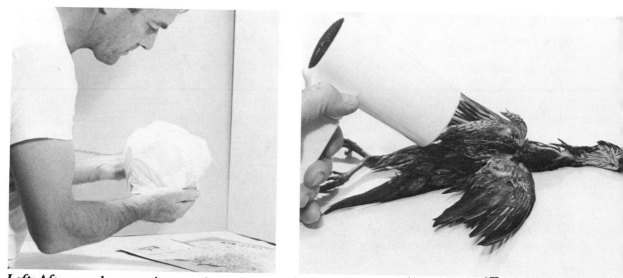

Left: After gently squeezing out the excess water, place the wet skin in a plastic bag containing several handfuls of sawdust. Shake the bag vigorously for a few minutes in order to work the sawdust into the feathers. The sawdust will absorb most of the moisture from the feathers. At this point the skin will look a disaster, but don't worry. You are making progress. *Right:* Using a hair drier, fluff the skin gently until it is dry. This will blow out any sawdust retained by the feathers, and the feathers will fluff up naturally. If you are patient, you will be happy with the results.

extremely wet, replace it with more dry sawdust. By tumbling the skin and feathers in sawdust, you should be able to remove most of the moisture.

Remove the skin from the bag and shake out as much of the sawdust as possible. Then put about two handfuls of powdered borax in the plastic bag and again tumble the skin. Some taxidermists prefer to use puffed borax rather than the powdered form because it does not cling to the feathers. Whichever form you use, the borax dusting is absolutely necessary. Not only does it remove much of the remaining moisture from the feathers, the borax also is a skin preservative.

After you have thoroughly fluffed the skin in the borax, remove it from the bag and shake out any extra borax still clinging to the skin and feathers. Then with a hair drier set on low heat, blow the feathers until they regain their natural fluffiness.

The skin is now ready for mounting.

MAKING AN ARTIFICIAL BODY

After you separated the natural body and neck from the skin, you either set it aside or refrigerated it until completing the skinning and cleaning of the skin. Now lay the neck and body on a piece of blank paper and trace an outline of the body and neck. Then turn the body on its back and draw an outline of this shape. Make any notes of body shape. And on the paper, mark the positions where

Measure the natural body and neck using calipers and tape. Record the dimensions and trace the bird from the top and side profiles. Also mark the points where the wings and legs will attach to the artificial body. These are shown by an X on the drawing and will be valuable guides later.

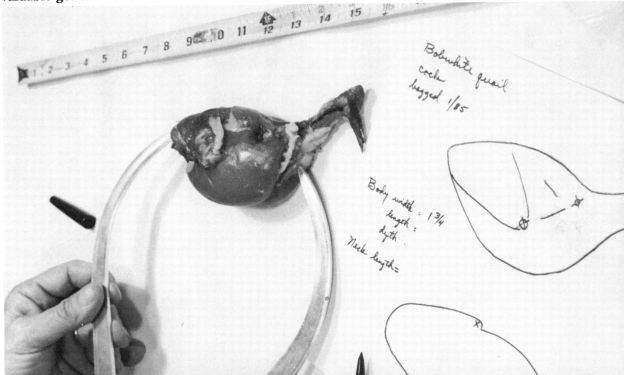

WATERFOWL

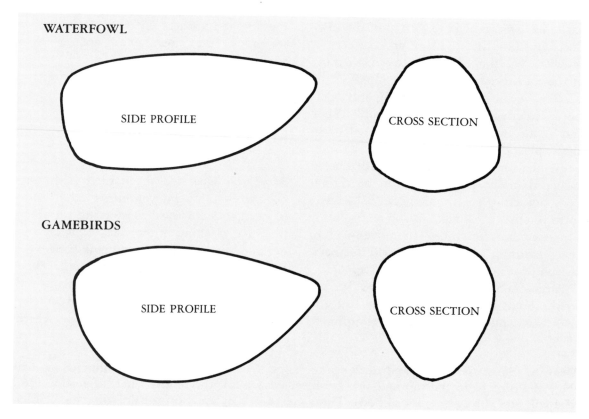

GAMEBIRDS

These drawings show typical body profiles of gamebirds. The upper profile and cross section are characteristic of waterfowl, which are flat breasted and typically wider at the breast than at the back. The lower drawings show the characteristic upland gamebirds, which have keeled breasts and bodies that are wider at the back than at the breast.

the legs and wings were separated from the body. It is also helpful to use calipers and record measurements of the neck and body.

You will notice that the body of your pigeon or quail is keeled so that the body is somewhat heart-shaped in cross section. On the other hand, waterfowl are flat-breasted and the body tapers toward the back. In order to pose your mount properly, the artificial body must closely approximate the original dimensions and shape.

An artificial bird body can be made from a variety of materials. It can also be purchased from most supply companies. As I show in the section that follows, award-winning bird taxidermist Jack Wilson prefers to carve bodies from high-density foam. However, it is best for the beginner to wrap a body from excelsior because excelsior anchors and holds wings and leg wires more firmly.

Begin by taking a wad of excelsior and squeezing it into a tight ball. Using nylon string—kite string is ideal—wrap the ball three or four times to hold the shape tight.

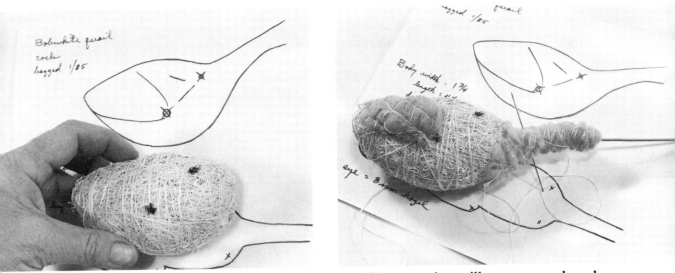

Left: Lightly wrap the excelsior body with string. This wrapping will serve to anchor the body wires. In wrapping, build the body up gradually to the same size and shape as your tracings. Note in this photo that I have marked spots on the excelsior to show the points of attachment for wing and leg wires. For this I used a felt-tipped pen. *Right:* To give fuller shape to this body, I added fiberglass thighs. Then I inserted the neck wire and wrapped the neck using fiberglass and string. Cotton, tow, jute, or fine excelsior can also be used for wrapping the neck. On upcoming pages, Jack Wilson describes a different technique.

Now begin to build up the body to the desired size and shape by adding additional wads of excelsior. Remember, you can't wrap the body too tightly, but you can wrap it too loosely. Continue to add excelsior and wrap until your artificial body reaches the size and shape of the natural body. Take measurements as needed, and regularly compare your wrapped body with the drawings you have made. When you are satisfied that the body is finished, tie off and clip the string.

Now insert the body into the skin and check for proper fit. The skin should close along the incision without requiring any stretching of the skin. If the body is too large, withdraw it from the skin and remove some of the excelsior. Better that the body be a little too small than too large. If the body is slightly too small, you can always stuff some cotton between the skin and body as a filler, but it is difficult to conceal an incision that does not close properly over a too-large body.

Now cut a piece of wire about one-and-a-half times the length of the bird skin and sharpen one end. For a bird the size of a pigeon or quail, use 14-gauge wire, which is about the size used for making clotheshangers. Push the sharpened end through the body, beginning at the tail and exiting at the point where the neck vertebrae join the body. Now, in order to build up the neck, wrap the neck wire with tow, cotton, or fiberglass insulation. Wrap the neck with string and continue to add neck material until you have the neck built up to the proper circumference and length. The string can then be tied off and clipped. The artificial body and neck are now complete.

BIRD MOUNTING TECHNIQUES BY JACK WILSON

[The procedures for skinning and cleaning a bird are standardized and followed by all taxidermists. However some taxidermists have the ability to mount award-winning birds, while other taxidermists are never able to. Jack Wilson of Brockville, Ontario, won a blue ribbon with the first mount he ever entered in a national competition, and he has been winning ribbons ever since. He has received the Award of Excellence from the National Taxidermist Association, and Wilson is a frequent judge of bird competitions. Interestingly, taxidermy is a second career for Jack Wilson; he is the retired Canadian National Hydroplane Champion. This illustrates that you don't have to begin taxidermy as a teenager in order to reach the top.]

When storing skins that you do not plan to mount right away, salt them rather than using borax. Borax will make a skin flint-hard if stored in a freezer and the borax is almost impossible to soften up later. When shipping a skin, it is also better to salt the skin rather than preserve it with borax. If there is a skin that I'm particularly concerned about, regardless of the species, I freeze it in a block of ice. To freeze a skin, fill a quart milk carton with water. Roll the skin up lengthwise and stuff it into the water-filled carton. Then freeze it into a block of ice until you are ready to mount the skin. The skin can be thawed out and will be full of moisture without any spoilage.

Award-winning taxidermist Jack Wilson won first place with this combination mount of brook trout and merganser at a National Taxidermist convention. He has developed a number of techniques that have enabled him to win numerous awards for his bird mounts. He is also highly skilled.

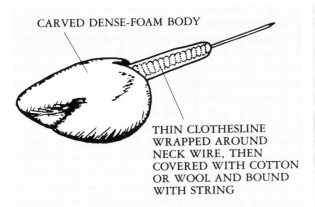

CARVED DENSE-FOAM BODY

THIN CLOTHESLINE
WRAPPED AROUND
NECK WIRE, THEN
COVERED WITH COTTON
OR WOOL AND BOUND
WITH STRING

Left: Wilson's unique artificial bodies contribute to his success as a taxidermist. He carves the body from dense foam to the exact dimensions of the natural body. He makes the neck by wrapping wire with small-diameter clothesline, as shown, and then covers this with cotton or wool wrapped in string. The clothesline acts as the neck vertebrae and produces very symmetrical curves. He also wraps the neck slightly less than natural size, then curls it up into the crop area for a pose with the neck pulled in. (Beginners often find foam more difficult to use than excelsior because the leg and wing wires tend to enlarge the holes that they make. Since the beginner spends more time adjusting these wires, these repeated adjustments may result in a "loose" mount. Wilson anchors the wires with a hot-glue gun. After you have become more adept at posing mounts, the foam body becomes easier to use.) *Right:* This compares a wrapped excelsior body and a carved foam body. Note the Jack Wilson technique of wrapping the neck wire with clothesline before applying the final cover.

I use a rather unusual method when drum-drying a washed bird skin: First, drum-dry the skin in ground corncobs. Then use paper clips to hold paper over the wing primaries and the tail feathers. Now put the skin in an onion bag which has very fine mesh, and tumble the skin in coarse, hardwood chips. This may sound hard on the skin but the paper and onion bag protect the skin and feathers. What I want to do is remove 80 to 90 percent of the water from the skin and feathers in 15 to 20 minutes. After tumbling with the hardwood chips, I blow-dry the feathers. If some of the feathers are particularly hard to reshape after being twisted during storage, hold the affected feathers over a steam kettle for a few minutes. Steam will restore the original shape of the feathers.

Begin first by carving the body from dense foam. I'm from the new school—I never used excelsior. I found foam worked a heck of a lot easier. I carve a fairly deep wing indentation in the body so that the wings will set properly against the body and give a smooth curvature. One other thing I do is carve a deep neck indentation. When you skin a bird you will see that the neck curls up into the body. Even if I am mounting a bird that will be posed with the neck and head low or pulled in, I still wrap the neck nearly full length and then fold it up into the cavity I have carved into the body.

Usually I make the neck about two-thirds as long as the body for an upland gamebird.

If the body is 5½ inches long, I make the neck 3¾ inches long. This doesn't have to be exact, but these proportions usually work out about right. When the neck is wrapped only as long as the neck will extend from the mount, you will end up with some extra skin, probably between the legs. By wrapping the entire neck and folding it into the body, you have a more realistic mount.

The reason I prefer to use foam bodies is the ease in adjusting the size and shape. There is not much that you can do with a wrapped body that is too large. With foam a rasp will change the size and shape in a minute or two. If the skin is too small, trim the body down. Also, if you are using a commercial form, buy one that is too large and trim it down. Never start with a small body and try to build it up with clay. It is not worth your time or the trouble.

For most upland gamebirds and small or medium-size waterfowl, I use 14-gauge wire for the neck and legs. This is about the right weight for birds of this size. For a mallard or larger bird, I might use 12-gauge wire. When in doubt, I will use a lighter-weight wire. I find that I get much better bends in the neck and legs with lighter wire. The heavier wire can sometimes be a real beast to crank around.

When I am working on a base, I'll bend the neck into the approximate desired location, then hold the body and neck on the base. With a little imagination you can visualize the position and shape of the mount. Then you can fold the neck into the approximate desired position. The neck will fold right back into the cavity that has been carved into the body. Next I'll insert the neck into the skin after it is already bent into shape. The neck might have to be loosened slightly if you are planning a very tight

fold, but you should minimize the movement because you will start pulling feathers out when you bend the neck.

The body is carved from 2- to 2½-pound foam, meaning fairly dense foam. If it is a little heavier, it will be a little more dense. This kind will sand down. Avoid the beaded foam because it will "float" and the shavings stick to everything.

Remove all of the meat in the skull and around the jaws, but do not disconnect the jaws. This makes it more difficult to shape the head. The jaw is the foundation of the skull, and keeping the skull in one piece will give you a more solid mount. Now pack the skull with potter's clay.

Make a hole in the front of the skull proceeding out the inside of the upper mandible (beak). Do not go out the top of the skull because this will tend to anchor the skin on top of the head and prevent moving the skin on the head. Also, rather than saw off the back of the skull, use snips and clip out the back of the skull to release the neck. Then trim this so that the artificial neck will just slip into the opening.

When skinning the head of a duck or bird with a large skull, I prefer to make the incision on the throat rather than on the back of the head. I find that this incision is easier for me to work through and then the feathers cover better on most mounts. It tends to be a problem on some species such as drake wood ducks because of the white throat patch which might get stained, but this is the method I prefer.

Wire the legs by inserting a sharp wire from the bottom of the foot and work it up the leg between the skin and bone. Remove the knuckle from the top of the femur (thighbone). Otherwise the knuckle tends to make the leg stick out too much from the artificial body. Then wrap the leg bone and

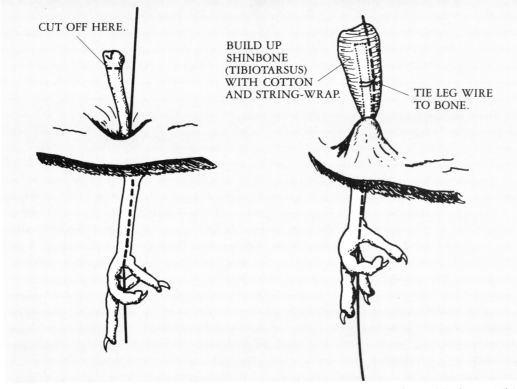

CUT OFF HERE.

BUILD UP SHINBONE (TIBIOTARSUS) WITH COTTON AND STRING-WRAP.

TIE LEG WIRE TO BONE.

In order to wire and wrap the leg, cut off the knuckle at the top of the shin bone (tibiotarsus). Then insert the sharpened wire into the bottom of the foot and work it up the back of the leg, as shown at the left. Be sure the wire is both straight and sharp before inserting it into the foot. When the wire is in place, tie the wire to the bone with a piece of nylon thread. Then wrap the leg (shown at right) with cotton or fiberglass.

wire with cotton, building it up to replace the meat that has been taken from the bone. When the leg is built up properly, wrap the cotton with more wool yarn. When finished, pull the leg back into the skin very carefully and smooth down the feathers on the leg. Then wrap the other leg in the same way. The leg wires should be pulled back flush with the end of the wrapped leg.

[Author's note: If you intend to inject the outer wing with a preserving fluid rather than completely skin out the wing, now is the time to make the injection. Using a syringe and needle, inject formaldehyde or

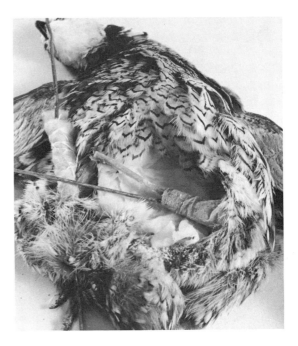

This shows the leg wires in place and the legs wrapped. Since I decided that this would be a closed-wing mount, the skin is ready for the artificial body and neck.

another preservative into various parts of the outer and middle wing segments. About 1cc (cubic centimeter) will be needed for each wing of a pigeon or quail.

If your specimen will be mounted with closed wings, you are now ready to insert the artificial body. However, an open-wing mount must now be wired and wrapped. Cut a piece of wire about 1½ times as long as the open wing and sharpen both ends of the wire. Insert the wire into the wing skin from inside the body after you have cut the large joint off the end of the humerus (upper arm bone) with a hacksaw. Since the wing has been skinned about midway past the radius and ulna (forearm), the wire will slip in easily. If you work the wire carefully the remaining length of the wing bones, it will exit from the skin near the end of the outer wing segment. Now pull the remaining wire out the tip of the wing until the opposite end is even with the sewn edge of the humerus. Then build up the wing along the humerus in the same way you wrapped the legs. Repeat the process for the opposite wing.]

Now you are ready to insert the artificial body and neck into the skin. Shape a nice, smooth curve to the unwrapped end of the neck wire and insert it into the skin. With your fingers, you should be able to guide the wire into the back of the skull and out the hole in the upper mandible (beak). Work slowly; don't be in a hurry. If you get in a hurry or get brutal, you are just going to pull out feathers. Work the end of the artificial neck up into the back of the skull, then clip off the neck wire about an inch from the mandible so that you don't stick yourself in the nose with it.

Lay the bird on the table, breast up, and insert the leg wires. Before you started to

mount the bird, the point where the legs will be connected should have been marked on the artificial body. For upland gamebirds, the legs should be attached in front of the midpoint on the body. For puddle ducks, I attach the legs about at the midpoint; diving ducks have legs attached to the body just a shade behind the midpoint. This is a rule of thumb that has worked well for me. When the legs are too far back, you are going to have a hard time balancing the mount.

Attach the legs by inserting the leg wire through the artificial body, bend a tight loop, and then pull the leg wire back through. Repeat this for the other leg. You can always tell if the legs are properly set by the way the tail skin fits over the artificial body. If you have a lot of slack and the tail just falls around the end of the body, the chances are good that the legs have been attached too far back. You should have to work the tail skin around the artificial body when the legs are anchored properly.

Sharpen the end of the neck wire. Then slowly work the wire up through the body and neck skin. Using your fingers as a guide, work the neck wire into the brain cavity and out through the roof of the mouth. Then work the end of the artificial neck into the back of the brain cavity and gently pull the skin of the neck over the wrapped neck.

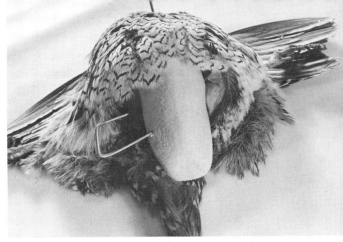

After the artificial body and neck are in place, push the leg wires through the body at the spots that you marked on the body and pull extra wire through the body. Bend a hook in the end of the leg wire; then pull it back into the body as shown on page 176. With the leg wire anchored by the hook, push the wrapped leg and bone up flush with the artificial body and bend the leg into position.

After you have pushed the femur (thighbone) flush against the artificial body, clip off the leg wires so they extend a couple inches beyond the foot. This will eliminate a lot of extra wire sticking out of the legs while you are sewing and posing the bird.

Before beginning to sew the incision, I like to stuff a little bit of cotton in the void where the crop was located at the base of the neck. Don't overdo it, just add enough to give the breast a rounded appearance.

Sew the skin with canvas or button thread. It's breakable, but it is tough enough to hold a bird skin together. A lot of taxidermists are using monofilament, but for me that is too springy. When I pull the stitch tight with my thread, it holds. Use a baseball stitch and each stitch should be about ½ inch apart. Take two or three stitches; then pull them tight. Begin at the breast and sew down to the anus. When the incision is sewn, grab hold of the neck wire sticking out of the beak and shake the heck out of the bird. This will help to make the feather packs fall into place. This step really reduces the time required for preening the mount.

The bird is now ready to be placed on the base. Whenever I mount a bird, I always mount it on the permanent base. I have tried to mount on a temporary base and then switch the mount to a permanent base later, but I'm never satisfied with the position of the legs, the balance, or anything else. So I always use the permanent base at the beginning.

[Author's note: Jack Wilson pioneered the swimming duck mount in which a diving duck is mounted in a simulated feeding pose. In order to effectively suspend the mount, Wilson twists two stout pieces of wire together and then glues them with epoxy cement. After sharpening the ends, he anchors the joined end of the two wires into the base with the wires extending like a two-pronged fork. After he finishes the mount, he positions the bird on the wires in a feeding position.]

With needle-nose pliers, bend an S-curve in the leg wire at the base of the foot. This will put a curve in the foot that looks more natural. It also conceals the wire better beneath the foot of the bird. Drill holes in the base to accept the leg wires. Then, working carefully, place the leg wires into the holes and push the wires down snug. Now begin to shape the bird. Don't be afraid to move it around and roughly position the feathers. Then you can get the balance point correct and adjust the angle of the head and neck. When you are satisfied with the general shape of the mount, pin the wings into place. This will get them out of the way while the rest of the bird is being shaped. This may not be the final wing set because it can be changed

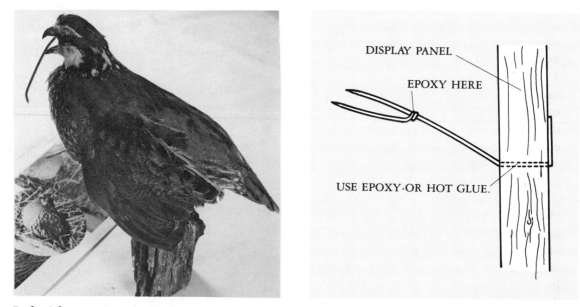

DISPLAY PANEL

EPOXY HERE

USE EPOXY·OR HOT GLUE.

Left: After sewing the incision, attach the bird to the base that you plan to use for the final mount. Here I used the top of a weathered fence post. Drill holes in the post for the leg wires; then add a drop of glue and push the wires into place. Do not use a temporary base if you can avoid it. Now you can begin the preliminary posing of the body. Always check your reference material while posing the mount. (The exposed wire may help you position the head. Thereafter, you can cut it off.) The wings are now ready to be pinned in place. *Right:* Jack Wilson uses a double wire to support some of his mounts, such as his merganser diving for brook trout, shown earlier. The main support wire has been anchored to the panel or base. A second, smaller wire is attached with epoxy to the main wire; the mount is then pressed onto the wires. This enables Wilson to give the mount a natural, suspended appearance without exposed wires.

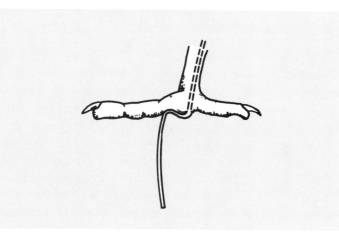

According to Wilson, the leg wires can be more easily concealed when an S-curve is bent into the wire at the bottom of the foot. This somewhat arches the foot and at the same time moves the point of attachment more directly beneath the foot.

easily later. However, since it is necessary to hold the bird firmly when pinning the wings, *this should be done before you spend a lot of time preening the mount.*

If the skin begins to dry out, use a small artist's brush and glass of water. Wet the brush and paint the inside of the skin with water. The brush can be worked in through the eyes or mouth to wet the skin. If the skin starts to dry before the preening is finished, *the feathers will never lay properly and the finished mount will look rough.*

After you are satisfied with the basic pose, turn your attention to the head. Since the head and neck feathers are short, this skin will dry more quickly than the rest of the skin, *so it is important to preen it first.*

Insert a tail support wire now. You might have to move it later, but it will support the tail for the time being.

Take a piece of 14-gauge wire and bend a loop at one end and round the other end on a file or sharpening stone. This is a very handy tool for adjusting the feathers. You

Clip off the neck wire flush with the roof of the mouth. Then fill the throat area by stuffing small pieces of cotton through the mouth and into the void at the base of the skull, under the jaws, and along the neck as needed. Do not overstuff. Simply fill out the neck skin as appropriate.

In most cases, the weight of the tail feathers will cause the tail to droop unless supported by a tail wire during the drying process. This T-shaped wire is sharpened at the base with the cross-T wide enough to support most of the tail feathers. Insert the T under the tail feathers at the angle in which you wish the tail to dry. For larger birds the tail wire can be left in place permanently; for smaller birds this wire is removed when the mount is dry.

can stick the rounded end through the eyes of the skin and rub the inside of the head and neck skin. Adjust the skin around the artificial neck. This will also stand up the feathers in their sockets and then allow them to drop smoothly into place. Then take small bits of cotton and work them down through the eyes and mouth around the throat and base of the skull. Don't overfill the neck or head, and try to keep everything as even as possible when working it under the skin with the looped wire. Examine the mount from all angles, including above and below. Fill all the voids. When a void is present, the skin will shrink around it and dry in an unnatural position—and this again will give a rough appearance to the feathers. So be sure that voids in the neck are filled completely. If you overstuff the neck, you can sometimes press the cotton back into a more natural shape; otherwise you will have to remove some cotton with forceps.

When you are satisfied that the skin has been filled properly, use wire cutters to clip

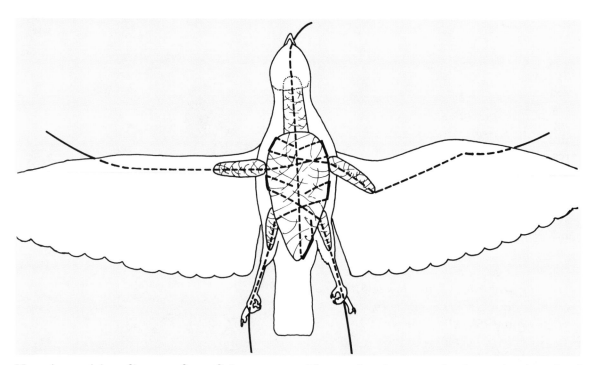

Here is a wiring diagram for a flying mount. The neck wire extends the entire length of the body and out the mouth. The leg wires go through the body and anchor on opposite sides, as do the wing wires. The wing on the left shows the initial wiring position. After the wing is bent in the proper position, as the wing on the right, each of the other wing joints must be bent too.

off the neck wire inside the mouth. Then run a thread through the nostrils of the bird and tie the beak closed. Some people pin the beak shut, others use a piece of masking tape. I find that a thread works as well as either of these methods.

Use a good quality eye, regardless of the manufacturer. The color of the eye can vary a great deal in wild birds. I have seen ruffed grouse from my part of Canada that have a very light hazel eye; the same species in other areas may have a very dark eye. Use an eye that is as realistic as possible for your particular area. Also, the pupil can vary, depending on the amount of sunlight, as in a human. Some photos show a very small pupil, but most wildlife photos are taken in bright sunlight. A small pupil simulates an angry

or aggressive attitude. On a cloudy day, dawn or dusk, a bird has a large pupil, and don't let anyone tell you differently.

Spend a lot of time getting the eyes in place. First mark the clay in the center of the eye socket as a guide for eye placement. Then clip off the end of the eye wire, leaving about ⅛ inch sticking out the back. Now put the eye into place and lift the eyelids with a needle or tweezers so they will overlap the glass eye. Don't be afraid to move the eyes around, making certain that they are level and lined up properly. Keep the eyelids wet during this process. When you are satisfied with eye placement, put a pin in the front corner of the eye, then use additional pins in the eyelids as needed on the bottom and back of the eye. Check the eye position

This chukkar has been fully wired but not yet posed. After the wires are anchored and the wing and leg bones forced against the artificial body, the wires are then bent into shape. Because they are not weight-bearing, the leg wires in a flying mount do not have to be as heavy as those needed for a standing mount.

After posing a flying mount, card the wings to hold the flight feathers in the proper position until the mount is dry. Without carding as the skin dries, the feathers may tend to pull out of position, resulting in an uneven appearance of the wings. To card the wings, cut strips of cardboard, such as from a milk carton, and staple them on both sides of the wings after you have spaced the feathers properly. Leave the strips in place until the mount is dry.

BIRDS MOUNTED BY JACK WILSON

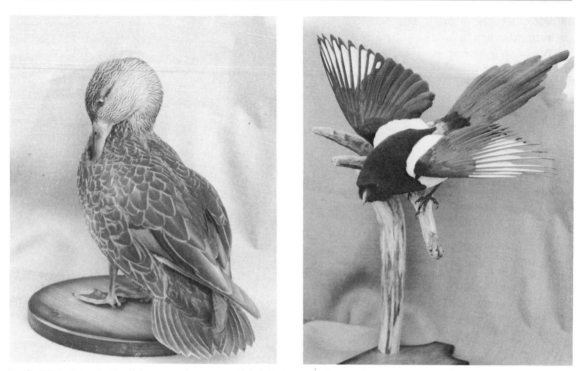

Left: This black duck's preening pose highlights striking feather patterns. *Right:* The black-billed magpie, a close relative of the common crow, was posed to emphasize the long tail and black and white colors.

The garganey duck is a Eurasion relative of the bluewing teal. Proper leg placement and balance are required to mount a bird on one leg. Wilson commonly uses driftwood bases for waterfowl. He recommends an airbrush for restoring faded colors on beak and feet.

from the front. Be sure that you can see the glass eyes from the front. It is surprising how frequently a bird is mounted with excellent eye position from the side but totally obscured from the front.

Now card the wings and tail, if necessary for the pose. (Pins, staples, or paper clips hold cards that sandwich the feathers in place.) Whatever the pose, make sure wing and tail feathers are equally spaced. This is particularly important for flying mounts in which the primary flight feathers should all be properly spaced. If the carding is not necessary, add a pin or two to the wings to hold them in place properly. Pin the toes in place to the base so that they will dry in a holding position.

You are now ready to begin the final preening of the feathers over the entire bird.

BALANCING
A BIRD MOUNT

Many beginning taxidermists, and a lot of old-timers as well, never seem to master the task of posing and balancing a bird mount properly. Most mammal mounts are posed with all four feet attached to the base. With a reasonably accurate artificial body, it is difficult *not* to pose the mount properly. Such is not the case with a bird mount. All too often the legs are attached improperly and the mount will have a totally unnatural appearance. The general tendency is to mount the bird with the legs too far to the rear. If you believe that posing a bird is easy, you probably are doing something wrong.

The key to a properly balanced mount is in recognizing the center of gravity of the bird. Four-legged animals have little problem with balance. Their weight can be shifted readily from one foot to another, as evidenced by the agility of squirrels, sheep, or even members of the deer family. Two-legged animals such as man and birds have a more formidable balancing problem. If you stand upright with heels together, your nose will be centered between your toes when looking at the floor. If you raise one foot off the floor and look again, your nose will be centered over the foot on which you are standing. Quite simply, you have unconsciously shifted your weight to one side in order to balance properly and keep from falling. A bird does the same thing. Often when the wires from the mount are attached to the base and the mount *seems* to be standing properly, it may only be an optical illusion. You can ignore the feathers when locating the center of mass because of the light weight of the feathers. This is illustrated in the drawing on the next page.

When posing a bird in a standing position, place the two feet side by side, with the center of gravity directly over the soles of the feet. The legs will be relatively straight beneath the body of the bird. If the weight of the bird is shifted by the pose, such as feeding or stretching, the center of gravity will shift also. With an outstretched neck, the birds' body weight will automatically shift to the rear to compensate for the position of the neck and head. When a bird is mounted in a walking position, the center of mass will roughly be located between the two legs.

The point of attachment of the leg wires to the artificial body will also change with the pose. In the accompanying drawing, the femur (A) is attached to the body in a ball socket of the pelvic girdle, and the knee joint rotates in an arc at the end of the femur. The point of attachment of the leg wire will

The position at which a bird's legs are anchored will depend on the pose of the mount. The thighbone (femur) *(A)* will rotate in an arc from *B* to *C*. In this particular walking pose, the front leg would be anchored at *B* and the back leg would be attached to the artificial body at point *C*. Also notice that the leg wires will emerge from the toes at a different position when the bird is "walking."

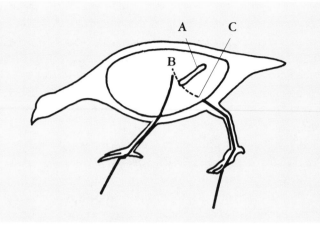

correspond to the position of the bird's knee in that particular pose. When a bird is standing, the knees will be quite high on the body, as at point **B** in the accompanying drawing. However when the bird is feeding, the forward leg could be attached at **B** whereas the trailing leg would be attached quite low at point C.

In summary, a properly posed bird mount requires that the taxidermist consider the center of mass of the bird's body and neck, as well as the anatomy of the legs. The mount won't look out of balance then, firmly attached to the base.

PREENING, WRAPPING, AND FINISHING

On most bird species, the feathers are not evenly distributed over the body. Rather, there are tracks of feathers which spread over the unfeathered areas of the body. So after the bird has been mounted and posed, the taxidermist preens the feathers in order to obtain a smooth, lifelike appearance.

Jack Wilson recommends that the bird be shaken vigorously after the incision is sewn and before the mount is placed on the base. This allows the feathers to fall into their natural pattern. Nevertheless there are always some unruly feathers that have become twisted or broken during the mounting process, and they must be straightened out. Remove any loose feathers that weren't blown free during the blow-drying process. If the feathers on the neck are particularly unruly, this is probably the result of twisted skin or baggy areas where the artificial neck is too small. Insert the wooden end of an artist's brush through the mouth of the mount and down along the neck. This will help to straighten the feather roots and will also help to eliminate any wrinkles in the skin. Then add additional pieces of cotton stuffing, as needed, to fill out the skin. The final preening must be one feather at a time, with either a needle or tweezers. In general, very little preening will be needed when the body and neck fit the skin properly. If the body is too large or is poorly shaped, then a great deal of preening will be needed and sometimes nothing will help.

The skin will shrink as it begins to dry,

This turkey was mounted by taxidermist Wayne Cooper of Milton, Florida. The mount was classed as the Best in Large Bird Category at a National Taxidermist competition. Posing large birds requires a thorough knowledge of anatomy and balance.

Left: After posing and preening the bird, wrap it with soft cotton string that will hold the feathers in place until the mount dries. Do not pull the string too tightly. Otherwise it will crease the feathers and produce an unnaturally "tight" mount. *Right:* Instead of wrapping, you can do as taxidermist Gary Senk does, cutting small pieces of paper about one inch square and pinning them onto the mount. Each pin prevents the shafts of feathers from shifting, and the paper holds the feathers down. In this way Senk is able to hold the feathers in low places, such as along the back, that cannot be reached by a string wrap.

and this will have a tendency to pull some of the feathers out of place. Therefore you will need to wrap or pin the feathers in place until the mount is dry. For a standing mount, double-check the position of the wings to ensure that they are properly seated in the feather pocket along the side of the bird. Then pin them into place with two or three fairly long pins. For larger birds such as pheasant, you can make your own large pins from 18- or 20-gauge wire and bend a short hook on one end that will grip the wing.

Then wrap the mount with soft, cotton string to hold the feathers in place. Don't wrap the string too tightly; otherwise it will make a permanent crease on the feathers. The string should be just tight enough to hold the feathers in place while the skin dries.

Taxidermist Garry Senk of Hales Corner, Wisconsin, pins small squares of paper on the mount rather than using a string wrap. He believes that the string has a tendency to hold all of the feathers too tightly against the body so that the mount does not have a

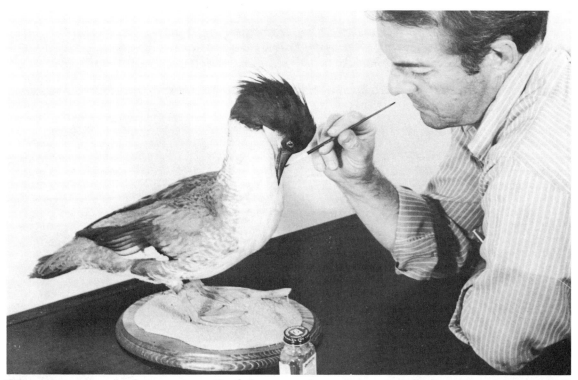

When the mount is dry, remove all of the wrapping or pins and fill in with mâché around the eyes as needed. Then using oil paints, restore the colors in the beak and on the feet. A very fine artist's brush may be needed to correctly paint the fine detail and spots on some birds, such as this hen common merganser. Here I selected a pose that would emphasize the crest of this strikingly colored species.

natural, fluffy appearance. By putting a pin in the center of a 1-inch square of paper, he is able to hold the individual feathers at the desired position.

The mount probably will require four to five days to completely dry, depending on temperature and humidity, and on the size of the bird. When the mount is dry, the wrapping can be removed, as well as any pins. However you should leave the pins in the wings in place, making sure that you have completely concealed those pins beneath the feathers.

You should restore the natural colors in the beak and fleshy parts of the bird with oil paints. Refer to your color notes and photos. Then mix the paints and apply them sparingly. You will notice very little color change in the feet and beak of quail and pheasant. But in some waterfowl, the color in the feet and beak may change drastically. Many taxidermists restore the colors of the feet with an airbrush, but artist's brushes can be used equally as well. Don't forget to paint the eyelids of the bird using a fine, No. 1 round artist's brush. After a week or two, check the bird again and alter the colors as needed if additional fading has occurred.

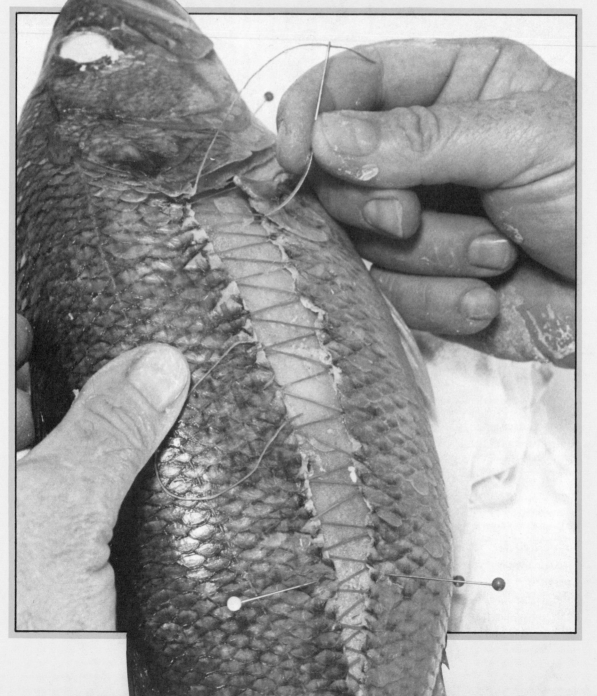

7 FISH TAXIDERMY

Fish taxidermy is an exciting art form that is not difficult to master. It has its challenges, with a thin unforgiving skin that requires an artist's touch to paint. But just as Rome wasn't built in a day, neither will fish taxidermy be learned in a day.

According to *Ichthyology*, second edition, there are more than 20,000 species of fish in existence, making them the largest group of vertebrates on earth. Fish come in all sizes and shapes and in all colors of the rainbow, so it is not surprising that there is an amazing variety of fish available. Fishing-license sales outnumber hunting licenses by two to one, and it has been estimated that as many as 27 million people fish for bass alone in a single year. This explains why so many fish are caught and mounted by taxidermists. In fact, the Archie Phillips studio in Fairfield, Alabama, mounts several hundred bass a month.

Taxidermists commonly classify freshwater fish as either warm-water or cold-water varieties. The warm-water fish include bass, perch, and members of the pike families. These fish are hard-scaled and generally free of grease. The cold-water fish include members of the trout and salmon families. These fish are usually greasy, and the scales are quite small or nonexistent. Since different skinning and mounting methods are required for the two varieties, I describe both methods in this chapter.

Here the incision on the "wall side" of a bass is partially closed by means of nylon thread and the baseball stitch, discussed in more detail later in this chapter.

The freshwater catfish and many saltwater species such as shark and billfish are virtually impossible to mount by conventional taxidermy methods. This is because these fish have a smooth, greasy skin that is extremely difficult to mount. Since World War II the availability of resins and plastics have enabled taxidermists to make plastic facsimiles of these species, in which none of the original trophy is preserved. I recommend that you steer clear of these fish until you are proficient in mounting bass and trout. Forget about catfish; they look better in a skillet than on a wall.

High-quality mounting of fish requires more practice than any other type of taxidermy. Although the fur or feathers on mammals and fish will conceal mistakes, fish scales can hide little. Also, any imperfections in the artificial body show through the skin of a fish mount, giving it an uneven or irregular appearance. Fish taxidermy also requires more artistic ability than other forms of taxidermy because all of the color in a fish mount fades when the mount dries. The mount must then be painted to restore the natural colors.

Regrettably, some taxidermists seem unable to master the painting, perhaps because they don't spend enough time painting or force themselves to practice. A beginner should spend a lot of time painting his first mounts and be willing to strip off the paint and do it all again. You can only mount a fish once, but you can paint it 50 times — and each time you will learn something and improve.

Fortunately for the beginner, some type of practice specimen is generally available. Warm-water fish, and particularly largemouth bass, are ideal. If you are unable to catch a bass or beg one, perhaps you can catch perch, crappie, or even carp. In coastal areas, practice specimens can usually be obtained from a boat captain or local fish markets. A 1- to 3-pound fish is ideal for mounting. Smaller fish require a little more care in handling, and larger fish require more muscle to mount.

FISH ANATOMY

As vertebrates, fish have many bones in common with birds and mammals. Many of the bones in the head and pectoral area are similar; others are unique to the fish. When a fish is skinned for mounting, the fins and much of the skull remain attached to the skin. Bones that are of particular concern to the taxidermist are the *mandible* and *maxillary bones* in the jaw, the *pre-opercal* and *opercal*, which act as gill covers, and the *branchiostegal rays* in the throat area. Bones that remain attached to the skin behind the head include the *cleithrum* and *postcleithrum*, which are part of the pectoral girdle. In addition to the *pectoral* and *pelvic fins*, most fish have a single or double *dorsal fin*, an *anal fin*, and always a *caudal fin*, which is commonly referred to as the tail. The *lateral line* is a sensory organ common to most fish.

The skin of a fish consists of two layers. The outer layer is the *epidermis* and the inner is the *dermis*, or *corium*. Scales, where present, are embedded in the dermis and covered by the thin but important epidermis. Most warm-water fish have scales; however, North American catfish are "naked." Many of the cold-water species have scales that are so small and/or deeply embedded in the skin that the species appear to be naked. On a scaled fish such as a bass, about 75 percent of the individual scales are embedded in the epidermis. When the fish is mounted, the skin must be stretched tightly and fit smoothly on the artificial body. If the skin is allowed to shrink, the scales will curl. The result will be a noticeably irregular surface on the mount.

Although the anatomical features are similar in all species, the size and placement may vary from warm-water to cold-water species. For example, the cleithrum is well exposed on a trout but concealed beneath the opercle on a largemouth bass.

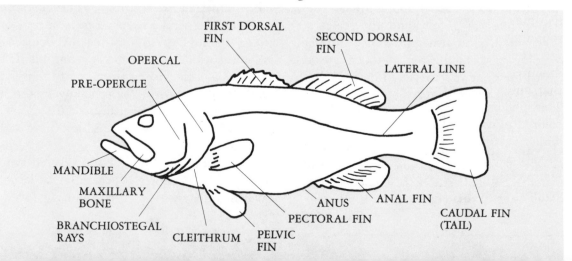

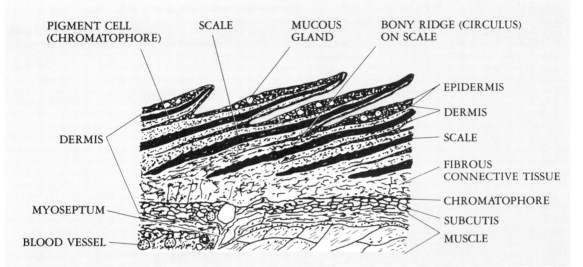

PIGMENT CELL (CHROMATOPHORE) SCALE MUCOUS GLAND BONY RIDGE (CIRCULUS) ON SCALE

EPIDERMIS
DERMIS
SCALE
FIBROUS CONNECTIVE TISSUE
CHROMATOPHORE
SUBCUTIS
MUSCLE

DERMIS

MYOSEPTUM
BLOOD VESSEL

The fish skin of a bass is surprising complex. Each scale is completely covered by a thin layer of skin. This skin includes both the mucous glands and the pigment cells that produce the color in the skin. In order to produce a smooth mount, flex the skin as little as possible during the skinning. (Adapted from General Biological Supply House drawing.)

Scattered among the flattened cells of the epidermis are numerous *mucous-gland cells* that extend into the dermis. The *pigment cells* (chromatophores) are also present in the epidermis. For most fish the background color pattern is similar: light on the belly with gradual shading on the side to a darker back. Other patterns are superimposed and serve as camouflage. The colors of an individual fish may change with age, season, the surrounding aquatic conditions, and even the gut content. However, when the fish is mounted, all of the coloration will fade so that only the light and dark hues remain. This phenomenon is similar to printing a colored photograph in black and white, in which vestiges of the color images remain in various tones of gray. Thus, a big challenge comes in attempting to restore the original colors with paints.

PREPARING FOR SKINNING

Selecting the Pose. Most fish are mounted so they can be hung on a wall. In this case the incisions and skinning are done on the wall side, and usually this side of the fish is only roughly finished. Yet in recent years, pedestal mounts have become more popular, particularly in taxidermy competitions. Pedestal mounts require that both sides of the fish be mounted as naturally as possible, and this requires a great deal more time and effort. As a beginner, you should probably concentrate on wall mounts until your skill is sufficiently perfected to justify the additional time, effort, and risk involved for a pedestal mount.

The pose you select may depend largely on the condition of the fish. Examine the fish carefully, taking note of any skin damage. Also examine the condition of the pectoral and pelvic fins. Frequently an improperly netted bass is damaged when brought into the boat or onto a pier. If some of the scales are missing on one side and not on the other, make the skinning incision on the damaged side. If none of the scales is missing, but a pectoral fin or pelvic fin is badly frayed, plan to mount the damaged fin against the wall.

As in other forms of taxidermy, good ref-erence material is essential in posing a fish, as well as in restoring the color. Unfortunately, good reference material on live fish is difficult to find. An aquarium can be an ideal source for reference, but rarely is a person able to find helpful photos of a leaping bass—the pose most commonly used by taxidermists. When you find good photos, value them like gold.

One good reference is the bass itself. Lay it on a table and lift the tail. You will notice that there is more flexibility near the tail

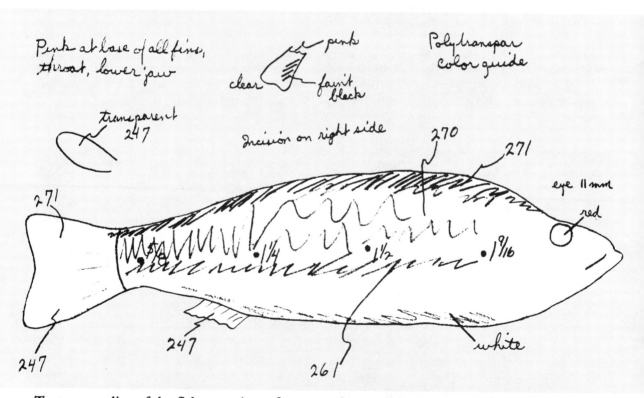

Trace an outline of the fish on a piece of paper and record the body thickness at a minimum of four places. The outline and thickness are much more useful than measurements of the circumference. As shown, record the size of the eyes and make color notations on the pattern. The numbers on this diagram identify specific colors from the Polytranspar color guide sold by Master Paint Systems. Since the colors of a fish mount will fade, your color guide notations become important references.

than at the head. Also notice the amount of arch that the body will easily take—and at what point the muscles and bones begin to strain. You will also see that there is very little flexibility of the fish vertically. For example, marine billfish are frequently mounted arched like a rainbow, but in life this is a physical impossibility. The spines on the top and bottom of the vertebrae greatly limit the amount of vertical flexing of the backbone. A fish's spine simply will not bend very much in that direction. Occasionally a trout or salmon may appear to arch when leaping from the water, but the apparent arch is really the arc of the trajectory of the fish rather than the shape of the spine. In short, when you consider the pose, know what your fish was physically capable of doing on its own.

MEASUREMENTS AND COLOR NOTES

Accurate measurements are very important. First trace an outline of the fish on paper. Butcher paper is best because it comes in large-enough sheets, but you can also tape two or more pieces of typing paper together. Then with a caliper make several measure-

By comparing the color guide with the natural color of the fish, you can determine and record the color codes most closely matching the natural colors. Even though there is a wide range of greens over different areas of a bass, the color guide will help you match each.

ments of the thickness of the fish and note these at the proper places on the drawing. Make any notations of size and shape on the paper, such as an enlarged belly, shape of head, or any other characteristics. These drawings and measurements will give you the size and shape of the artificial body and the amount of filler needed to properly mount the bass. Don't depend on circumference measurements. Otherwise, you may carve a body that has an accurate circumference but has the wrong cross-sectional shape. With an accurate profile and accurately measured thickness, the circumference will probably turn out right anyway.

A word of caution: As much as you might like to enlarge the fish, forget it. There is very little stretch in a fish skin, and if you try to add pounds or inches, you will create insurmountable problems.

On your drawing make any notations of the fish's coloring. A fish will begin to fade as soon as it is removed from the water, and this fading increases with time. By the time you are ready to mount the fish, the colors may significantly differ from those when the fish was alive. Also, some fish fade more completely than others. Thus, a good color photo of the fish soon after it was caught is your best guide. Lacking a good color photo of the freshly caught fish, be sure to at least note colors on the drawing that you have made. Either you can describe the colors yourself, or you can use a number-coded color key such as that sold by Polytranspar Paint Systems. Using this system, you simply note the number of a particular color on your drawing. Then when you finally begin to paint the fish, you will have some color guidelines to follow. But you can also make some adjustments so the coloring conforms to your published references. Be sure to mea-

sure and note the eye diameter in millimeters and color of the eyes too.

TOOLS AND SUPPLIES

The tools needed for mounting a fish are different from most of those used in other kinds of taxidermy. Short-bladed, heavy-duty scissors are needed to make the incision and do some of the skinning. You also need a fish-skinning knife with a serrated blade as well as a fleshing tool designed for fish. Curve-bladed pruning shears serve effectively as bone snips.

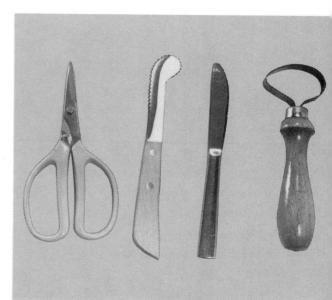

The tools needed for fish taxidermy are different from those used in other kinds of taxidermy. A kitchen scissors (left) and fish-skinning knife are perhaps the most useful tools. A table knife and the Jim Hall fish scraper (extreme right) are also very useful. Many taxidermists use a garden pruning shears to cut the bones in a fish. Before you begin to skin a fish, lay out all the tools.

For supplies, you will need glass eyes and water-based paints. The body can be carved from dense foam purchased from a taxidermy supplier. You may also prefer to use a fish mix that you can either concoct yourself or purchase. The few needed chemicals are discussed more fully later in this chapter.

REMOVING THE MUCUS

Normally, you will want to freeze a fish until you have sufficient time to skin and mount it. Although it is better to remove the mucus, or slime, from the fish before you freeze it, you can also "de-slime" the fish after you have thawed it.

To de-slime a fish, wipe it with soft paper towels or paper napkins, removing as much mucus as possible. Pay particular attention to the areas beneath the jaws, beneath the *operculum*, and at the base of the fins. Since much of a fish's fishy odor is caused by the mucus, be sure to dispose of the paper when you are finished. Then lay the fish on a piece of newspaper and coat the entire fish with deiodized salt or powdered borax. If you intend to freeze the fish, you can leave the salt (or borax) on. However, if you are ready to skin and mount the fish, leave the salt (or borax) on the fish for 10 to 15 minutes; then rinse it off and wipe the fish dry. Check over the fish to be sure that you have removed all of the mucus. If not, apply another coat of salt (or borax) and wait a few more minutes. When you are satisfied that the fish is free of mucus, it is ready to skin. (Note: If you plan to eat the fish be sure to use only salt and not borax.)

SKINNING THE FISH

Lay the fish on a piece of oilcloth or other nonabsorbent material. This will help you when cleaning up your workbench later. Then align the fish, tail toward you, with the body as straight as possible and with the damaged side (wall side) of the fish up. Insert the tip of your scissors at the point where the lateral line reaches the tail, about ¼ inch from the tail. (Scissors or snips are best for making the incisions in a fish skin. They will cut through the scales, leaving them in place. On the other hand, a scalpel will pull the scales out, giving the finished mount a rough appearance along the seam.) Cut a smooth line along the center of the body until you reach the *cleithrum*, which is the arcuate bone at the front of the body and beneath the *operculum* (gill cover). With bone snips, cut through the cleithrum to the base of the gills. Then return to the tail and make an incision with the scissors perpendicular to the body incision along the base of the tail. These are the only incisions needed to skin a bass, except where the skin is freed behind the gills.

Using a fish-skinning knife, pick up the skin along the body incision and work the knife between the skin and body. Now lay your free hand on the outer surface of the fish and work the skinning knife along the underside of the skin. A fish-skinning knife is quite dull, but the serrated edge literally tears the connective tissue that holds the dermis to the underlying muscle. The sound of skinning is distinct. So you will hear, as well as feel, the difference if the knife digs too deeply into the muscle. Work the knife along the upper side of the fish until you reach the dorsal fins. Then skin the lower side until you reach the pelvic fin.

HOW TO SKIN A BASS

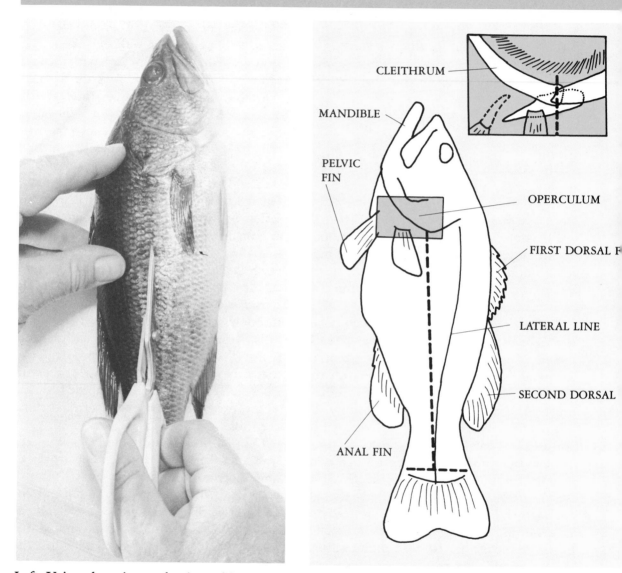

Left: Using the scissors, begin making the body incision at the tail and then cut forward to the cleithrum, the circular bone beneath the gill cover, or opercle. The scissors is much more efficient for making this incision than a scalpel. Remember: Make the incision on the side of the fish that will face the wall. This is usually the side that is less attractive, usually as a result of damage. *Right:* Begin the T incision about ¼ inch in front of the tail and then follow the midline of the body to the gills. The short cross-T cut will enable you to lay the skin flat. Clip out the roots of the tail bones along the scale line separating the body from the tail, and this forms a shallow pocket.

Left: Lift the skin gently and work the skinning knife between the skin and the body. The knife itself is dull, but the serrated edge rips the connective tissue between the skin and the body. Work carefully and avoid flexing and stretching the skin. *Right:* When you reach the anal and dorsal fins, use the scissors to cut the fin roots free from the body. Keep your fingers behind the skin so that you can feel the movement of the scissors and so can avoid puncturing the skin. After cutting the fin roots free from the body, cut the body free at tail.

(Continued)

(Bass Skinning continued)

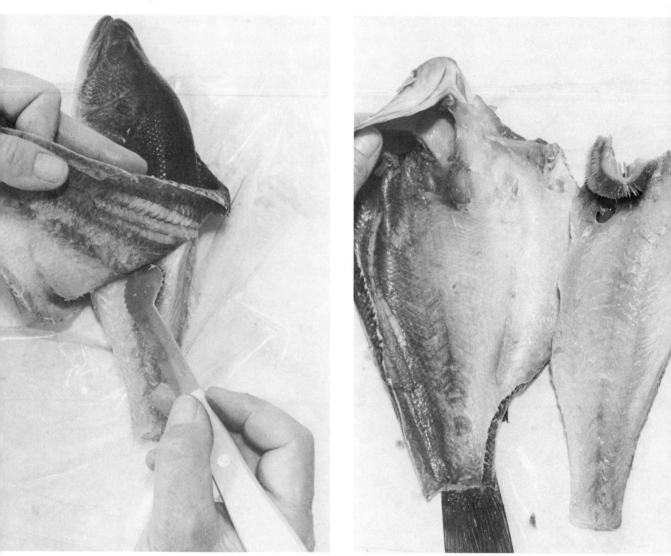

Left: Turn the fish over and gently lift the tail, working the skinning knife along the side of the body. Let the weight of the fish body act as a "third hand" so that you can work the skinning knife carefully. Since all of the fins have been separated from the body, the fish can be skinned all the way to the head. *Right:* In this photo, the body has been completely skinned and remains joined to the skin only at the pelvic fin. Note that the whole body has been removed in a single piece with the gills attached. If you wish to leave the gills in the mount, you should leave the body skin attached to the head beneath the gill cover.

Turn the fish so the tail is towards you, then skin below the cleithrum in front of the pectoral fin. Work the skinning knife slowly along the bottom edge of this bone and then forward to the base of the gills. With scissors or a scalpel, cut the skin free from the body along the back edge of the gills. You should now have the skin free on both sides of the incision to the dorsal and pelvic fins, as well as along the head behind the gills.

There is a small, pointed bone called the *basipterygium* that joins the pelvic fin to the skin. Work the point of your scissors under this bone and snip it off close to the base of the fin. Work carefully so that the point of the scissors does not break through the skin. Often it helps to keep your fingers pressed against the outside of the skin so that you can feel the location of the scissors beneath the skin. This will prevent undue damage to the skin.

The fish is now skinned on the "wall side" to the dorsal and anal fins. Bass and members of the perch family have two dorsal fins. One is called the first, or spiny-rayed, and the other is called the second, or soft-rayed, dorsal fin. Beginning at the back of the second dorsal fin, work the point of your scissors or snips behind the fin and gradually snip the roots of the dorsal fins free from the skin. Again, keep your fingers along the outside base of the fin so that you can guide the scissors accurately and not puncture the skin. Now repeat the same procedure with the anal fin by starting at the front of the fin and working toward the rear. At the same time, you will cut through the intestine at the anus. If you have not already done so, clip off the basipterygium that joins the second pelvic fin to the skin. Finally use your scissors or snips to clip the bones around the edge of the tail.

Turn the bass over with the show side up. Grasping the tail, lift the bass gently and begin to work the skinning knife along the unskinned side of the fish. Avoid careless handling or folding of the skin, which would cause the scales to pop out of their sockets along the fold and create an uneven surface on the mount. Skin forward until you reach the cleithrum. Then work your skinning knife under this bone and forward to the back edge of the gills. With scissors or a scalpel, cut the skin free around the back edge of the gills. The body will still be joined at the throat where it forms a "V" between the mandibles. Skin the area carefully; then clip through the small bone in the middle of the throat muscle, leaving the skin intact. The body has now been completely skinned, but it is still joined to the skin at the back of the head.

Gently lay the bass on its back so you can see where the bony roof of the mouth joins the softer part of the mouth and esophagus. With shears, cut through the spine at this point and then clip away any remaining flesh around the back of the skull. The body will come free, leaving the head attached to the skin. The body can now be discarded or eaten if it is sufficiently fresh and if you have been using salt rather than borax.

The eyes must now be removed and the cheeks skinned out. To remove the eyes, make a small wire hook and insert it under the front of the eye. Lift gently and with a scalpel cut the muscles that control eye movement. After removing the eyes, work a dull scalpel or screwdriver through the eye socket and along the edge of the cheek. First work the tool along the inside of the skin, then work it under the muscle along the bony surface below. These are the muscles that control the jaws and must be removed or else they will decay, causing shrinkage. After you have

After removing the body, you must remove the eye and the muscle from inside the cheeks. After removing the eye, work a blunt knife through the eye orbit and under the muscle. You will be able to feel the area where this jaw muscle is located. Scrape the meat free from the bone and pull it out through the eye orbit.

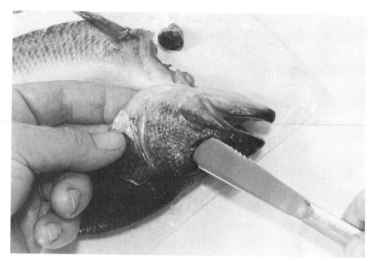

loosened the muscle on the top and bottom, reach through the eye socket and grasp this piece of muscle with needle-nose pliers. You will be able to pull the bulk of the center of the muscle free; however, muscle fragments will remain attached at both ends. With the center of the muscle removed, you can work the screwdriver in behind the remaining muscle and scrape it free. This completes the skinning process.

Leaving the Gills In. With the skinning method described above, you remove the entire body, including the gills. With some mounts, and particularly bass, you may wish to retain the gills in the mount. When you want to leave the gills in the fish, *do not* cut through the skin at the base of the gills and in front of the cleithrum. Instead, when you reach the base of the gills, you are also against the back of the mouth. Working carefully, cut downward with your scissors or a scalpel along the skin that forms the inside of the mouth and the esophagus. This task may appear to be somewhat messy. However, this

will leave the gills attached to the skin, allowing you to create an "open-gill" mount. Since the open-gill mount requires advanced skills, be sure you first master the skinning of a fish without gills.

FLESHING, DEGREASING, AND PRESERVING

Scraping the Skin. After you have lifted the body out of the skin, there may be a considerable amount of scraping to do, depending on how cleanly you removed the skin. You can scrape your first fish or two using the edge of a tablespoon or a blunt butter knife. But the best tool available is the Jim Hall scraper, which removes the adhering flesh cleanly and quickly. When properly used, this tool will not tear the skin.

Work the scraping tool parallel with the muscle lines on the skin. These are diagonal lines running from the belly back toward the midline of the skin. Occasionally it is necessary to scrape from tail to head, but *never* scrape a fish skin from head to tail. This will cause the scales to "stand up" in the sockets and ruin the mount.

After you have removed all of the flesh from the flat surface of the skin, use scissors to trim all meat away from the fin roots. Work slowly and carefully, and keep one or two fingers beneath the area that you are trimming so that you will not jab the point of the scissors through the skin. There is likely to be some meat in the throat skin. Also use snippers to clip away any meat in the skull cavity. Remove the brains with a screwdriver or some type of brain spoon. Now turn your attention to the tail and trim any bone away from the tail roots along the edge of the scaled area of the tail. Work carefully on this area, and again be sure to use your fingers on the outside of the skin so that the point of the scissors will not break through the skin.

The head is another problem area. Be sure that you clean it out. If you left the gills in the skin, pay special attention along the back of the skull, esophagus, and mouth area. After you have removed all of the flesh from the skin, fins, and tail, rinse the skin in cold

Use a fish scraper to flesh the skin. Always move the scraper parallel to the ribs and **NOT** from head to tail. The skin will be easier to flesh if you apply a little bit of powdered borax. Use a scissors to trim the flesh away from the tail and fin roots. Also remove as much meat as possible from the head and throat area, and remove the brains.

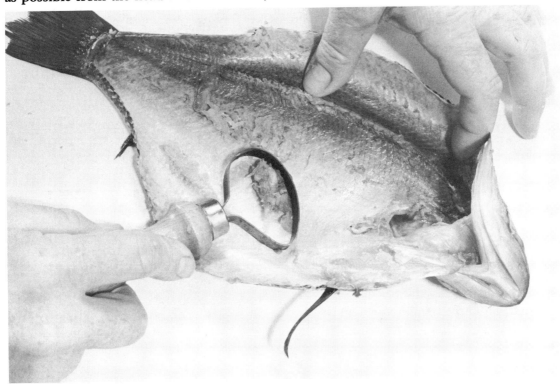

running water to remove any remaining scraps of flesh or bone.

DEGREASING METHODS

Most fish have at least a small amount of fat beneath the skin. During the skinning process, you will inadvertently transfer some of the grease from this fat from the body to the skin. If there is any grease left on the skin, it may discolor the mounted skin and fail to take paint properly. So all fish skins should be degreased regardless of the species. As Jim Hall will explain later in this chapter, the cold-water species may be extremely greasy. Degreasing not only improves the quality, it will also increase the longevity of your mounts.

A number of compounds will work satisfactorily to remove the grease from a fish skin. These include white-gas camp fuel, mineral spirits, and the commercial products sold by various supply dealers. Many of these have a high flash point but are nonetheless dangerously flammable, so be sure you use them outdoors away from spark or flame and where there is plenty of ventilation.

Place the skin flat in a glass or ceramic tray and pour the degreasing solution over it. Stir gently to be sure that the entire skin is covered and that no air pockets remain inside the tail, skull, or mouth. A warm-water fish skin, such as that of a bass, should be left in the degreasing solution for 30 minutes to an hour. This will be enough time for the solution to dissolve any oil from the skin and around the bones. Now remove the skin and lay it flat on a piece of newspaper. Blot the remaining solvent from both sides of the skin. The remainder will evaporate quickly. You can return any remaining de-

greasing solution to a metal container and reuse it until it becomes dirty or discolored.

While soap or detergent will remove grease from a bird or small mammal skin, it is unsatisfactory for fish skins. Soap will help remove any oil or grease from the surface of the fish skin itself, but it will not draw the fat out of the joints or bones in the head. This fat may later bleed through the paint to the surface of the skin and discolor or ruin the mount.

PRESERVING THE SKIN

There is a variety of methods that will satisfactorily preserve fish skin. The most commonly used is a borax solution similar to that used for small mammal skins. Borax is recommended for warm-water species by Archie Phillips, owner of one of the largest fish-mounting studios in the world, and by Jim Hall, who is world-renowned for his cold-water fish mounts. On the other hand, award-winning bass taxidermist Tom Sexton urges that all fish skins be tanned and preserved in Edolan U. If you are a beginner, you probably will find that the borax solution produces good results. Nevertheless a tanned skin treated with Edolan U will probably ensure a longer-lasting mount.

Borax. Dissolve ½ cup of powdered borax in 1 gallon of lukewarm water. If some of the borax fails to dissolve, the solution is saturated and sufficiently strong. Dissolve more borax as needed. Next add 3 to 4 drops of formaldehyde, using an eyedropper. (Too much formaldehyde will cause the skin to stiffen and become difficult to mount.) Stir the solution and allow it to cool to room temperature before placing the skin in the

After applying borax to the skin, soak the skin in a borax-formaldehyde pickle solution. Mix these solutions only in a plastic container and be sure the solution is saturated. The skin can then remain in the solution for several hours or longer. However, if you expect some delay in mounting the skin after pickling it, remove and freeze it.

mixture. Allow the skin to soak for 2 to 3 hours, until the small amount of flesh on the bones of the fins has turned white. You may also leave the skin in the borax solution overnight if needed, but I do not recommend that the skin be left in solution more than 24 hours. If you are unable to mount the skin by the time the flesh on the bones has turned white, remove it from the solution and freeze it until you are ready to mount it. After removing the skin from the borax bath, rinse the outside of the skin in cool running water. This will remove any borax that might have crystalized on the skin while it was in the solution. Crystalized borax on the outside of the skin will result in a sand-paperlike surface on which the paint is applied rather than the slick, smooth surface that you want on a fish.

Tanning and Mothproofing. A fish skin should be tanned and mothproofed too. There is no question that a skin treated in this manner will last a long time. If you are a beginner, however, practice is more important than the longevity of your mount, so on practice mounts you may choose to ignore the tanning and mothproofing techniques. But it would be wise to incorporate the techniques into any mounts you will value.

Purchase one of several commercial fish-tanning solutions that are available from the various supply companies. Follow the directions included with your solution. In most cases the skin must be soaked for several hours to a day or longer and then removed from the fish tan and rinsed in clear water. The skin can then be soaked in an Edolan U solution. This is one of the best mothproofing agents on the market. Again, follow the directions included with your Edolan U. Since very little chemical is required (the amount based on the dry weight of the skin), you can treat several skins at the same time. Also, you can store this solution for reuse once or twice. However since the Edolan U will bond with the skin, the solution will gradually weaken and so must be replaced. Caution: Always use rubber gloves when handling this mothproofing agent; otherwise it will mothproof your skin as well as the fish.

MOUNTING A WARM-WATER FISH

Carved-Body Technique. There is a wide variety of ways to mount a fish skin. Some taxidermists wrap an artificial body with excelsior in the same way I described in earlier chapters for birds and small mammals. While excelsior is potentially good, many taxidermists find it too time-consuming to wrap an anatomically accurate fish body. Also, if the fish is large, excelsior results in a relatively heavy mount. Many stuffing methods have also been developed. Today commercial fish mix is used. It has replaced the sand-filled fish mount that produced a hollow fish skin attached to a panel. In fact, some feel that there are as many methods for mounting a fish as there are taxidermists. This probably is not too far from true because each taxidermist usually develops some modifications of a standard technique.

For practical purposes, I recommend that beginners start by carving an artificial body. This develops your understanding of fish anatomy and body shape, and it is fast and inexpensive. After you have perfected your skill in carving bodies, you can adjust your techniques in order to improve your mounts. Because stuffing a skin with fish mix is becoming very popular, I also describe this method later in this chapter.

As a guide for carving your first fish mount, use a commercial form. There are a number of anatomically accurate polyurethane, or dense foam, fish bodies offered by various supply companies. Three award-winning fish taxidermists—Matt Thompson, Archie Phillips, and Jim Hall—have all sculpted a line of fish bodies that are relatively inexpensive. When you place an order for taxidermy supplies, order a fish body for a 2- or 3-pound bass. You will then have this as a reference, and you will see what the experts do. For a beginner, the

Although you should develop the skill of carving a foam body, I recommend that you purchase a commercial form to use as a guide. Here a form by the Archie Phillips Supply Company is ready to be fitted to the skin. Always begin with a larger body, which you can carve down, rather than try to fill in with papier-mâché.

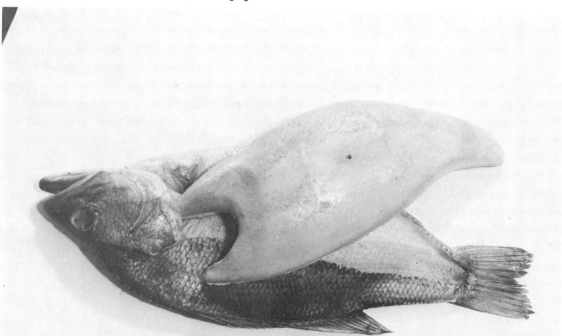

disadvantage of using a commercial body is that the form probably will not fit his fish skin. Most bodies are made for a particular species, such as largemouth bass, and the bodies are usually graduated in one-pound increments. If the body is too big, you must sand it down; if the commercial form is too small, you have to add a layer of papier-mâché. So for the beginner, it is best to simply carve one's own artificial body accurately, using a commercially produced form as a reference.

Before you began skinning the specimen, you traced an outline of the fish on paper. You made several measurements at that time too. Using this profile as a pattern, trace the outline onto a piece of dense foam that is at least as thick as the greatest thickness of the fish. Be careful not to destroy your pattern if you have written the color descriptions on it. Now with a keyhole or a band saw, cut out the side profile of the fish. Then, using the thickness measurements you made, draw a top view of the fish on the upper side of the foam side profile. If you wish to put a smooth curve in the body, include it in this top profile. Then cut out the top profile.

With the body roughed out of foam, you can now carve it and sand it to the proper size and shape. Begin by cutting the corners off the body with a filleting knife. As is explained by Jim Hall in the following section of this chapter, try to work on opposite sides of the body at the same time. In other words, trim the left side of the back first and then the right side of the back. In this way you will be able to achieve better symmetry. Throughout the trimming process, continue to check the size of the body, using the actual fish skin. When you begin, there will be a wide gap along the side incision. But as you carve and trim, this incision will

FITTING THE SKIN

Test fit the skin on the artificial body for size. For the fish shown, body length is correct but the gap along the side indicates that the body is too large through the middle and so must be shaved down. For proper fit, it is not absolutely necessary that the incision be completely closed as long as the dorsal and anal fins are properly seated along the body.

(Continued)

(Fitting the Skin continued)

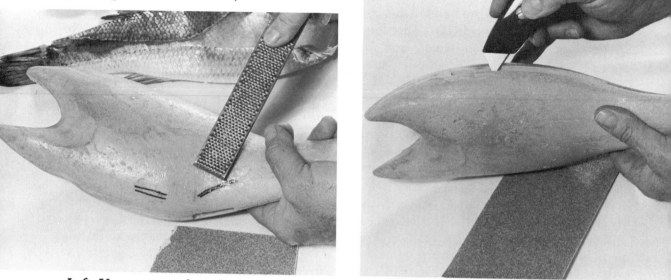

Left: Use a rasp and sandpaper to bring the artificial body down to the proper size and fit. Work slowly. You will make up the amount of time you spend in fitting the body properly during the actual mounting of the skin. *Right:* Mark the location of the fin roots on the body and cut a recess in the body to accommodate these fin roots. The groove will also help you align the fins on the body when you put the skin in place. During the mounting you will fill the groove with papier-mâché.

After you have carved the artificial body for the fish, inset a small piece of ¼-inch plywood on the BACK of the artificial body. A hot-glue gun gives a fast, permanent bond to the polyurethane form. The plywood serves as an anchor for the screws which attach the mounted fish to the panel.

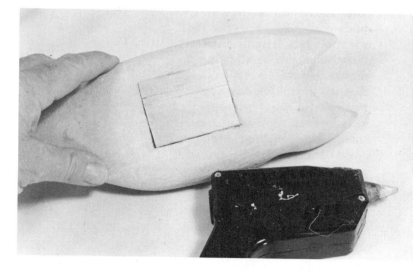

gradually close. When you have reduced the incision gap to an inch or less, do the final shaping and trimming with rasp and sandpaper. This will eliminate any ridges left by the knife, and it will also enable you to put some detail into the belly, around the fin butts, and in the throat area. The artificial body is finished when the incision will close over it.

During the final phases of trimming the artificial body, cut a groove along the back for the dorsal fin roots and on the belly for the anal fin butt. Make sure that the body fits smoothly into the tail area of the skin where a small pocket of skin will be left after the trimming of the tail butts. There should be a small indentation in the belly profile where the pelvic fins are located. Make sure that the head area of the artificial body fits snugly into the skull and that the throat of the artificial body fits smoothly between the mandibles.

The final step in preparing the artificial body is to insert a wooden block that will anchor the mount to a panel. When the body is carved to your satisfaction, cut a piece of ¼-inch plywood about 2 inches square and draw its outline on the back of the fish body. Then, using a knife, cut away enough of the foam to allow the small piece of wood to fit into place. With carpenter's glue or a hot-glue gun, put the wooden block in place. The location, size, and shape of the wooden block will vary with the pose and size of the fish.

The skin is now ready to be mounted. Spread the skin flat on the workbench and, after mixing a small amount of papier-mâché, stuff a small wad of mâché into the brain cavity and around the base of the skull. Put a small amount of mâché on the roots of each of the fins and in the tail. Then give the artificial body a coat of hide paste. (I use the same hide paste for mounting fish that I use

MOUNTING THE SKIN

After laying the skin flat and making a final check to be certain there is no remaining muscle or bone clinging to the skin, mix some mâché to the desired consistency and spread it along the roots of the fins and tail. Also put some mâché in the throat area and behind the skull. The mâché should be fairly quick-setting. Since the skin will begin to dry immediately, the mâché should set up within about 2 hours and before the skin shrinks and otherwise deforms the mâché.

(Mounting the Skin continued)

 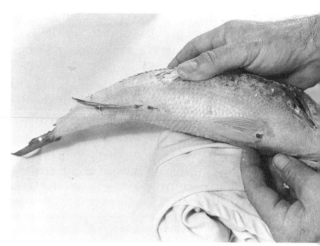

Left: After carving the artificial body to the proper dimensions and after preparing the skin, apply hide paste or glue to the body. The paste will fill the pores of the foam and also hold the skin in place while it dries. Here carpenter's glue is being used. This glue is water soluble as well as light colored. If the hide paste is dark colored, it will read through the skin somewhat, making the fish more difficult to paint. *Right:* With the concave side of the fish resting on a roll of damp rags, pull the skin into place and line the fins up with the centerline of the artificial body. At this time insert a couple of pins as shown, at the tail, the anal fin, and the dorsal fin. One or two pins in the throat area help hold the skin before you begin sewing the incision.

Begin sewing with nylon thread at the tail and work toward the head. Here a baseball stitch is shown, as illustrated on page 127. Since nylon thread easily tears the fish skin, you may not be able to draw the incision completely closed by sewing. Anyway, the incision need not be completely closed, as long as you have lined up the fins properly.

for deer heads. Most supply companies sell hide paste. The paste sold by McKenzie Supply works well for both game heads and fish.)

Now you are ready to assemble the mount. With the skin lying flat, flesh-side up, insert the paste-covered artificial body. Begin by inserting it into the tail area and then into the head and throat. The fit will be a little snug because the papier-mâché has occupied some of the space. Work slowly and carefully, working the extra mâché out to the incision where it can be scraped away. Push the fin roots into the indentation that you cut into the body, and smooth out any lumpy areas caused by the mâché by working your fingers over the skin. Throughout the process it is a good idea to have a damp rag handy. Wipe the skin from time to time in order to keep it moist. Be certain that the fins do not dry out either. You can also use the rag to wipe any hide paste off the outside of the skin. When the skin fits over the artificial body, put three or four pins into the skin along the incision to hold the skin in place.

Turn the mount over, incision down, and you will have a chance to examine the show-side of the fish. Check to ensure that the fins are properly set, particularly the dorsal and anal fins. Then lift the operculum (gill cover) and put a row of pins along the skin in front of the cleithrum. Line up the skin on the throat as it is pinned in place. You may also want to put a pin or two into the base of each fin and into the anus so that those parts will be held in place while the hide paste is drying. When you are satisfied with the show-side of the fish, moisten it with your damp rag and turn the fish over.

A wet rag or towel can be rolled up and the fish laid on it. Assuming that you have some curve in the body, the mount cannot be laid incision up unless the middle of the body is supported by a rag or towel.

Now pin the skin along the throat, on the incision side of the mount, and also pin the fins as needed. Pin the pectoral fin flat against the body so that the panel will fit properly. You are now ready to sew the incision. I use a baseball stitch. Also, if the artificial body is dense enough, many taxidermists simply staple the incision closed. Since appearance is not a factor on the wall-side of the mount, use whichever system works best for you. If there is still a little wobble where the head joins the artificial body, stuff some papier-mâché through the mouth and into the junction of the skull and throat area with the artificial body.

After you have carved a few fish bodies, you may decide that you prefer to buy precast commercial forms. Always order the body slightly smaller than you will actually need. Then after you have modified the body, such as carving grooves for the fins or reshaping the head as needed, spread a thin layer of papier-mâché inside the fish skin as if spreading peanut butter on bread. After you have sewn the incision closed, work the skin with your hands to move the papier-mâché as needed. Remember, a commercial form is easier to use when you build it up with mâché than when you try to shave it smaller with a knife or sandpaper.

At this point, you have mounted the skin on a carved or commercial form. There is a considerable amount of detail work left to be done, but this is the same regardless of the mounting technique. The following section describes fish mix techniques and is followed by a section explaining the finishing of tail, fins, and head.

THE FISH-MIX TECHNIQUE

The use of fish mix is as close as a taxidermist ever comes to "stuffing" a specimen. Meyer Fish Mix Company in Cincinnati, Ohio, is the originator of this material, and subsequently Ballard and other suppliers have developed their own variety of mix. Regardless of the manufacturer, fish mix is a lightweight, inert filler and paste that is literally stuffed into the prepared fish skin. Most fish mix contains ground high-density foam, pearlite, or similar substances and a water-based glue. Beginning taxidermists can make their own by grinding foam with a rasp or sanding disk. When you have ground about 1 cubic foot of foam, add 1 cup of papier-mâché and 1 cup of wallpaper paste. For best results, put all of the ingredients into a small plastic bag and shake thoroughly. The mâché and paste will mix with the ground foam more uniformly this way.

Now prepare the skin using the same techniques I described earlier for using the carved body. The skin must be scraped, degreased, and preserved. Then lay the skin flat and put the papier-mâché into the base of the tail, fins, head, and throat. Now sew the incisions, beginning at the tail, about halfway up the body toward the head. Use a baseball stitch and make the stitches close together, but not too tight. Don't pucker the skin along the incision, simply draw the two edges together. You can also use a pliers-type stapler.

One cubic foot of mix will be adequate for a bass weighing about 2 pounds. Assuming that your fish is about that size, pour half of your fish mix into a large mixing bowl and add about 1 cup of water. Mix it thoroughly. The mix should be about the consistency of cookie dough. If the mix is too dry, add more water. When it is thoroughly mixed and can be squeezed into a ball, the mix is ready to be stuffed into the sewn portion of the fish skin. Use a tablespoon or just push small amounts into the skin with your fingers. After you have about 2 inches of the skin filled, use a dowel, such as a short length of broom handle, and tamp the mix tightly into the tail area of the skin. Continue this process of stuffing and tamping until you have filled the skin to the end of the sewn incision. *Do not overstuff*! You want the skin to look like a fish and not like a sausage. Next sew the incision forward until you have about 2 inches of the incision still open. Repeat the stuffing and tamping process, but this time be sure that you work the mix up into the head area and into the throat. Cut a 2 × 2-inch piece of ¼-inch plywood and slip it through the incision, working it back to the middle of the body directly under the skin. Now close the remaining part of the incision up to the cleithrum.

Turn the fish show-side up and work the skin with your hands in order to properly shape the fish. There should be a smooth union of the body skin with the tail, and the dorsal and anal fins should be centered on the top and bottom of the mount. Work some shape into the skin around the belly and anus, as well as at the junction of the head and body. You may also wish to prop up the head and tail with wedges of dense foam. If the skin is overstuffed, use a spoon to remove some of the mix through the mouth. If you need additional stuffing, push the mix into the mouth with a spoon and then tamp it back into the body with the spoon or dowel.

When you are satisfied that the fish is adequately stuffed, you need to block the inside of the mouth in order to keep the fish mix in place. Assuming you have removed the gills and esophagus, wet a ball of newspaper and stuff it into the back of the mouth against the mix that has filled the body. The paste in the fish mix will bond to the wet paper, forming a permanent block for the body and throat. If the gills were left in place, then a wad of *dry* paper should be stuffed into the back of the mouth until the fish dries. This is a temporary block and will be removed later.

Two aspects of using fish mix require constant attention: (1) keep the skin and fins wet so that they remain soft and flexible while the skin is being stuffed; (2) don't overstuff the skin, which would cause the fish to lose its natural shape.

FINISHING THE MOUNT

Both the carved-body and the fish-mix techniques will produce good results for the beginner. Some people find that it takes as long to stuff the fish as it does to carve a body. However the stuffing method has the advantage that the pose can be changed at any time, whereas the pose is established as soon as you begin to carve the body. No matter which method you choose, the same techniques are used to finish the mount.

Now that the fish is mounted, the tail, fins, and head require some additional attention. Moisten both sides of the tail, and then spread it smoothly into the desired position. Do not overspread the tail; otherwise it will look extreme and out of shape. Using snips, cut a piece of ⅛-inch hardware cloth the approximate size and shape of the spread tail. It is better to have the hardware cloth too large than too small. Place the hardware cloth on the back of the tail and put a strip of plastic milk carton on the front of the tail. Then hold both pieces together with large paper clips, or with alligator clips from an electric supply house, or even with staples. (Later, you can fill the staple holes with papier-mâché.) If you staple, be sure the staples go through the edge of the tail so that it cannot shrink while drying and draw the tail closed. Brace the tail with a piece of heavy wire inserted along the back of the tail and into the artificial body. This will hold the tail in a smooth curve with the body, and the weight of the hardware cloth and clips will not pull it out of position.

Use this same procedure for the other fins and the branchiostegal rays along the throat. You may want to temporarily pin a small scrap of foam under the pelvic and pectoral fins in order to hold them in place away from the body rather than using a wire. As the fish is drying, watch the fins and tail to make certain they are not drying out of shape. If this begins to occur, remove the hardware cloth and dampen the fin and the skin at the base of the fin. Then readjust the fin and sandwich it in place again.

The final step is finishing the mouth. Take a wad of papier-mâché and stuff it into the cheek through the eye orbit. Fill out both cheeks. Avoid overfilling the cheek area. This is a common mistake by taxidermists, and the result is that the artificial eye will not fit properly. One way to avoid this mistake is to make a measurement of the thickness of the head at the cheeks before you begin skinning the fish. Then you can stuff it back to the proper dimension.

Since some skin shrinkage will occur around the eye orbit, stuff the cheeks up to the eyes. Since the artificial eyes will be set later, the eye area can be built up properly

SETTING THE FINS

While drying, the fins and tail have a tendency to shrink closed. So they must be backed with 1/8-inch hardware cloth and sheet plastic from milk cartons, that keep them spread. Use the snips to cut the cloth slightly larger than the fins and tail. These pieces can be used repeatedly and will last for years.

Left: To keep the tail properly spread during the drying process, use a pliers-type stapler to hold the edges of the tail to the hardware cloth. *Right:* With the hardware cloth pressed against the back of the fins and tail, paper clip the plastic sheeting against the front. This combination of materials will enable you to see that the fins and tail are properly spread. Also, the air will reach the back, through the hardware cloth, allowing proper drying.

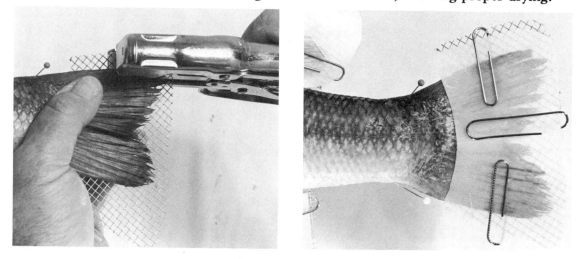

As a final step, stuff the cheeks. Use a butter knife or other instrument to work papier-mâché through the eye orbit into the cheek area. The area should be filled but not overstuffed. Many taxidermists mistakenly use too much mâché in the cheek. This exaggerates the dimensions of the cheeks and forces the eye orbit out of position.

after the skin is dry.

Brace the mouth open with a piece of wood such as a short length of dowel or a broken pencil. Do not overstretch the mouth. Make it natural. After all, it is possible to open a skinned fish's mouth far wider than the fish could ever have opened it in real life. If you have skinned the fish with the gills in place, put a small spacer between each of the gill rakers so they are properly spaced.

The mount is now finished and can be set aside to dry. I recommend that the mount be laid on a rack that will allow air to circulate freely and completely around the fish. This will allow uniform drying so that abnormal shrinkage in one area does not disfigure the mount. A flat frame of 2×4s covered with hardware cloth works very well. Another option is to screw a piece of lath to the back of the fish and hang the mount from the rafters. Either way the fish will dry uniformly.

Give the mount a thorough examination three or four hours after you have finished. Check to make certain that the fins are spread properly and that they are supported at the proper angle. Has the tail maintained a smooth curve with the body or is it drooping out of position? Are the branchiostegal rays correct? They have a tendency to draw up under the operculum as the fish dries. If the cheeks are beginning to look lumpy, you may need to adjust the papier-mâché filler. You can reduce any lumps on the body by tapping them with a small tack hammer. Since the outer surface of a fish dries rather quickly, this may be the last time you will be able to make changes in the mount. So be thorough.

The final drying time of a fish mount will vary with a number of factors: the size of the fish; the temperature of the drying room; and the relative humidity in the air. A fish skin mounted on a carved body will dry more quickly than a skin stuffed with fish mix, and most warm-water species will dry more quickly than cold-water species. As a general rule, I recommend that a fish be allowed to dry for at least a month, but you must use your own judgment. I suggest at least a month because any shrinkage that occurs after painting will crack the paint and place you

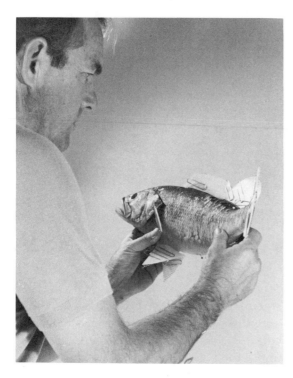

Make a final inspection of the mount before setting it aside to dry. Be sure that all of the fins and the tail are properly backed and that the mouth has been propped open. Add pins as needed to hold the fins and the branchiostegal rays in place. Work your fingers along the edges of the fins and tail to smooth any papier-mâché that may have worked out of place. If the mâché is lumpy, work the excess toward the incision and scrape it away.

Left: When the mount is dry, back the fins in order to strengthen them for the final mount. In this photo the tail has been backed with a fin-backing cream that supports the tail while retaining the natural serrated edge. This makes the tail look natural and somewhat flexible, though still susceptible to damage. *Right:* I backed this tail with a thin sheet of mylar plastic and carpenter's glue. I later trimmed the plastic to the natural configuration on the tail. This backing technique makes the fins and tail more durable and produces a more finished appearance. Most professional taxidermists employ this technique.

This is the finished mount ready for painting. I have set the eye in papier-mâché and backed all of the fins and the tail and allowed them to dry. Note the smooth lines of the fish, the natural curvature of the body, and the natural spread of the fins—not overextended. Avoid opening the mouth unnaturally far.

back to square one. If you try to rush the drying time, you will probably regret it.

When the skin is thoroughly dry, prepare it for painting. Remove the tail and fin backing, and fill any pinholes with papier-mâché. Also use papier-mâché to reshape the inside of the mouth after you have removed the extra paper block. (In order to speed the drying time of the mâché, mix some plaster with the mâché before adding the water.)

Two methods are commonly used to back the fins. Most taxidermists glue a backing of clear mylar plastic film behind each fin and the tail. This gives a smooth edge to the fins and tail. It also fills any tear that has occurred in the fins. Carpenter's glue works well. Instead of using plastic, you may prefer to coat the back of the fins and tail

with a "fin-backing cream." This will retain the natural serrated edges of the fins and tail, but it will not mend any damaged areas, and it is not as strong as a plastic-backed fin.

You should now set the artificial eyes. These should be the same size as the natural eyes. Most supply companies sell eyes for various species and in different sizes for each species. If there is too much dried mâché in the eye socket from stuffing the cheeks, cut it out with a scalpel. Then make a bed of mâché in the socket area and push the glass eye into place. Use reference photos when setting the eyes. Also, when both eyes are in place, examine the mount from various angles to ensure the eye positions are symmetrical. Set the mount aside a day or two to allow the glue and mâché to dry.

PAINTING A BASS

Painting a fish separates the basic taxidermists from the artists. With a little time and practice, anyone can mount a fish properly, but not everyone seems able to master the technique of painting a fish. Nevertheless, with a good color guide and practice, most taxidermists can master the techniques of painting those species that are most commonly found in their region.

Not only are largemouth bass among the most common and wide-ranging gamefish, they are also among the easiest varieties to paint. The markings are distinct, and the three primary colors are white, yellow, and green; so this is another good reason for the beginner to start with bass.

Probably 90 percent of all fish painted by pros are painted with an airbrush, yet few beginning taxidermists have an airbrush available. For the first few fish you mount, simply use watercolors and brushes. You can get satisfactory results with a little practice. If you plan to mount many fish, you should consider using an airbrush, because an airbrush applies very light coats of paint that dry quickly and it allows you to blend the colors more accurately. If you make a major mistake, the paints are easier to remove or overpaint with an airbrush. Nevertheless, the painting tool is a matter of choice, and some outstanding fish have been painted with just an artist's brush.

As to paints, there are a few fundamentals that you should understand. First, paints made by different manufacturers may react when the paints are mixed, so it is a good idea to stay with a single manufacturer. There are several good lines of fish paints available from different supply dealers, but stick with a single source. Second, I recommend that the beginner use watercolors rather than oil-based paints because cleanup is easier and because mistakes can be corrected more easily with watercolors. The other advantage is that if you eventually begin using an airbrush, watercolors can be used safely indoors and there is no need for an exhaust fan or respirator. Prolonged exposure to the fumes of lacquers can be very harmful and should be avoided. Finally, apply your paints in thin coats so the natural character of the skin and scales shows through the paint. Painting a fish is *not* like painting a wall where a heavy coat is best. The natural spots on the side of the bass are good indicators of paint density. If your paints are hiding these spots, you are applying the paint too heavily. *The purpose is to "tint" the fish rather than actually paint it.*

Also, taxidermists use several specialty paints that you are not likely to find in your local art supply store. The mounts must first be sealed so that the surface of the fish will accept the paints uniformly. Part of the mount is actually dried skin, part is exposed scales, and part may also be fillers such as papier-mâché. All parts are going to be painted at the same time. Each part has a different porosity and will absorb the paint differently. Therefore you must apply a sealer to the entire fish, front and back, before you begin to paint. The taxidermist also uses "pearl of essence," which actually contains microscopic fragments of freshwater pearl. This reproduces much of the iridescence that you see on live fish. Finally the painted mount is finished with a gloss to give the mount a wet appearance. All three of these coatings—sealer, pearl, and gloss—can be obtained from a taxidermy supply dealer.

Taxidermy Instructor Ralph Garland, of Piedmont Technical College, in Roxboro,

Many outstanding fish mounts have been painted with artist's hair brushes. But an airbrush, as shown, is the painting tool of choice among professional fish taxidermists. The airbrush can apply light coats that dry quickly, and it allows you to blend colors accurately.

North Carolina, wrote a painting schedule for largemouth bass that was published in *American Taxidermist*. Although originally written for use with an airbrush, the painting schedule also applies when you use an artist's brush. With a brush, the procedure is just slower and requires more skill in blending the paints.

After the fish is thoroughly dry, check it carefully for shrinkage or cracks around the mouth. If some filling is required, such as around the base of the fins, use papier-mâché. Allow this to dry. Finally, wipe the skin with a damp cloth to remove any dust or dried mâché that may have accumulated. Again allow the fish to dry. Apply a coat of water-based sealer (for a sealer compatible with watercolors) over the entire mount. Apply sealer to both sides of the fish, on the fins and tail, and inside the mouth. When this is dry, the fish should begin to show a definite clear covering. If you do not see this, apply a second coat. Master Paint Systems has developed a fungicidal sealer that not only seals the surface; it also retards mildew and bacterial action.

As shown in **Part A** of the accompanying drawing, apply white paint to the inside of the mouth, the lower part of the operculum, the belly, and the throat.

Use pearl of essence in the same area that you applied the white, but it should be painted up the sides of the bass to about the lateral line. It should be heaviest in the throat area.

As shown in **Part B** of the accompanying drawing, apply yellow along the side, blending it with the white below and upward to the dark part of the back. Do not cover the dark markings on the side of the fish; these should show through the yellow. The yellow also goes on the operculum and up near the eyes.

As shown in **Part C**, apply medium green on the back and upper part of the body. This medium green should fade out and blend with the yellow at the lateral line.

Mix a very small amount of black with the medium green and apply it to the back of the fish, the top of the head, and the dorsal fins and tail. This is a similar area to that shown in **Part C** but does not extend down to the lateral line.

Now you should intensify the spot pattern of your mount with black. Darken the back of the fish, the fins, and tail as needed. Then, as shown in **Part D**, go over the spot pattern on the flanks of the bass, its head and cheeks. Some bass have faint black spots on each scale below the main patterns, and these extend almost to the white belly. The lower mandible will also need some black. By painting this carefully, you will actually bring out the original pattern in your mount so that it is

BASS PAINTING SCHEDULE *(Described in accompanying text)*

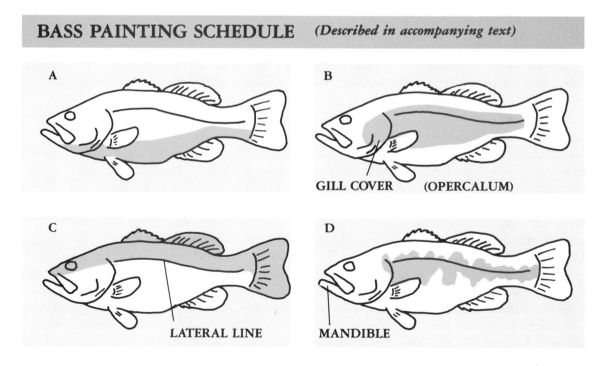

A

B

GILL COVER   (OPERCALUM)

C

LATERAL LINE

D

MANDIBLE

My finished largemouth bass. Literally millions of bass are taken each year, and they are excellent specimens for mounting and display. Such a mount can help an angler recall the episodes related to the catch.

unique, original, and one-of-a-kind.

Now restore the pink that is found at the base of the anal, pelvic, and pectoral fins, as well as in the throat area. You can also add a little pink inside the mouth along the base of the tongue and faintly at the esophagus. Two parts white mixed with one part red will make the right color for most fish. Also, if you mounted the fish with the gills in place, paint the gills bright red.

Apply two gloss coats. The first is primarily a sealer of the paint. A second coat, and third if needed, should be applied to produce the glossy or wet look. If you apply these coats too heavily, the gloss may run and ruin the appearance of the mount. It is best to gradually build up to the intensity of gloss that you desire rather than try to apply it in a single coat. The paint job is now complete.

Notes Along the Way. Remember to work slowly and allow each color to thoroughly dry before adding the next color. You will gradually learn to blend the colors so you can apply them more quickly. A fan, circulating the air in your painting room, will hasten the drying process.

Mounted by Matt Thompson of Lovejoy, Georgia, this largemouth bass was awarded a blue ribbon at a national competition. The fins have a plastic backing. And the mount was painted with Polytranspar paint. (Joe Sebo photo)

MOUNTING COLD-WATER FISH

By Jim Hall, Idaho Falls, Idaho

[Author's note: Since national taxidermy competitions began in 1977, thousands of fish have been entered and many have won ribbons. For every 10 bass entered in competitions, only about one trout or salmon is likely to be entered. Historically, if that cold-water fish won a ribbon, it was probably mounted by taxidermist Jim Hall or by one of his students. Hall has "written the book" on taxidermy of cold-water fish through his extensive travels, study, and experimentation. This part of this chapter is based on notes I made in Hall's studio in Idaho Falls, Idaho, where he conducts seminars and classes on the techniques of mounting cold-water fish.]

I recommend using the carved-body method for mounting all cold-water species. This works well because a lot of different things can be done with the carved body that cannot be done when mounting fish any other way. The carved body gives a smoother surface because no mâché is between the skin and the artificial body. Extreme curves are possible with this method also. It is possible to carve the body in any shape that you wish to obtain; then you can actually try the skin on the body for proper size before the mounting proceeds. The carved-body method also has been the most successful in producing winning entries in competitions.

The disadvantage is that the carved-body technique requires more homework. Since you are actually carving a reproduction of the fish body, you have to know what the original body looked like in order to carve one properly. You have to look at details:

the dorsal fin, the front edge of the dorsal fin, the position of the anal fins. Look at the body carefully. The highest point on the fish is at the leading edge of the dorsal fin; then there is a change in the slope of the fish. Another change in angle occurs at the adipose fin. The adipose fin is a rayless, fatty fin between the dorsal fin and the tail. The lower line of the belly changes at the anus in front of the anal fin. Note how the branchiostegal rays lie under the mandible. The only way to properly mount the fish is by knowing how these various features look on the fresh fish.

Before you begin skinning the fish, lay it flat on a piece of butcher paper and trace an outline of the profile by holding the pencil vertical along the edge of the specimen. Then with a caliper, make four measurements and record them on the profile:

1. Gill covers
2. Just ahead of the dorsal fin where the body thickness is greatest
3. At the vent or anus area
4. Just ahead of the tail.

As an additional guide, sketch cross sections of the fish at these points so that you will have a guide to the body shape. You will find that the fish is generally egg-shaped through the body, but the "point" of the egg is towards the belly at the gills and anus and toward the back at the dorsal fin. The tail area is generally a uniform oval rather than egg-shaped. Record the size of the eye on your sketch too.

The most difficult part of skinning a fish is separating the body at the head and throat. When using conventional skinning techniques, there is a lot of stress and flopping of the skin at this phase of the skinning process. Since cold-water fish damage easily,

HOW TO SKIN A TROUT

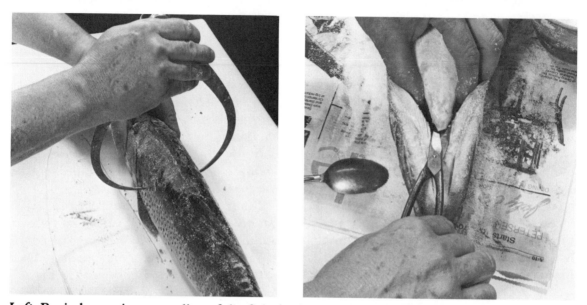

Left: Begin by tracing an outline of the fish, both top and side views. Use a calipers to verify and document the dimensions. All of this information is essential for accurate carving of the artificial body. *Right:* Make the first incision by rolling the fish on its back and cutting through the throat latch with a snips.

This is an actual fish pattern drawn and used by Jim Hall for the mounting of the brown trout photographed in this sequence.

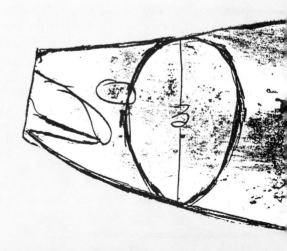

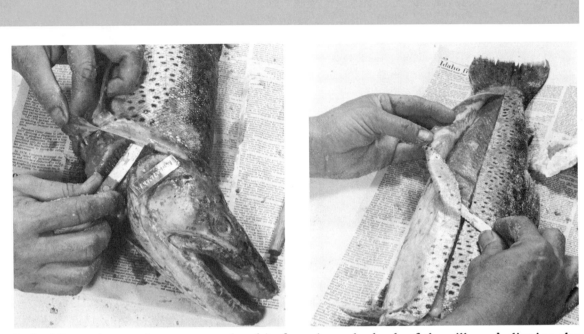

Left: After using a scissors to cut the skin free along the back of the gills and clipping the spine free from the skull, lay the fish on its side and begin working the skinning knife back under the cleithrum and skin as far as possible along the body. At this point much of the head area has already been skinned without creating an exposed cut in the skin. *Right:* Now make the conventional body incision aiong the wall side of the fish and begin skinning along the sides. Work the skinning knife between the body and skin, listening for the "crispy" sound. It is not necessary to lift the skin.

(Continued)

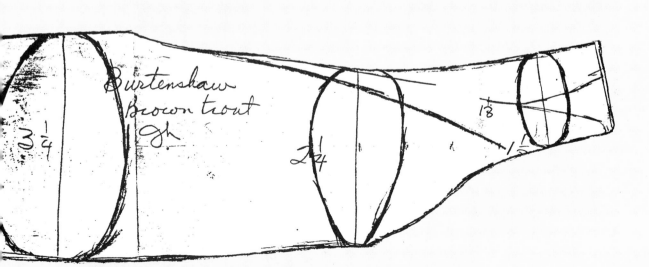

(Trout Skinning continued)

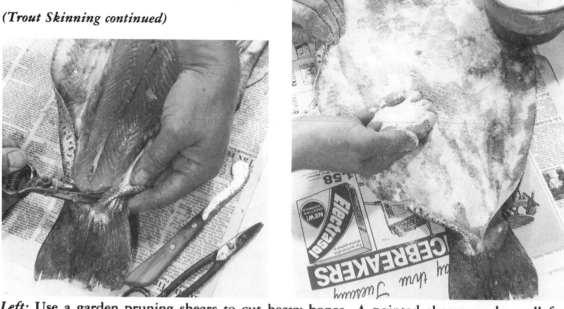

Left: Use a garden pruning shears to cut heavy bones. A pointed shears works well for removing the roots of the tail bones. *Right:* Apply a liberal amount of powdered borax to the skin before you begin to flesh it. This will tend to soften the meat and ease the scraping.

Left: Insert the point of your scissors between the jaw and the tongue and cut along the inside of the lower jawbone. Since there is a great deal of grease in this area, you must thoroughly clean and flesh it. *Right:* Cut the skull out of the head skin with a scissors. By working carefully under the skin with a scissors, you can remove the skull in a single piece, complete with eyes and brain case. On lake trout, the head skin is firmly attached to the skull, so additional care is required.

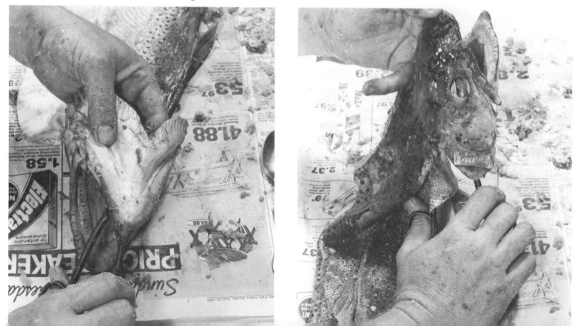

I have developed a technique that simplifies skinning the head area. First, dust the fish lightly with powdered borax so that the fish is easier to grasp. Then hold the fish on its back and cut through the throat latch at the point of the "V" behind the lower jaw. Now cut the skin behind the gills from the throat to the top of the gills at the head. When you have done this on both sides of the head, work your skinning knife under the skin and work back toward the body. The cleithrum or collarbone must be removed, so work the skinning knife between this bone and the skin. When you reach the pectoral fins, snip the bones close to the skin. With a conventional skinning knife, you should be able to skin about 2 inches of the body behind the head. Repeat this operation on the other side of the fish. At this point you have completely skinned the fish at the head and throat.

Turn the fish show-side down and make an incision along the middle of the body from the head to about ½ inch in front of the tail. Then make a short, vertical incision in front of the tail. Work the fish-skinning knife under the skin and begin skinning along the sides. Use as little lengthwise movement of the knife as possible. Otherwise, the movement tends to stretch the skin and pop out the scales. Whenever possible, the skinning motion should be from back toward the incision rather than from tail to head. With a little experience, you can actually hear a "crispy" sound as the knife skins properly between the skin and the body. If you don't hear this sound, you probably are leaving too much flesh on the skin.

Sever the fins as close as possible to the skin. Using scissors, and with your fingers placed along the base of the fin on the outside of the skin, slowly cut the fin roots underneath. Use this procedure for severing the dorsal and anal fins, then snip through the intestine at the anus and cut the tail free. Cut the ventral fin free from the skin on the show-side. The skin is now free from the carcass except at the head. Roll the fish on its back, and with your snips, cut through the spine at the back of the skull. Then sever the remaining muscle behind the head. The skin will now be free from the body.

Most of the skinning has been done without ever lifting the skin. Instead you have simply worked the skinning knife between the skin and the body while watching the movement of the knife beneath the skin. In other words, the skinning has all been done by "feel," including clipping the fin roots free. By doing this you have minimized the amount of movement of the skin and allowed the weight of the body to act as a "third hand."

Examine the skin. All that remains is to clean out the tail section and the head, and scrape the remaining flesh from the inside of the skin. Put powdered borax inside the skin where the body fluids and water will form a paste. Not only will this act as a preservative, borax also helps to soften the flesh adhering to the skin and will make scraping easier. Then scrape the inside of the skin with a fleshing tool, but avoid lengthwise movement as much as possible.

The basipterygium, a small bone behind the pectoral fin, must be removed. Lift it up away from the skin as far as possible and snip it off. Then trim all of the fins so that they will seat properly against the artificial body. Skin out the tail by using scissors and cut the bones and flesh by following the body contour where the body joins the tail. This area is usually too tight to insert a skinning knife, so any trimming will have to be done with scissors. When this piece is removed, work borax into the tail-pocket area.

Start cleaning out the head on the lower

jaw by removing the tongue with an incision along the base of the tongue. Work your scissors back along the bone while watching from the outside so that the point of the scissors does not tear the skin. When the incision has been made along both sides of the jaw, the tongue and muscle will come free in a single piece. This is a very oily part of the fish and must be removed.

To skin the inside of the head, insert the point of your scissors inside the double row of teeth and work the scissors between the skin and the head. Unlike a bass, most coldwater fish can be skinned over the skull, although on lake trout the skin is more firmly attached to the skull. Once the scissors is inserted, clip the skull free by working toward the back of the skull; then repeat the process on the other side of the head. Now turn the fish and skin forward along the skull to the forward point of the head. Then skin the roof of the head with scissors, working the tips under the skin slowly and with care all the way forward. The skull should come out in one piece with the eyes attached.

Scrape the head and work borax into the skin. One area that a lot of taxidermists ignore is between the pre-opercal and the opercal. Rub borax into these areas and then mechanically work the flesh out of the area. Clean out the cheek at this time by cutting away the muscle from inside the head. When the meat has been roughed out, put borax on the area and then work the remaining flesh out of the cheek. The inside of the lower jaw is a concave surface—scrape the bone and work borax into that area. The more meat that you remove from the head, the cleaner will be the mount and the less odor you will have while drying. If the cleithrum is still attached to the skin, it should be removed. Then apply borax to the entire skin. The skinning process is finished.

There is some latitude in changing the shape of a fish. For example, if you have a very snaky-looking fish, it is possible to shorten the length about an inch while increasing the width. This allows you to give the mount a more symmetrical appearance. However, you only have a limited amount of latitude before you begin to run into problems with scales being forced out of their sockets, with resultant uneven appearance.

Carve the body from a piece of dense foam, such as polyurethane, that is thick enough to accommodate the maximum thickness of the body, plus any curvature in the body. Use the outline that you made on butcher paper before the fish was skinned. Then add the thickness dimensions along the top of the foam block. Mark the centerline of the body on the top, head, and tail to act as guides while carving. Since flat surfaces are easier for the eye to compare, cut a series of flat slices off each corner. It is simply a case of cutting off the corners of the block. The belly of the fish is generally round. Behind the head, a fish is oval, but this changes to a pointed shape that leads right up to the dorsal fin. Keep this in mind when you are carving. Carve both sides of the belly first, then both sides of the back. Don't switch from belly to back, then to the belly again. When the body is roughly shaped out, switch to a rasp to remove the additional material. Rasp with long, smooth strokes and touch up the rough spots. Do not rasp around the body. This will create a wavy surface that will be apparent on the finished mount.

Finish the shape of the back first, then the belly. This will allow you to shape the contour of the back, getting the dorsal fin properly set. Then finish the belly, removing small amounts from the form with the rasp.

SHAPING THE BODY

Pin the body pattern to a piece of foam. The shape can be cut out with a bandsaw or other tool. Cut out the top profile first, then the side profile as shown here.

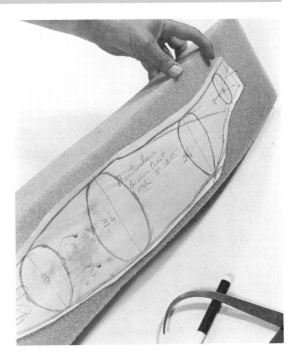

Left: After you have "squared out" the body with the saw, use a filleting knife to carve the foam. Begin by carving the belly. Then turn to the back. Don't switch back and forth. *Right:* Once you have roughed out the body, use a rasp and sanding screen to produce the final shape. Note that the centerline on the back of the artificial body acts as a guide for shaping. Carve and sandpaper lengthwise, watching symmetry, never around the body.

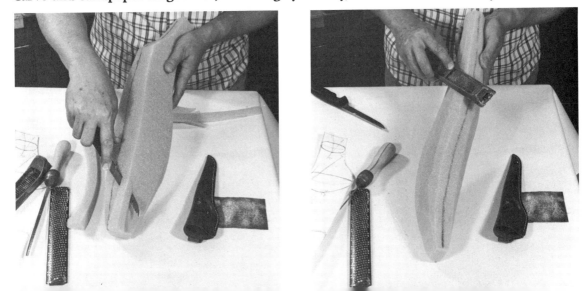

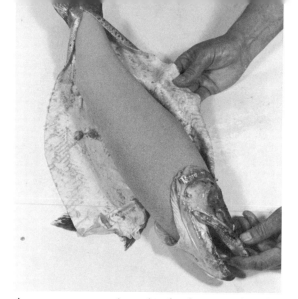

As you are carving the body, occasionally check-fit it with the skin. Remove foam slowly, because it is better to have the body too large than too small. First put the tail skin in place, then the head, and finally wrap the skin around the sides of the form.

When you have the skin fitting properly, with about a ¼-inch gap along the incision, you are ready to sand the form to the final shape. Use hardware-store screen cloth that is used in finishing drywall. Go over the entire fish, removing any ridges caused by the rasp. The centerline is the last thing to be removed.

There are three reference points that should guide you in carving an accurate body:

1. There is a change in body shape at the leading edge of the dorsal fin. If your body has a smooth curve along the back, it is inaccurate.

2. The shape of the belly changes at the anus.

3. The configuration of the overlay between the operculum and cleithrum should be correct; if not, the body is either too short or too narrow.

Test-fit the skin on your artificial body and see if it fits properly at the reference points. All reference points must be in exactly the correct place. If the skin doesn't fit properly, then parts of the skin will be improperly located on the artificial body. Remove the skin from the body and make the necessary adjustments with sanding cloth. Take your time and check as often as necessary to get the proper adjustment. The time you spend in shaping the body will be saved in the mounting process.

When mounting a fish that has been skinned in this manner, it is necessary to rebuild the mouth if the mouth is to be open. Several artificial mouths are available, or you may want to purchase an artificial tongue and rebuild the upper part of the mouth with papier-mâché. Whichever method you prefer, the mouth should be cut into the artificial body at this time. The top of the form determines the upper position of the mouth. The correct angle of the mouth should align with a straight line drawn from the center of the mouth to a point about one-third the distance from the anus to the head. Rough out the mouth, then rasp the lower line of the jaws, keeping in mind that all of the curves are smooth. Final adjustments can be made later, and the final position of the mouth can be changed with clay or mâché.

While you are carving the body, soak the skin in a degreasing solution of some hydrocarbon solvent, such as mineral spirits or white gas. Several good ones are on the market. These are high flash point solvents and can often be purchased in bulk. Although it is possible to leave the skin in a degreasing solvent for several days, soaking overnight is usually adequate if the skin has been properly fleshed. Remove the skin from the solvent and rinse it in a cool, soapy solution. After the soapy solution has been rinsed away,

Since the mouth was completely removed to allow degreasing the head, put an artificial mouth (shaded) in place. Carve the opening in the artificial body after finishing the rest of the body. The angle of the mouth depends on the top of the head. As a general rule, the artificial mouth should line up with a point about one-third of the way from the anus to the tip of the lower jaw. This is roughly in line with the ventral fins. After setting the artificial mouth in the body, fill around it with papier-mâché.

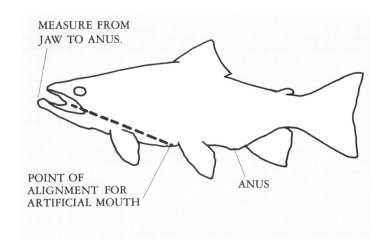

MEASURE FROM JAW TO ANUS.

POINT OF ALIGNMENT FOR ARTIFICIAL MOUTH

ANUS

This shows the artificial mouth ready to be set in place. Several commercial mouths are available, including those from Jonas Bros. (shown here), Master Paints, and Mohr. Each is designed slightly different, so the mouth opening in the body should be carved accordingly.

soak the skin in a saturated borax solution for one to two hours.

When the skin has been degreased and preserved and you are satisfied that the skin accurately fits the body, you are ready to proceed with the mounting. You need a quick-drying mâché—1½ to 2 hours—so that it will set up before the skin starts to dry and shrink. Find a mâché with the consistency you like, then add plaster or filler to adjust the setting time. Mâché should be almost puttylike so that it will stay in place after being modeled under the skin.

A ¼-inch-thick layer of mâché goes into the head to compensate for the shape of the skin and the form. Then fill the cheek pockets. Don't overfill them; if anything they should be underfilled so that the drying skin will not shrink around a lump of mâché and give the appearance of overfilling. A small layer goes on the base of the dorsal and anal fins. Put a little into the base of the tail just to compensate for the difference in bone length. Avoid letting mâché get anywhere that there are scales on the fish; this is particularly important at the junction of the head and body along the back. Again fit the skin to the form and make sure you have not added too much mâché; then remove the form and make adjustments as needed in the amount of mâché. Don't get too much mâché in the tail area.

Paint a layer of paste on the artificial body. Although this is not absolutely necessary, it acts as a lubricant in moving the skin; it also fills the pores of the foam. Your paste should be compatible with the foam and it must be light colored so that it will not create a dark background beneath the white belly skin. A linoleum-type paste made by Elmer's works well, as long as it is light colored. Apply it with a stiff paintbrush and work it into the pores of the foam. Multi-purpose flooring adhesive used for carpeting may also be used.

When you start to place the skin on the paste-covered form, work slowly from head to tail and concentrate on one area at a time. Don't let your attention jump around from head to tail to dorsal fin. Slip the head skin onto the form, adjust the mâché as needed, and then pin the skin into place. Adjust the lower jaw at this time. With the head finished, pull the tail skin into place. When it is positioned correctly, put a pin or two on the back side of the tail so that the skin will not move when the rest of the skin is being pulled and adjusted.

Put a layer of old, damp towels on your workbench. This will form a nice soft surface on which to lay the fish. Any dry, foreign material on the workbench at this time will dent the show side of the fish while you are adjusting the skin.

Now pull the dorsal fin up where it belongs. A couple of temporary pins can be inserted along the seam; then turn the fish over and work the show side. Wet the skin and smooth it gently with your hands to work any air bubbles out from under the skin toward the back seam. Position the anus and anal fin and insert a pin in each to hold the skin in place. Then roll the fish onto its back and pull the throat skin into position and pin it permanently. Also put a row of pins under the operculum where the skin was severed at the base of the gills. Finally sew the seam with waxed dental floss and close the skin as closely as possible. Fancy stitching is not necessary since it will be covered. You can also staple the skin, but sewing tends to pull the skin together more neatly and helps remove bubbles under the skin.

Look over the skin again. Check the head. Insert a long pin into the corner of the mouth to hold the mouth skin in position on both sides. If this is not done, the eyes will appear to be set too high. Any lumps caused by bone attached to the head skin can be tapped with a small hammer so that it will set properly. Pin the gill covers into place, and push excess throat skin up under the lower jawbone. Be sure that there is a smooth curve between the head and body.

At this time, attach a temporary mounting board which can be put into a vise; this will act as a "third hand" while you are finishing the mount. Then rinse off the fish again. This will keep the fins soft while they are being pinned.

Card the fins and tail using ⅛-inch wire cloth and clear plastic. Cut the wire cloth about the same shape, but larger than the fins and tail. Cut similar pieces of clear plastic from milk cartons. Use large paper clips

MOUNTING THE SKIN ON THE FORM

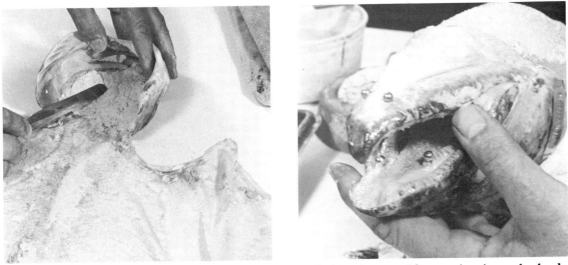

Left: Spread a layer of papier-mâché inside the head skin, but avoid smearing it on the body skin. The mâché will then be molded under the headskin to form a smooth bond between the head and artificial body. *Right:* After painting the artificial body with hide paste, slip the tail into place and then the head. After inserting pins at the top and bottom of the tail to hold it in place, add at least two pins in the lower jaw and also inside the mouth. These pins will hold the skin in position at each end so that you can adjust the body skin.

Left: Use a baseball stitch to sew up the body incision (illustrated on page 127). This is a good stitch for cold-water fish mounts. Each stitch forms a loop so that the skin is pulled directly across instead of being stretched as in the baseball stitch. *Right:* Here Jim Hall makes a final inspection of the mount before setting it aside to dry. Double-check to see that all of the fins and the throat skin are properly aligned. Since the papier-mâché will begin to set up quickly, adjustments must be made promptly.

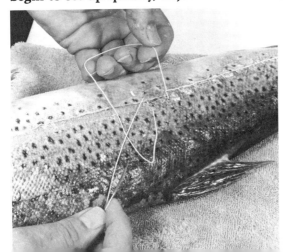

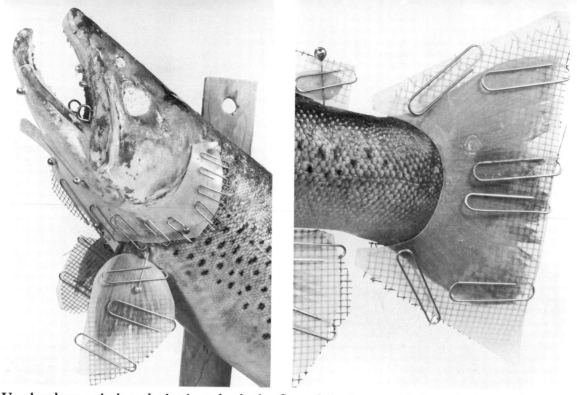

Use hardware cloth and plastic to back the fins while they are drying. Add as many pins as needed to hold the head skin in place. Also note that the branchiostegal rays are carded for drying. A long pin clipped to the hardware cloth will keep the fins from being pulled off center while drying.

to hold the wire cloth against the back of the fins and the plastic on the front. This carding technique allows the fins to be shaped and then watched during the drying process; the wire cloth allows air to reach the fins and tail so that they will dry more quickly. Try not to overspread the tail. Then support it so that it will not droop while drying.

I open the gill cover about ⅛ inch. When the fish dries, a crack will develop in the paint along the gill line if it is completely closed. When the gill cover is left open slightly, your mount will not develop a crack, and the customer still cannot see construction inside the mount.

No matter how accurately you carved the body, some shrinkage will always occur on top of the head. After the mount is thor-

oughly dry, cut away the skin on top of the head, down to the middle of the eye orbit and above the upper jaw, and discard the skin. Then using a carvable resin, build up the head to the natural configuration. It can then be sanded smooth before you begin to paint the mount.

The fish is now ready to be painted. The painting techniques for cold-water fish are identical to those of warm-water species. Whether you use an artist's brush or an airbrush, whether lacquers or acrylics, restoring color simply requires time and experience. Don't be afraid to make a mistake. Just wipe off the color and start again. With a little practice and experience, as well as good reference materials, you will soon be pleased with the results.

MOUNTING DO'S AND DON'TS BY JIM HALL

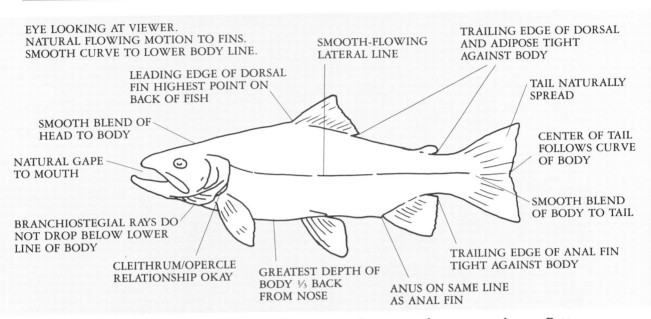

EYE LOOKING AT VIEWER.
NATURAL FLOWING MOTION TO FINS.
SMOOTH CURVE TO LOWER BODY LINE.

SMOOTH-FLOWING
LATERAL LINE

TRAILING EDGE OF DORSAL
AND ADIPOSE TIGHT
AGAINST BODY

LEADING EDGE OF DORSAL
FIN HIGHEST POINT ON
BACK OF FISH

TAIL NATURALLY
SPREAD

SMOOTH BLEND OF
HEAD TO BODY

CENTER OF TAIL
FOLLOWS CURVE
OF BODY

NATURAL GAPE
TO MOUTH

SMOOTH BLEND
OF BODY TO TAIL

BRANCHIOSTEGIAL RAYS DO
NOT DROP BELOW LOWER
LINE OF BODY

CLEITHRUM/OPERCLE
RELATIONSHIP OKAY

GREATEST DEPTH OF
BODY ⅓ BACK
FROM NOSE

ANUS ON SAME LINE
AS ANAL FIN

TRAILING EDGE OF ANAL FIN
TIGHT AGAINST BODY

Top: **This shows the key areas to check for a correctly mounted trout or salmon.** *Bottom:*
**Here are common mistakes made in the mounting of a cold-water fish, but they may also
apply to many other species. Frequently the taxidermist exaggerates the pose, making the
mount look unnatural. Good reference material is the key to a properly mounted fish. And
remember, a poorly mounted fish cannot be corrected by an outstanding paint job.**

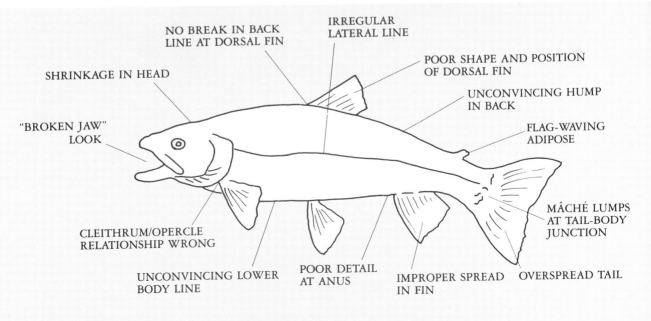

NO BREAK IN BACK
LINE AT DORSAL FIN

IRREGULAR
LATERAL LINE

POOR SHAPE AND POSITION
OF DORSAL FIN

SHRINKAGE IN HEAD

UNCONVINCING HUMP
IN BACK

"BROKEN JAW"
LOOK

FLAG-WAVING
ADIPOSE

MÂCHÉ LUMPS
AT TAIL-BODY
JUNCTION

CLEITHRUM/OPERCLE
RELATIONSHIP WRONG

UNCONVINCING LOWER
BODY LINE

POOR DETAIL
AT ANUS

IMPROPER SPREAD
IN FIN

OVERSPREAD TAIL

GALLERY OF MOUNTS BY JIM HALL

What the grayling lacks in size is made up in beauty. The large dorsal fin does not require any special efforts other than carding. The driftwood makes an attractive hanger and adds to the rustic beauty of the mount.

Above: This brook trout has a deep, flat-sided body. The quality of Jim Hall's mounts begin with his ability to carve an accurate replica of the natural body. *Below:* This brown trout is mounted in a swimming position with mouth open at a natural, feeding angle. Hall avoids creating extreme body curves and unnatural, widely gaping mouths.

8 MOUNTING A SNAKE

Having lived in New Mexico since the mid-1960s, I have developed a healthy respect for all kinds of reptiles. They are not all venomous, but most have teeth and know how to use them. In addition, I have found that all reptiles are basically angry, at least when I find them, or vice versa. As a consequence, I have reached an agreement with reptiles: I leave them alone, and they leave me alone.

Not all taxidermists avoid reptiles. Ralph Garland is an Instructor of Taxidermy at Piedmont Technical College in Roxboro, North Carolina, where reptile taxidermy is part of the curriculum. In addition, Garland has presented a number of seminars on snake-mounting techniques at various taxidermy conventions. Garland is an expert at mounting a snake. The following is based on his instructions:

Rattlesnakes are common taxidermy subjects in many parts of the country. These are not the pygmy rattlers and sidewinders. If a person intends to mount a snake, it is usually a diamondback or an equally dangerous species, such as a copperhead or water moccasin.

Avoid being careless when dealing with any kind of snake. Whether you caught the snake yourself or whether it was brought in by a friend, get a positive identification from a snake expert. In the event that you are snagged by a fang while handling the snake,

In a taxidermy competition, this timber rattler would be admired for its realistic pose. But judges would certainly have to disqualify it. Reason? The rattles are rattling. (Leonard Lee Rue III photo)

you will need positive identification to ensure that you receive proper medical treatment. Also, it is smart to check with your local hospital first to be certain they have an antivenin on hand for the species you will deal with, especially if the snake is not a local variety. Don't tempt fate and regret it later. While most bites from venomous snakes are not fatal, they are very painful and frequently lead to paralysis of an arm or finger, or to other complications.

The best way to kill a snake for mounting is to freeze it solid while alive. (Note: Before you place a protectively boxed, live rattlesnake in the freezing compartment of your refrigerator, be sure to make some prior arrangements with your family members!) Freezing the snake kills it while preventing damage to the skin. Like a fish, a snake is covered with scales, and even the smallest hole requires attention. If you have to shoot the snake, use a shotgun from enough distance to kill without blowing the skin apart. If you have only a .357 Magnum handy, forget about mounting the snake.

Once the snake thaws out, decide the pose that you want. I recommend that your first couple of mounts be in simple, relaxed poses. You can try the more dramatic, coiled pose later. You can carve a relaxed-pose body from foam. Several supply companies sell artificial bodies for coiled rattlesnake poses.

The first task is to remove the fangs. (*Caution*: Avoid puncture wounds from fangs and avoid allowing venom to contact your eyes, or abrasions or open skin.) Lay the snake on its back and carefully open the mouth. Then, with a scalpel, make an incision in the roof of the mouth beside each of the fangs. With

LIVE-SNAKE REFERENCE PHOTOS (By Leonard Lee Rue III)

The top two photos show a timber rattler. Note the heat-sensing pit located between the eye and the nostril.

Like its cousins, the rattle-snakes, this copperhead is a pit viper. However, a copper-head has no rattles to warn you of its ill humor.

The eastern banded water-snake has no venom glands but tends to give most people pause anyway.

This pilot blacksnake has just eaten all of the baby wrens in the birdhouse. Such a scene offers the taxidermist a crowd-stopping, yet realistic, pose concept.

needle-nose pliers, push the muscle away from the root of the fang and break the fang off below the gum line. After you have removed the second fang, place the fangs in a shallow dish of alcohol until the mount is completed. To remove venom from the two venom glands, cut into the roof of the mouth into each venom gland and blot the venom with absorbent material.

Begin by stretching the snake out full-length on newspaper and drawing an outline of the body. This will serve as a guide to the approximate dimensions and the length of the snake when you make the artificial body.

Begin the skinning process by making an incision along the inside of the lower jaw from one corner of the mouth to the other. Separate the skin of the throat from the muscle in the lower jaw. After skinning the throat to the back of the head, use scissors or snips to carefully cut through the neck and detach the skull from the spine without cutting the skin. Then carefully skin forward along the head, past the eyes to the nostrils and the heat-sensing pits. You will actually skin-out the head through the mouth. Next cut the skin free along the inside of the upper jaw. The head is now completely skinned-out, leaving only the jaws attached to the skin. With scissors, trim as much of the meat as possible away from the jawbones and the skin of the head. Measure the eyes at this time also.

There are two options available for skinning the body. Since most venomous snakes are mounted in a coiled or striking position, at least part of the belly is exposed on the mount. In order to avoid an exposed seam, Garland skins the snake through a belly incision that is 8 to 10 inches long at the widest part of the body. This part of the mounted snake will be flat on the base, thus concealing the incision while the tail and forward portion of the body are raised off the base. When the snake is to be mounted in a relaxed pose with the belly close to the base, the belly incision should begin at the thickest part of the body and extend all the way to the tail. The longer incision will simplify the skinning process, and the incision will not be visible.

After making the incision, skin around the body with a skinning knife or scalpel, and then cut the body in half so the two halves remain joined by the skin. Grasp the front half and turn the snake inside out as if you were removing a stocking. Repeat the process with the back half, skinning carefully around the anus and the nearby scent glands. On a rattler, the tail should be cut free when you have skinned back to the rattles.

The skin should be fleshed in the same way that I described the fleshing of a fish, beginning in Chapter 7. Also tendons along the back must be removed, and the dark line along the belly, which is a sensory organ, also must be scraped. Preserve the skin with powdered borax by working it into all parts of the body and head. Now take a small amount of tanning cream or neat's-foot oil and rub it into the flesh-side of the skin along the back. This will prevent the skin from excessive shrinkage after it is mounted. Do not put the cream on the inside of the belly skin.

Next, you prepare the artificial body. Assuming that you are mounting a rattlesnake, purchase an artificial body from one of the supply companies that has a form of the approximate dimensions. Order a body that is the correct thickness, or slightly large, and then modify the length to match your

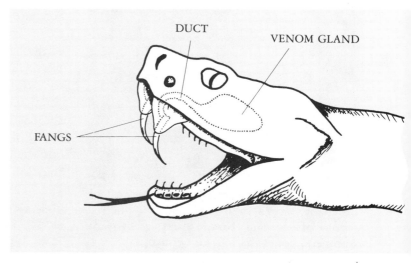

This shows locations of venom glands relative to the fangs.

HOW RALPH GARLAND SKINS A SNAKE

The fangs should be removed from any venomous snake before you begin skinning. Here instructor Ralph Garland of Piedmont Technical Institute in Roxboro, North Carolina, lifts the fangs from a large diamondback rattlesnake so that they can be removed with a needle-nose pliers. (*Caution:* Because venom remains potent after a snake dies, wear protective gloves if you have open sores on your hands. Eye protection is also recommended.)

Garland stretched out this 6-foot diamondback so he could trace a profile. The profile is used as a guide for carving the artificial body. The rattles are removed at this time so they will not be damaged during skinning and mounting.

(Snake Skinning continued)

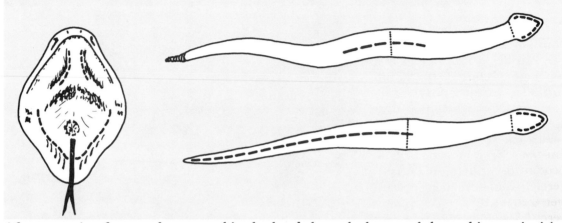

After removing fangs and venom, skin the head through the mouth by making an incision inside the lower jaw. Then work your skinning knife backwards between the skin and throat. Sever the flesh and spine behind the head, and then skin forward to the heat-sensing pits between the nostrils and eyes. For a coiled, striking pose, use the short incision shown. If the pose will keep the back half of the body on the base, a long incision, extending from the thickest part of the body all the way to the tail, will make skinning easier. (*Venom reminder:* Wear hand and eye protection).

After making the belly incision, Garland skins around the back of the snake. He then cuts the flesh and spine in half, leaving the skin intact. Both halves of the body are removed through the belly incision in much the same way you might pull a sock off your foot.

You can either carve an artificial body or use a commercial form. If you opt for a commercial form, order a form that is slightly oversized and then trim it to size. A commercial form can be modified by adding or removing sections and then joining the sections with a hot-glue gun. Here Garland puts the final touches on a body he has carved.

skin. The commercial body should be carved and fitted in the same way I described for a fish body in Chapter 7. Use sandpaper to thin the body down to the proper dimensions; the length can be changed by adding or removing sections from the body. If your artificial body is too long, cut one or two sections out and join the ends with a hot-glue gun. If you wish to add a few inches, cut the body and glue-in a section of dense foam. Then sand-down the added piece to the configuration of the body.

If you wish to carve your own body, trace it from a paper cutout tracing onto a piece of foam to the approximate configuration of the snake. Cut this out with a saw, then begin shaping it with fillet knife, rasp, and sandpaper. The snakeskin is more difficult to fit than a fish skin because the snakeskin will stretch lengthwise during the skinning process. When carving a body, you will have to depend on your tracings for proper di-

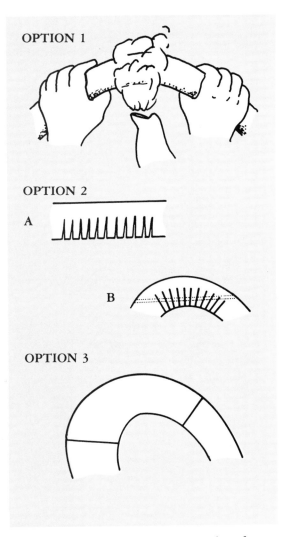

There are three ways to put curves in a dense-foam form. *Option 1:* Heat the form over steam. This will temporarily soften the foam and allow you to put a shallow arc in the body. *Option 2:* Drawing A shows a number of cuts sawed into the body. They can be widened with sandpaper. Drawing B shows wire through the curve that holds the shape of the bend. *Option 3:* For a very tight curve, simply cut your body form cross sectionally, carve a curved segment to match, and glue it between the first two.

mensions. Remember that the shape of the body varies with the attitude of the reptile, and this must be considered when carving the body. For example, there is usually a ridge on the back of a snake when it is relaxed; the body will flatten when the snake is alarmed. (Author's note: The backs of all snakes I've come across were flattened.)

Now is a good time to prepare the base. If you plan to mount the snake in a coiled, striking position, the base should be reasonably flat. However, if you want the snake to be relaxing on a limb or rock, the base should be constructed with the limb or rock in place.

The carved body can be shaped to the limb or rock using several techniques developed by Garland and his students, as shown on the previous page. When foam is heated with steam or hot water, it can be reshaped to a limited extent. Simply heat the artificial body over a steam kettle, then hold the body in the desired position until it cools. The heated and bent body can be chilled more quickly if you hold it under cold water for a minute or two. If more drastic bends are needed, saw a series of cuts about $\frac{1}{16}$ inch apart and halfway through the body. You can apply a spot of hot glue in each of the cuts and bend the body into a relatively tight curl. A final anchor is made by inserting a wire in the curved portion to hold the curve in place,

Here Garland puts the finishing touches on the rattler. He works the final detail into the head before the clay hardens and sets the eyes later. When the mount is dry, Garland glues the rattles on with superglue.

A snake mount looks best in a habitat setting. Since snake mounts are rather fragile, extending leaves or a dried bush can help prevent too much touching by admirers.

as shown on the previous page. Very tight curves can be made by carving the curved part of the body from a scrap of dense foam. Cut a straight segment out of the form and glue the curved piece into place. Using these methods, you can shape a relatively flat body into a surprisingly lifelike form that will conform to the shape of your base.

The snake components are now ready for mounting. Begin by cutting the artificial body into the three pieces equal to the natural body that you removed during the skinning process: the head, the back half, and the front half. Put a wad of soft potter's clay into the tail skin so that the rattles will seat

properly on the form. Now give the tail portion of the artificial body a smooth coat of hide paste before slipping the form into the skin. With the tail skin worked slowly onto the form, model the clay around the rattles so there is a smooth junction between rattles and body skin. Avoid pulling the skin with your hands because this tends to stretch the skin lengthwise while reducing the circumference. Instead, use an ice pick or a fork and gradually work the skin over the form. Line up the centerline of the color pattern with the axis of the back of the form. Then work the skin with your hands to eliminate any wrinkles in the skin. The scales should line up in rows, and the belly scales should not show on the sides of the mount. If you find air pockets, use a hypodermic needle and syringe to draw the air out from beneath the skin. When the tail half of the artificial body is in place, insert a couple of pins along the belly to hold the skin in place while you mount the front half.

Now repeat this process with the front half of the artificial body. Apply a coat of hide paste before slipping the front half of the body into the skin through the belly incision. Before you begin to align the skin, use a hot-glue gun to join the two body halves. Now, using a fork or ice pick, move the skin into position. When all of the scale patterns line up, either sew or staple the belly closed.

Only the head remains to be mounted. Opening the mouth skin, fold the head skin back over the neck portion of the artificial body. Then with a hot-glue gun, attach the artificial head to the neck. A long pin can be pushed through the head and into the neck for added strength in joining these pieces. Now pull the head skin forward and into place and check for proper fit. You may want to add some potter's clay onto the artificial head in order to shape it more accurately. Check to be sure that the lips fit snugly together without tucking the lips.

Garland here finishes another rattlesnake habitat. If the snake is mounted with open mouth, various methods can be used to reconstruct the inside of the mouth. For safety, most taxidermists remove the fangs before skinning and reglue them when the mount is finished. Reasonably good fang simulations can be fashioned from the ribs of a fish.

When you are satisfied with the fit, fold the head skin back over the body again and give the artificial head a coat of hide paste before pulling the head skin back over the form. A couple drops of superglue will hold the lips closed until the skin dries.

Now make a final check of the mount. Use a nail-set to indent the heat-sensing pits in the head. You can use a pin to open the nostrils. Again check the alignment of the skin with the artificial body, and check for air bubbles and wrinkles.

If the snake is to be mounted with the mouth open, the same skinning and mounting process is used as I described for a relaxed-pose mount. However, the jaws should be glued to the rim of the mouth in the artificial body; then the configuration of the mouth can be modeled with Sculpall, mâché, or clay. When this is dry, replace the fangs with a drop of superglue. (If you would prefer not to use the natural fangs, rib bones from a large fish make a reasonable substitute.)

When the skin has totally dried, use an electric hand grinder such as a Dremel tool, or simply the point of your scalpel, to grind out the eye sockets. Be careful not to damage the skin or the eyelids. Then set the eyes in papier-mâché. Go over the entire skin with an art gum eraser, *working from head to tail*, and pop all of the scales out of their sockets. You must remove these scales in order to have a smooth surface on the mount. The scales of the snake are a transparent protective scale that are similar to the human fingernail and they must be removed because they serve no function on the mount and will only curl and deform. An eraser is the best device for removing the scales, and the underlying color patterns will be unaffected. You can then paint the mount following the color patterns on the skin. Attach the mount to the base with a hot-glue gun or some other paste, and the mount is finished.

You are now the proud owner of a mounted serpent that not even God appreciated.

9 SPECIAL TECHNIQUES

In the previous eight chapters, I covered the core topics and skills that seem to be of prime interest to most taxidermists and would-be taxidermists. In this chapter I cover important miscellaneous techniques that may apply to one or more of the previous chapters. Here you will find techniques for construction of bases and habitats, skull cleaning, various antler mounts, special mammal mounts (half-lifesize, open-mouth game head, novelties), and follow-up trophy maintenance and care.

MAKING BASES AND HABITATS

In the earlier chapters, I explained the importance of planning the complete mount. Before you even begin skinning a specimen, you rough-out the base for the freshly mounted specimen. It is not always possible to have the base completed, nor is it always advisable. Nevertheless the mount should be posed on the rough base at least before it dries because the pose cannot be changed later. A squirrel or bird temporarily mounted on a flat board probably will not fit properly on a limb after the mount has dried.

A base does not have to be complex. In fact, some mounts are hung directly on the

This remarkably realistic base was made by Fata's Taxidermy Studio in Pownal, Maine. The ice was made from fiberglass resin. The rock shapes were created from chicken wire and were covered with laminated paper and glue. A base should be of appropriate size for the mount and not overpowering.

wall. Most fish are mounted on a hardwood panel that serves only to attach the trophy to the wall. Most large saltwater fish are hung directly on the wall without a panel. This is true of game-head mounts, as well.

When a base is needed, it should be designed to be simple and yet accent the specimen. It should also be of natural materials. If, on the other hand, you want to depict the specimen in its natural surroundings, a habitat appropriate for that species must be constructed.

Keep the base simple and in proportion to the trophy. The top of a wooden fence post makes an excellent base for a quail or dove. And a short length of wooden fence post is about the right size for a squirrel. You can attach the fence post to a wooden panel and add a little moss or grass to the post's base. However, avoid using a big chunk of wood that will dwarf the mount and otherwise make it difficult to handle. The base should help emphasize the mount and lend atmosphere to it, not detract from it.

Keep the base realistic and logical. Don't put a shell fragment from an almond or Brazil nut in a fox squirrel's mouth. Likewise don't mount an Arctic fox stalking a ringneck pheasant. Ducks are seldom found standing on shore, but you can design a base that looks like a shoreline. Also for ducks you can place driftwood near them. While a duck may never set foot on a piece of driftwood, at least the bird and the base occur naturally together.

Habitat, as base, is intended to go a step beyond the simple, realistic base. This is an attempt to duplicate the natural environment of the mount. Bases may be as large

FENCE-POST BASE

Left: The base should be simple but appropriate for the species. This bobwhite was mounted on the top of a wooden fence post affixed to a hardwood panel. An irregular scrap of foam surrounds the bottom of the post. *Right:* After the foam was coated with carpenter's glue, dried moss was pressed onto it, followed by insertion of several dried sunflower tops and a few pieces of grass.

or small as appropriate for the mount. The habitat can also be as complex as you have the time and interest to construct. Taxidermist Tom Ridge of Blaine, Tennessee, has prepared a number of award-winning habitats for specimens ranging from fish, to birds, to bears. Some of the habitat-construction methods Ridge has described in *American Taxidermist* are given below.

Artificial Rocks. In using rocks for habitat construction, begin by carving the rocks from dense foam to the desired shape. Use a sharp knife for this purpose. Most of the rocks used in a water scene should be rounded and relatively smooth. Rocks used in other types of habitats are generally rough and irregular. Ridge found that different supply companies offer papier-mâché that has different char-

The fence post was screw-mounted to the panel through the panel bottom. All base elements are from quail habitat. A bell jar protects the fragile elements and wards off dust. Total construction time: 10 minutes.

acteristics. Some mâché is a very fine and therefore gives a very smooth surface when coated over a foam rock. Other mâché is very coarse and produces a rough surface that is more appropriate for dry-land scenes. After the mâché has dried, paint the rocks as needed, but most mâché has a natural, earthy color when dry. Apply a very heavy coat of sealer to produce the "wet" look on a rock.

Pine Limbs. Many of the artificial Christmas trees on the market look realistic. When you find one you like, buy it, and take it apart. You will find that it is made in sections. Find a natural pine limb, about the same size as the artificial one, and attach the artificial tips to the natural branches. Since the pine needles generally become more sparse on the inner part of the natural limb, use a dab of hot glue to replace these. Gradually you will create a very natural-looking branch. Of course, some touch-up with paints may be needed.

Lily Pads. Obtain some scrap aluminum house siding. Frequently this is available in large sheets of "seconds" at a nominal price. First draw a pattern for your lilies on a piece of cardboard. Transfer this to the aluminum. Cut out the lily pad with shears and include a small tab where the pad would attach to the stem. Now cut a piece of wire the length of the stem desired, and attach the aluminum pad to the wire with a small amount of auto-body putty and crimp the tab around the wire. Next insert the wire into a piece of ¼-inch plastic tubing, into which you have put a small amount of glue. When this is dry, paint the lily pad with an aluminum primer paint before doing the final painting.

Foam Accessories. Mushrooms, cacti, cattails, and a variety of other items can all be made from dense foam scraps. Mushrooms can be carved with a sharp knife, first the cap and then the stem separately. The cap and stem can be joined with a hot-glue gun. These can then be sanded into shape and coated with a thin layer of mâché.

You should build a foam prickly-pear cactus, pad by pad. Cut thin sheets of foam and carve or sandpaper them into shape. For a

To the display panel for this chukkar mount, I added a calendar picture showing a bobcat flushing a pair of chukkars. The diorama-like background may have been a factor in the mount's receiving a place ribbon in national competition.

more realistic appearance, hold the pads — one at a time — over a heat source and bend them into more realistic shapes. Use a hot-glue gun to attach the pads together. After coating the cactus with a smooth papier-mâché, paint it before affixing the natural spines with the glue gun.

A cattail can be carved from foam and then sanded. Cattails have a naturally rough surface so they don't need any mâché. After painting the cattail, apply spray adhesive to affix a tuft of natural cattail fluff, giving the appearance that the cattail has gone to seed. Use a ¼-inch dowel for the stalk.

When painting any of these accessories,

use latex or water-based paints. Most foam will dissolve when painted with enamels.

Collecting Natural Materials. The next time you are out scouting for deer, carry along several Zip-lock plastic bags and a knife. Collect lichen, moss, acorns, and leaves, as well as any other items that would look attractive on a habitat mount. When you return home, spread these out on a shelf to dry. Avoid placing the items in direct sunlight because that will fade the natural colors. Lichens generally retain their natural colors but moss will fade; however moss can later be dyed with Rit dyes. Attach lichens to your rocks or limbs with carpenter's glue or spray adhesive. Moss that has been soaked in a mixture of glycerin and water after being dyed will remain soft and lifelike for a long time. Natural cattails can be dried in the shade and used. To prevent the dried cattails from shattering, dip them in a very thin shellac and allow them to dry. The shellac acts as a sealer and helps to keep the cattails from rupturing.

Two-Part Epoxy. This material is available under various trade names. Although it has a wide variety of uses in taxidermy, its value in habitat preparation is often underrated. Two-part epoxy can be obtained from auto parts stores, where it is sold for auto-body repair. It is useful for modeling stumps or for smoothing the attachment of limbs to a base. Epoxy can be sanded and painted. It can also hold leg wires and screws where strong attachment is needed. If you mix a drop or two of enamel paint in the epoxy, you can trim or sand the epoxy without losing the color. This saves work later when the final touch-up is done, according to Ridge.

Building a Habitat Base. A base should be made with plywood and covered with a piece of dense foam. Tom Ridge recommends that, for a base, a piece of plywood, either ¼-inch or ⅜-inch thick, be cut to the size and shape desired. Then cut a piece of foam to go over the plywood. The two can be attached with a hot-glue gun. When making a base representing soil, mix equal parts of papier-mâché with hide paste. Add sufficient water to obtain the proper consistency and spread a layer of the mixture over the foam. While the mixture is still moist and sticky, sprinkle a liberal coat of sand or dry soil onto the

surface. Pat gently with your hands to work the sand-soil into the hide paste/mâché mixture. Allow this to dry. You will now have a realistic base coated with sand or native soil.

Now place the mount—or the un-mounted form if the base is being constructed in advance—on the base and determine where the leg wires will be attached. Drill holes the proper size. Begin adding the other habitat materials to the base, keeping clear the area for the mount. Place the largest items first, such as a stump or large rock; then add the smaller items. Finally you can fill in the empty space with grass, moss, or other ground cover. A hot-glue gun works well for attaching the smaller items. The bigger items can be glued in place, but a screw or two added from the bottom, through the plywood, will add support.

If you want to reproduce a snow scene, prepare the foam base as described above. Spray the foam with an adhesive and sprinkle a layer of artificial snow. Repeat this process until you have obtained the desired effect.

Many habitats made for fish require the use of fiberglass resins. This subject has been studied extensively. Larry Goldman of Hide and Beak Taxidermy and Supply in Saginaw, Minnesota, has published an authoritative manual on the subject. Entitled *How To Create Water and Ice and Other Good 'Stuff'*, Goldman's book can be purchased from most supply companies for only a few dollars. For the beginning taxidermist interested in using resins, this book is certainly a good investment.

Bases and habitats definitely require an imagination and additional time. However, you are likely to find the results rewarding, adding an extra dimension to the trophy.

SNOW-COVERED FIELD HABITAT

I created this winter habitat for this coyote, which is also shown being mounted in Chapter 3. *Left:* To create a similar habitat, cut a piece of 1-inch Styrofoam insulation to the dimensions of the plywood base. Use a fillet knife to cut holes that will make the paws appear to sink into the supposed snow. *Right:* Glue the Styrofoam to the plywood base. Then insert dried, natural grass, in this case a desert bunchgrass. After spraying adhesive over the base, sprinkle ground Styrofoam "snow" from the can. This gradually builds up a layer of soft snow shown in the next photo. *Below:* The finished mount, which I called "First Snow," won 2nd Place in a recent National Taxidermist Association competition. It is now part of a habitat display in the New Mexico Museum of Natural History.

GALLERY OF OUTSTANDING HABITATS

Taxidermist Ron Reynolds of Bath, Ontario, has won a number of awards for fish habitats. His bases usually include a number of "rocks" carved from foam. Also, he uses stumps and weathered antlers quite effectively.

(Continued)

Jay Neilson, Chief Preparator for the Utah Museum of Natural History, made this brook trout habitat from papier-mâché and artificial snow. The "water" is a sheet of clear plastic. Note the realistic appearance of the water-warn roots in relation to the snow-covered vegetation.

This Pawlesta Classics mount of blue (scaled) quail is a model of simplicity. Taxidermist Paul Provenzano and his wife Ester Mae of Missouri City, Texas, constructed a base of papier-mâché, including rock fragments and weathered cactus. The unique cholla cactus wood is native to the scaled quail country.

In 1984 this coyote diorama won 10 awards in taxidermy competition. The mount, named "Hard day's night," was done by Tim Winter of Cold Spring, Kentucky. The base is surprisingly simple but effective. It is composed of a natural stump and moss, sprinkled with pine needles and a few leaves.

CLEANING SKULLS

One of the most unpleasant, and often nauseating, tasks is the cleaning of skulls and other bones. Bear and cat skulls are the basis for trophy measurement in the Boone and Crockett Club and the Pope and Young Club programs. In order to preserve a natural skull for entry into records book competition or just for display, you must clean and cure it. As I pointed out in Chapter 5, it is impractical to use the natural skull and teeth when making a rug, but you may still want to preserve the skull and teeth separately.

First strip the meat, eyes, and brain from the skull. Using a sharp knife, cut along the inside of the lower jaw so that all of the muscle and tongue will come free in one piece. The rest of the muscle is located between the zygomatic arch (cheekbone) and the cranium (braincase). Clean this area too and remove the eyes. Then bend a hook on the end of an 8-inch piece of sturdy wire and work the brain out of the skull through the opening where the skull and the neck join.

At this point the skull will still have a considerable amount of flesh attached. Place the skull in a large pail or bucket and cover it with hot tap water. Do not boil the skull. Boiling tends to loosen the seams of the skull, and it will also tend to split the teeth. However, by repeated changing with hot tap water, you will effectively cook the flesh so that you can scrape it off the bone.

After scraping the bone again, place the skull in a protected location for several months where insects have free rein and where larger birds and animals are kept off. An unused bird cage is ideal for this purpose, or you can make a "cage" from ½-inch hardware cloth. Because you have removed the brains and most of the flesh, odors from the skull will be minimal. If you place the skull where it will receive direct sunlight, such as on a roof or in a tree, you will probably not notice any odor. Allow at least three months for the skull to become thoroughly dry.

The skull is now ready to be bleached. In a plastic bucket large enough to completely immerse the skull, mix equal parts of laundry bleach and water. Place the skull in this solution. It is safe to leave the skull in the bleach solution for the following approximate times: bear, 7 to 15 days; coyote, bobcat, and fox, 6 to 10 days; small skulls, 1 to 3 days. Even bird and snake skulls can be cleaned in this way, but they should be watched carefully. All skulls should be completely immersed; otherwise any portion protruding and unbleached will take on a different color. Immediately after placing the skull in the solution, you will see a chemical reaction take place. A sudsy foam will form on top and some of the flesh that had been adhering to the skull will rise to the surface. However you will find that after several days the solution loses its strength and needs to be replaced.

Upon extracting the skull from the bleach, rinse it thoroughly in cold water to remove any bleach remaining on the bone. In most cases you will find that there is still some cartilage around the teeth, ear, and nasal ducts. Pare this off with a scalpel. Now place the skull in a large kettle and add about a teaspoon of liquid detergent. Cover the skull with water and bring the water to a slow boil for about 15 minutes. This will remove any grease or fat that the bones have absorbed. Then remove the skull from the water and allow it to dry thoroughly. (Before you throw out the water, ensure that none of the teeth have fallen out during the boiling pro-

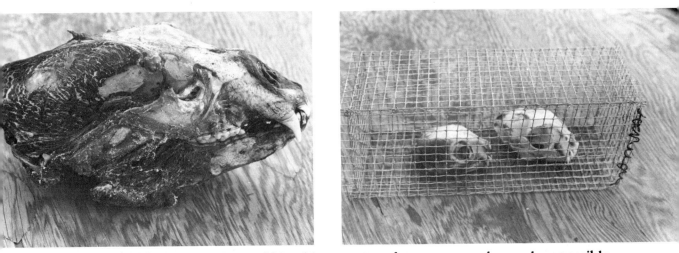

Left: As the first step in cleaning and bleaching, carve and scrape as much muscle as possible from the skull. Pull the brains out of the back with a hooked wire. Soften and remove additional meat by soaking the skull in hot tap water. However, a fresh skull should not be boiled because that will weaken the bone sutures (seams). *Right:* A wire "cage" made from ½-inch hardware cloth will allow the skull to dry when exposed to the air. It will also prevent damage or theft by neighborhood cats and dogs. If the skull was adequately cleaned before being put into the cage, it will emit relatively little odor while drying.

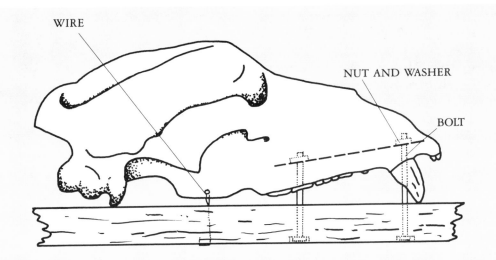

WIRE

NUT AND WASHER

BOLT

A skull can be wired or bolted to its display panel. This drawing shows both methods. One bolt is adequate for cat and small animal skulls. Two bolts should be used for heavier skulls. In most cases, the lower jaw is put in place before the skull is attached to the panel.

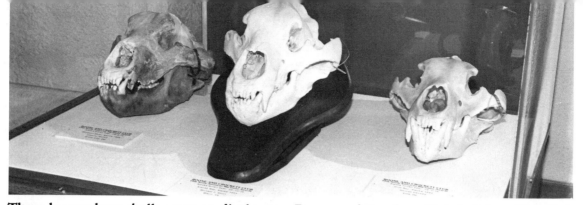

These brown bear skulls were on display at a Boone and Crockett Club judging. The Club scores bear and cat skulls by adding just two measurements: greatest length (without lower jaw) and greatest width.

cess. After the skull has dried, give a slight tug on each of the teeth and glue any that are loose.)

A single bolt provides one of the most convenient methods of attaching the skull to the panel. As shown on the previous page, the bone that forms the roof of the mouth extends from the nose to the eyes. The nasal passages form a rather large cavity above this bone. Drill a hole through the panel that lines up with this passage, and extend the hole through the bone. Put the lower jaw in place, then slip a washer and nut into the nasal passage and tighten down.

European-Style Mounts. When making a European-style horn or antler mount, cut the crown of the skull considerably larger than is normally needed for a conventional antler mount. After you have severed the crown and antlers from the rest of the skull, clean the bone as well as possible; then salt and allow it to dry in your shop. When the bone has cured for several months, set the skull plate in a shallow pan and pour enough bleach and water into the pan to cover the bone. If you are not careful to keep antlers or horns above the bleach, they will lose color too. If parts of the horns are inadvertently bleached during this process, the horns can

usually be touched up with a flat, black paint. Bleached antlers should be stained with walnut wood stain. Mounted on a dark or black panel, the horns or antlers make an unusual and striking mount.

European-style horn mounts require that the skull be cleaned. Since the bleach will whiten the horns and antlers, the skull plate should be placed in a shallow plastic dish. Bleach-water mix should be added only to the level of the horns or antler burr.

ANTLER MOUNTS

The styles of antler mounts are about as diverse as taxidermists. Most supply companies offer kits, which make mounting quick and simple. In preceding paragraphs, I explained the method of making a bleached-skull antler mount. Another common technique is to cover the skull plate with plaster of paris and allow this to harden. The plaster can then be sanded smooth and covered with buckskin or velvet. For best results, drive a screw through the top of the skull plate and into a piece of ¼-inch plywood beneath the skull plate. This allows easier attachment of the antler mount to the wood panel.

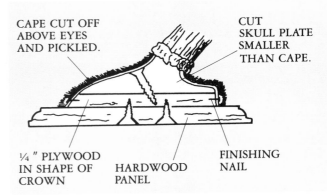

CAPE CUT OFF ABOVE EYES AND PICKLED.

CUT SKULL PLATE SMALLER THAN CAPE.

¼ " PLYWOOD IN SHAPE OF CROWN

HARDWOOD PANEL

FINISHING NAIL

A simple but rustic antler mount can be made by leaving the crown of the scalp attached to the antlers. The scalp must first be pickled and tacked to a piece of plywood, as shown, before attachment to the display panel.

Horn mounts are an economical display. To do this, temporarily screw-mount the skull plate to a scrap sheet of ¼-inch plywood cut to the shape of the crown. Then mold plaster over the bone and plywood. Cover the plaster with buckskin or velvet. After the plaster dries, attach the mount to a display panel. Since the horns of a pronghorn would otherwise protrude almost perpendicular to the wall, mount them at an upward angle.

One of the more rustic antler mounts can be made using the actual crown of the skull with the cape (skull hide) attached. Make an incision around the crown of the scalp at about the level of the upper eyelids and the top of the ear butts. Then peel the scalp back to the antler burrs and saw off the top of the skull *above* the eye sockets. You now have the antlers joined by a thin skull plate with the somewhat larger scalp crown still attached at the antler burrs. Clean the skull plate of all attached muscle and work with a dull knife or screwdriver between the skull plate and scalp.

Thoroughly salt the skull plate and scalp crown, and allow them to cure for two or three days. Place the skull and crown in a shallow pan of pickle solution as I described in the skull cleaning section. After about 8 hours, remove the antlers and rinse them thoroughly. This is also a good time to clean the antlers.

Set the antlers on a piece of ⅜-inch plywood and draw the approximate outline of the skull plate. If the skull plate is somewhat crooked or irregular, this can be compensated for in your outline on the wood. Saw out the piece of plywood and attach the skull plate to it with one or two screws. You can also fill in around the edges of the skull plate with papier-mâché or potter's clay. Then tack the scalp around the plywood with brads, as shown on the drawing on the previous page.

Hang the antlers aside until the scalp is completely dry; this may require a week or more. Some shrinkage will occur, so you may need to move brads or add others in order to hold the scalp firmly against the plywood. Finally, trim the excess scalp from around the base of the plywood and then attach the antlers to a panel so they won't rotate. This finishes the rustic antler mount. This method is quicker than using buckskin or velvet, and equally attractive. Furthermore, it is completely bugproof and long lasting.

SPECIAL TAXIDERMY MOUNTS

There is no end to the variety of items that can be made from animal parts. Even prehistoric Indians used deer antlers for everything from decorations to miner's picks. Modern man has been equally inventive. Many of these items are only curiosities and not considered taxidermy; nevertheless there are three special types of mounts that require the skill of a taxidermist: half-lifesize mounts, open-mouth game-head mounts, and foot novelties. Most of these can be made from the information I presented in earlier chapters, but they nevertheless warrant special mention here.

Half-Lifesize Mounts. In this day of apartments, condominiums and four-plexes, living space is frequently limited. Nevertheless, there are occasions when a hunter would like to have a life-size mount but simply does not have the room. A half-lifesize mount may be the answer. Mountain sheep and goats are particularly attractive when mounted in this manner.

Most supply companies will sell a half-

A half life-size Barbary sheep mount is an impressive display, with long neck mane and "chaps." Such a mount will extend from the wall about 3 feet but still requires far less space than a full-body mount. Sheep and goat mounts are attractive half life-size.

lifesize form for about 60 to 75 percent of the cost of a full form. You should order the form that most nearly fits your trophy while having the entire skin tanned. A backboard is put into the form 2 to 3 inches behind the front legs. The front legs are attached to a small, artificial base usually resembling a rock outcropping. Mount the skin in the same manner that you would mount a life-size sheep, and the remaining back half of the skin can be used for a rug or other novelty.

Your biggest problem in mounting a half-lifesize trophy may be in locating a supplier who has a form to match your animal. In some cases it is necessary to fabricate the proper form by using the shoulders of one form and the head of another. In most cases, the extra work is worth the striking results.

Open-Mouth Game-Head Mounts. This type of mount is a cross between a conventional head mount and a rug. Bear and mountain lion are frequently mounted in this way. Also, it is not uncommon for a bull elk to be mounted in a bugling pose. This requires an open-mouth mount. Order a headform according to the nose-to-eye and the nose-to-back-of-skull dimensions. In some cases you may also need the neck circumference. The artificial jaws must be ordered to fit the form. For carnivores such as bears and cats, you may need to specify a medium- or large-size jaw set. For bugling elk, one jaw set fits all sizes because only mature bulls bugle.

Set the artificial jaws following the directions I give in Chapter 5 for setting jaws in a rug shell. After you have anchored the jaws in place with hot glue or pins, sand the headform using the techniques I described for conventional headforms and rug shells.

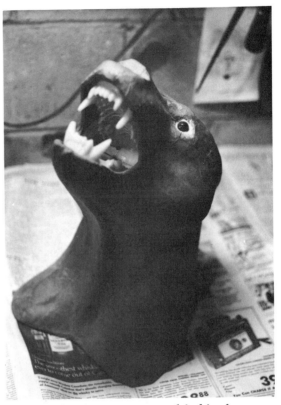

Wall head mounts are assembled in the same way that a rug shell is prepared. The jaws are anchored in the form and the eyes are set at the same angles I illustrated in earlier chapters for life-size and rug mounts. Shown here is an older-style paper form which must be waterproofed with shellac before the skin can be mounted.

Set the artificial eyes; then coat the entire headform with hide paste, including the inside of the mouth. Slip the cape over the headform and work the nose and skin of the lower chin into place.

Hold this skin in place with a couple of pins and tuck the lip skin inside the mouth between the jaws and the form. A pliers-type stapler works well for anchoring the lip skin inside the mouth. Assuming that you

G. Schroeder

If a bear hide is badly rubbed, making it unsuitable for a rug or a life-size mount, a shoulder mount can be a good alternative. This Montana grizzly was mounted by Gerry Schroeder of Bozeman, Montana.

put plenty of hide paste inside the mouth along the inside of the form, this should be adequate to hold the lips until they are dry. Then use Sculpall, mâché, or some other filler to model the inside of the mouth in order to build up the gums between the teeth and the lip skin. The mount should be completed using the same methods required for a game head or an open-mouth rug.

The open-mouth mount takes a little more time than a conventional game-head mount, but the results are well worth the effort.

Foot Novelties. With the exception of the head, perhaps no part of a big-game animal is used more frequently than the feet. Deer-foot gun racks have been common for many years and they serve a useful function. Through modern innovation and technology, feet are now being used in making lamps, stools, and even coffee tables.

Although there is very little meat inside a game foot that will deteriorate, the bone should be completely removed from the foot and the hoof, and leg skin should be pickled and mothproofed. First, split the skin down the back of the leg from the joint with the upper leg to the dewclaws. Skin the leg down to the dewclaws, and then cut through the joint at the top of these claws. Continue

Barbary sheep legs were used to make this desk lamp. Legs and feet are probably the most common novelty items made by taxidermists, and their usefulness is limited only by the imagination of the taxidermist. Many supply companies offer kits for making foot novelties such as this lamp. (Photo courtesy of the Northwestern School of Taxidermy)

stop yielding when you reach the hoof, but the bone will be firmly attached to the hoof. Using a heavy screwdriver, work down inside the hoof and into the joint between the hoof and the leg bone. You can then use heavy scissors or a scalpel and cut the cartilage and tendons that join the hoof and bone. After you have separated both bones from the hoofs,

skinning down to the hoofs. The skin will salt and dry the leg skin. After the leg skin is dry, soak the skin and hoofs in a borax and formaldehyde pickle solution for 8 to 24 hours. Then dry or freeze the skins until you are ready to mount them.

Purchase the forms for whatever novelty you want, whether it is a gun rack, lamp, or other item. Since mature animals have approximately the same size legs, one form size usually fits all feet of the same species. Insert a small amount of potter's clay into each hoof and paint a moderate amount of hide paste on the leg form. Then slip the

This photo shows the steps for making a bearpaw ashtray. First, skin the foot all the way to the last joint of each toe (left). Then pickle the skin in a borax-formaldehyde solution. Next cut the pad off the bottom of the foot. Cut a form from 1-inch plywood (bottom right) and also cut a hole in the top of the paw to accommodate the ashtray (bottom left). After packing potter's clay into each toe, insert the wooden block and glue the ashtray into place, as shown at right. Fill the skin with lead shot. Then sew a pad of buckskin to the bottom to replace the pad.

form in the hoofs and pull the skin up around the form. Work the clay in the hoof into place. Next line up the color pattern on the leg form. Most deer and other big-game animals have a dark strip down the front of the leg. Be sure that this is centered on the form and is straight. Three or four pins will hold the skin in position while you work the rest of the leg skin around the back of the form. The skin on deer feet should be sewn tightly, but the forms for lamps may simply require that the back edge of the skin be pinned in place and allowed to dry. Lamps should be assembled and then allowed to dry so that they will sit level when the lamp is completed.

When the leg is dry, polish the hoofs with jeweler's rouge. This is a polish designed for fine metals that will add a deep gloss to the natural hoof. If there are any deep scratches, you can reduce them by using 220-grit sandpaper before polishing the hoof. A paste wax will add a final sheen.

FOLLOW-UP TROPHY CARE

Care for a mounted specimen does not end when you hang it on the wall. On the contrary, continued care is necessary to maintain its beauty and durability. After all, if we bring these beautiful creatures into our homes, we should make every effort to preserve them so that their beauty can be enjoyed for a lifetime.

Game heads need to be vacuumed periodically so that dust does not accumulate on them. The vacuum should be equipped with a soft brush that enables you to work gently over the head and back of the neck. Watch for dust on the back of the ears. Also cobwebs sometimes accumulate in the eyelashes. The antlers will need little attention with time. They should be dusted, and antlers can be brightened up with a light coat of furniture polish. Do not apply anything to horns. Unlike antlers, horns will absorb polish or oils and will become unnaturally dark. If you have used black paint on the horns of pronghorns or African antelope, this can be repainted with "flat" or "semi-gloss" black paint.

If properly used, a vacuum cleaner is the most effective tool for cleaning big-game trophies. Shorthaired species such as deer, sheep, antelope, and caribou should be vacuumed using the furniture attachment. Always move the vacuum in the direction in which the hair lies. After you have thoroughly vacuumed the fur, remove the attachment and carefully vacuum the eyes, ears, and nose. Remember that the short mane on the pronghorn antelope and some African specimens should stand up. Clean the eyes with a soft, lint-free cloth, being careful not to apply so much pressure that you disturb the eye. Longhaired animals such as goat, bear, and wolf may be vacuumed *against* the hair before reversing the procedure to lay the hair down properly. A coarse-tooth comb will help to fluff the hair. A comb may be used regardless of whether the longhaired trophy is a head mount, a life-size mount, or a rug.

When a rug becomes extremely dirty, hang it over a clothesline and beat it with a switch or a lath before vacuuming. Under no condition should you wash the rug; this would remove the oils that keep the rug soft. Some commercial dry-cleaning establishments can clean the lining without damaging the head, but be sure that the firm has extensive experience before you turn your once-in-a-lifetime trophy rug over to them.

Occasionally hairline cracks may develop from shrinkage in the face and must be filled. If there is a gap in the crack, you may want to fill it with papier-mâché or Sculpall before touching it up with paints. Restore the sheen on the nose with spar varnish after the painting is done.

Bird mounts are quite fragile and must be cleaned with care. Use a feather duster to clean bird mounts. Or on very dirty mounts, use the soft brush attachment of a vacuum cleaner. If the mount has become spotted for any reason, a mild detergent and ammonia should be adequate to remove the spots. A cotton swab works well for cleaning the eyes, beak, and feet, although you should take the trouble to remove any lint that may have been left by the swab.

Like birds, fish are very delicate and should be handled as little as possible. The fins are quite fragile even though they may have a backing. Consequently avoid moving the fish after hanging it on the wall. Dust the fish lightly with a feather duster. If this does not remove all the dirt, wipe the fish with a damp cloth. Then dry it with a lint-free rag. You can brighten the wood panel behind the fish with a light coat of furniture polish.

INDEX

Grolier also offers merchandise items.
Please write for information.